OHIO'S CRAFT BEERS

For Mark Wilson Kimble,
Il mio compagno di birra

gordon biersch
hoppin' frog
TOXIC BREW
Willoughby
ACTUAL
findlay
indigo imp
Lager Heads
Great Lakes
THE BREW KETTLE
ELEVATOR
KELLEYS ISLAND
J.A.F.B
Main Street
BARLEY'S
Jackie O's
Ohio Craft Beer
Weasel boy
catawba island
thirsty dog
STAR CITY
PORTSIDE
HOOF HEARTED
ROCK BOTTOM
Rivertown
Market Garden
50 WEST
blank slate
MT CARMEL
warped wing
COLUMBUS
yellow springs
Rhinegeist
bad Tom
Four String
Listermann
MadTree
PLATFORM
NORTH HIGH
Eudora
SEVENTH SON
lock 27
BUCKEYE LAKE
Put-In-Bay
Cornerstone
CARILLON
LUCKY STAR
WOLF'S RIDGE
Zauber
madcap
Rockmill
SMOKEHOUSE
FAT HEAD'S
Rocky River
maumee bay
ZAFTIG
MOERLEIN LAGER HOUSE
PORTSMOUTH
Father John's

Ohio's CRAFT BEERS

* DISCOVERING THE VARIETY
* ENJOYING THE QUALITY
* RELISHING THE EXPERIENCE

PAUL L. GASTON

 ™

Black Squirrel Books™
Kent, Ohio

Publisher's Note: In an industry as dynamic as craft brewing, changes occur frequently. The author and publisher have made every effort to ensure that the information presented in *Ohio's Craft Beers* was current at the time of publication. The author would like to hear from readers about the latest news on craft brewing in Ohio. Contact him at plgaston3@gmail.com.

Text copyright © 2016 by The Kent State University Press, Kent, Ohio 44242
Photographs copyright © 2016 by Paul L. Gaston

Library of Congress Catalog Card Number 2015036097
ISBN 978-1-60635-275-5
Manufactured in China

Black Squirrel Books™
Frisky, industrious black squirrels are a familiar sight on the Kent State University campus and the inspiration for Black Squirrel Books™, a trade imprint of The Kent State University Press.
www.KentStateUniversityPress.com

Library of Congress Cataloging-in-Publication Data
Names: Gaston, Paul L.
Title: Ohio's craft beers : discovering the variety, enjoying the quality, relishing the experience / Paul L. Gaston.
Description: Kent, Ohio : The Kent State University Press, [2016] | Includes bibliographical references and index.
Identifiers: LCCN 2015036097 | ISBN 9781606352755 (pbk. : alk. paper) ∞
Subjects: LCSH: Beer--Ohio. | Breweries--Ohio--Directories.
Classification: LCC TP577 .G36 2016 | DDC 663/.309771--dc23
LC record available at http://lccn.loc.gov/2015036097

20 19 18 17 16   5 4 3 2 1

CONTENTS

FOREWORD

My mother always told me not to give advice when it's not asked for. But she died before I wrote this foreword, so I'm doing it anyhow.

But first, a few words about this book. Paul Gaston has written a book that serves two purposes for the craft beer enthusiast. On the one hand, it is a snapshot of craft brewing in Ohio at mid-decade, useful for navigating the multitude of brewpubs and microbreweries in the Buckeye State. As time passes, this purpose will diminish and it will transform into one of a more historical nature.

On the other hand, this book is a general reference of the lay of the beer land and beer-related terms. The introduction and first chapter set the tone. This use is timeless.

Both are welcome, so kudos to Paul for taking the immense time that it takes to write a book of this magnitude. It's a thankless task.

I have been involved with craft beer in Ohio since almost the beginning, having opened my first brewpub in 1992, almost a quarter century ago. Much has changed, and much remains the same. With more than one hundred craft breweries in Ohio today, and the commensurate cast of characters who make up the craft beer industry, it is literally a community unto itself.

While I read these pages, several thoughts came to mind. Considering these thoughts is a useful frame of reference as you read this book for yourself.

There are scores of beer styles, with many more substyles. Moreover, like a talented jazz musician, craft brewers riff on styles more than at any time in the history of this iconic fermented beverage. A couple of decades ago, there was no such thing as an American pale ale. Imperial IPA? Unheard of until a virtuoso in the American craft community came up with one. Now, it's a sought-after style around the world.

So it pains me when I hear someone say, "I don't like dark beers," or, "I only drink hoppy beers. The more the better." For all the variety out there, and for all the going-out-on-a-limb experimentation that's happening in our craft beer community, some of us are in a rut. That's not a good thing.

When you've been drinking craft beer as long as I have, sometimes it's easy to get into a rut.

I also go through periods where this beer or that beer is my "go to." I get too comfortable with the routine. That's bad, because it can lead to boredom, and craft beer is not boring! Sometimes I even have to take a (short) break from beer. That's when I'll turn to a Manhattan or a vodka tonic to reset my palate.

Don't get in a rut!

We are blessed. There are a staggering number of microbrews we can now get that are fresh. And local.

The American craft beer scene came on because we didn't have a variety of beer to choose from. A quarter century ago we all bought yellow, fizzy beer made by macrobreweries because we liked the label. Or we had a fetish for Clydesdale horses or clear mountain water. These are not bad beers by any standard. Put simply, though, the richest nation in the world was lacking choice.

Today, in addition to the macrolagers that are still with us, we have available to us a cornucopia of beer choices. Today is a virtual beer renaissance in this country. Do not take this for granted. One day, perhaps within a generation, we may have fewer choices again.

Those of us in the craft brewing business want to brew beer you'll buy. We also want to make a profit on the beer we painstakingly create. The downside to this is clear, and it is already happening. Given enough time, craft brewers will predominantly make the most popular beers. On a tour of Founders Brewing Company, for example, I was startled to learn that 70 percent of all beer they brew today is All Day IPA, a session IPA. Others of us will succumb to an "offer we can't refuse." Red Hook, Goose Island, Widmer Brothers, Kona, 10 Barrel and Elysian, among others, have already cashed their checks. In time, beer selection could be decided for us again.

This is not so much a prediction as a cautionary tale to not take what we have today for granted. This is a minor reason, though, to add variety to your beer sessions.

The real reason not to get into a beer rut is because you'll be doing yourself a favor.

What you thought was a great beer last year is now "meh" for you. You curse the brewery that brewed it, knowing they changed the recipe. Perhaps more likely, though, you have been drinking the same style for a year. Guess what? Your taste buds are likely fatigued. You're bored. Do you remember why you started drinking craft beer in the first place? It's because you were bored with the beer you were drinking then.

To combat "taste bud apathy," I offer a few suggestions for injecting some new life into your craft beer experience.

- **Take a Couple of Days Off.** Sometimes you just have to give your palate a rest. When was the last time you ordered a single malt? Or a glass of red wine? Is it heresy to suggest a glass of nonalcoholic root beer on the rocks? Recently, I had my first ever single malt mixed with vermouth and bitters. Heresy? I liked it and was mind-blown. Did I ask someone if I was supposed to? Nope. A couple of days off is all it takes for everything to taste fabulous again. Remember the first time you watched *The Wizard of Oz*, and the movie turns to Technicolor? Isn't that the experience you want from the craft beer in your pint glass?

- **Drink Local.** As much as I love many of the craft breweries from around the country, I ♥ our Ohio craft scene. We have more than one hundred craft breweries in Ohio now. Try some of the new ones. Rediscover some of the old ones. There is such a diversity now that it's a shame if you don't try them.

- **Drink Real Ale.** Don't turn your nose up at that cask-conditioned ale drawn from a beer engine, or that firkin sitting on the bar. Every real ale is an Adventure with a capital *A*, just like Alice's Adventures in Wonderland. Softer notes, low carbonation, dry hopping. That's just some of the beer roads less traveled. Have you ever had a nitro? Really, never? They don't make this stuff in Saint Louis. Celebrate it.

  If you've never had a cask-conditioned ale, you know why you should? Because it's awesome! And fear not the firkin. This is the playground where craft brewers try out new and out-there stuff.

  Firkins represent how beer was consumed pre-Industrial Revolution. If you can order a pint and instantly connect to our forefathers and their beer experience, why wouldn't you? Party like it's 1699!

  Beer engines came into being with the invention of hydraulics during the Industrial Revolution. For the first time in human history, beer was served in a closed system. No more air getting into the beer, spoiling it within a day. The cask could also be relocated to the cellar where now, on a ninety-degree day, you could enjoy seventy-degree beer!

- **Try a New Beer Every Week.** Yeah, I know. You might order something you don't like. So what? It's about the adventure. Tell me, Explorer, is it more fun to follow the road less traveled, or to constantly circle a cul-de-sac? Every new experience makes you that much more, uh, experienced. It will make your favorite stand out that much more. Get together with your friends for the express purpose of going out and trying something new. Just like when panning for gold, you may go a long time before you strike pay dirt. But you'll never find your next nugget if you're not panning.
- **Introduce Someone New to Craft Beer.** Don't be greedy. Share your knowledge. Someone turned you on to craft, so return the flavor. But please don't do it as a beer snob. No one likes a know-it-all. And don't turn your nose up at someone who's drinking a beer you haven't had since 1997. Everyone starts somewhere. Usually with the cheapest stuff they can find. You left that station and so will they, as long as they don't think you're an asshat.

If we stayed in a rut at the Smokehouse, we would have never branched out into Belgians. Or multiple styles of IPAs. We would have never researched how to make nitros. We would never have put our ale in a bourbon barrel.

Right now, we have a bourbon barrel of sour beer that we don't know what we're going to do with. We also have a carboy that is full of wild yeast, pulled out of our brewery air. Why do we do this? It's for the same reason you shouldn't get in a beer rut—we want to explore!

Shake that tendency of same-old, same-old. It's good for your taste buds. It's good for your life. After all, that's why you picked up this book. Now go grab an Ohio-brewed craft beer. No, the other one.

Cheers!
Lenny Kolada
Owner, Smokehouse Brewing Company
Columbus, Ohio

ACKNOWLEDGMENTS

Anyone who writes on Ohio craft brewing owes an immense debt to Rick Armon. I did not read his *Ohio Breweries* (2011) as I was preparing this book, so as to avoid the "anxiety of influence" and any possibility of inadvertent narrative echoes, but now that I feel free to do so I will doubtless find information I should have cited and insights I should have shared. Rick's reporting on beer in the *Akron Beacon Journal* is always thorough, judicious, and deliciously readable. Rick continues to make a special contribution to craft brewing awareness in Ohio through his Beer Blog, a daily clearinghouse for news on craft brewing and a treasure of his and others' stories on trends, openings, and new releases. In a notable "anthropological experiment" (his term) in 2014, Rick reported on every ounce of beer he had tasted in the course of the year and took a selfie to record each occasion. I'd call his experiment a success! Because the priorities of this book and those of *Ohio Breweries* are somewhat different, there should be little overlap between the two, but I am grateful for his reporting, his advice, and, above all, his example.

Similarly, through his weekly recommendations Marc Bona at the *Cleveland Plain Dealer* has pointed me and many others to good brews. He and Rick are friendly competitors in northeast Ohio, which is fortunate to have two experts who wear their expertise lightly.

I am grateful also for my appointment as Trustees Professor at Kent State University. My position provides ample motivation for my more traditional scholarship in English literature and higher education administration while allowing some latitude for less traditional scholarship. The university exemplifies a commitment to excellence, and I like to think of this book as itself a celebration of excellence—that pursued by the entrepreneurial, creative, and quality-obsessed craft brewers of Ohio. Although I did not seek or receive support from the university for this project, I am grateful for an environment that encourages scholars to try something different from time to time.

I thank the many good friends who have encouraged—or have at least tried to understand—my lifelong fascination with good beer. I suspect that some do not share my interest in arcana such as wet hopping, cask conditioning, and service on nitro, but for the most part they have at least made a show of interest. While I have enjoyed many a beer while traveling by myself, beer always tastes better when enjoyed with friends. Eileen, my wife, has been an especially valuable ally. When we travel, she sometimes has sought out the good brewpubs before I have even begun to think about lunch. And her proofreading! Superb.

This book would not have been possible without the gracious assistance of Ohio's craft brewers—including, of course, Lenny Kolada, who wrote the foreword. Without exception, they welcomed me to their breweries, showed me around, provided small samples of their beers for me to taste, and shared with me their love for what they do. I offer special thanks to the executive director of the Ohio Craft Brewers Association, Mary MacDonald, who has kept me up to date on the expanding list of Ohio's craft brewers and who has made it possible for me to become acquainted with the Ohio Craft Brewers Association. In fact, I inaugurated work on this project at the fall 2013 meeting of the OCBA in Cincinnati. To celebrate my completion of this project, I now wear the OCBA T-shirt: "Drink Beer Made Here."

Finally, I thank Will Underwood and his associates at the Kent State University Press. As the craft brewing industry in Ohio has evolved (and continues to grow) at a precipitous pace, I have had to modify—then modify once more—the intent and focus of this book. Their counsel at each stage has been invaluable, and their patience with necessary deadline extensions has enabled me to work with a sense of urgency without succumbing to panic.

INTRODUCTION

A first-time visitor to a taproom or brewpub is often well advised to order the sampler, a judicious selection of a few taster glasses that represents the range of what the brewer offers. A sampler is not meant to be comprehensive or definitive, nor does it rank the beers according to their quality. It's a sampler.

SAMPLING OHIO'S CRAFT BREWERIES (AND BEERS)

That's what this book is—a generous sampler of Ohio craft brewing. Although the sample should provide a representative overview of Ohio's craft brewers, it describes in detail only some of those listed. As the title suggests, the emphasis is less on providing an inclusive record than on discovering the variety, appreciating the quality, and relishing the experience of Ohio craft beer. Each of the profiles reports on my visit to the brewery or brewpub that is described, the beers described in terms of tasting notes are ones I have tasted, and the photographs are ones I have taken. I was not able to visit those listed under "Consider Also," but they are not necessarily any less worthy of attention than those profiled.

Speaking of beer, my commitment to drinking "responsibly" dictated that I sample only a few of the available beers when visiting a brewery. Occasionally, when visiting two or three breweries in the course of a day, I had to pace myself carefully. But I have attempted to offer a perspective on a representative range, and, in addition to those I describe, I list many (though far from all) beers that I would have enjoyed if it had not been for dear prudence. Some brewers can point to a historical list of well more than fifty varieties, and there are new ones released virtually every day.

Of course, because a brewery will have in production at a given time only a small percentage of the beers in its book, you may want to call or consult its Web site concerning what's being poured before making a visit. Or you may simply trust to finder's luck. Any visit to a craft brewery can be an adventure.

Few industries are more dynamic than craft brewing. Breweries introduce new beers and discontinue others. Brewers move from one brewery to another—frequently. Brewing systems and packaging lines expand. Menus express new priorities in the kitchen. Hours change. Production breweries open taprooms, and craft breweries that have brewed only for their taprooms undertake production. Within twelve months, to take one example, Rivertown in Cincinnati expanded its brewing and bottling systems, made changes in personnel, introduced new beers, and revised the graphics on its cans. Dayton offers another example of dynamic change. The proposal for this book asked whether Dayton's few breweries should be included in the Columbus chapter or the Cincinnati chapter. A year later, the growth of craft brewing in Dayton demanded its own chapter.

Given such an exciting but volatile environment, I attempted in the final days of this project to contact the breweries profiled one final time so as to verify current information. I am grateful for all those that responded, but two did not. That is another reason for you to verify the crucial details, especially days and times of opening, before paying a visit. Most challenging of all have been the start-ups with modest capitalization and uncertain timelines. Because any new brewery requires a leap of faith, I have taken several such leaps myself by including in the "Consider Also" listings projects that may not come to fruition. Again, a quick phone call or a check of the Web site would be a good idea prior to a visit.

As you will discover, while this book reflects the variety of craft brewing in Ohio and offers an appreciation for its quality, it provides no rankings—not in the profiles, not in the "Consider Also" listings, not in the "Ten Great" lists. The order is alphabetic within categories: profiled brewpubs, profiled breweries with tasting rooms, and "Consider Also." Instead, I want to suggest the pleasures to be found in visits to breweries and brewpubs from Portsmouth to Toledo and from Willoughby to Cincinnati. Frank Peters, who won the 1972 Pulitzer Prize for music criticism, described one overriding goal. His 2007 obituary in the *St. Louis Post-Dispatch* recalled his response to the prize: "In writing about a good concert, I want to make them wish they'd been there." Similarly, if I have enjoyed a brewery or brewpub, I want to make the readers of this book consider a visit.

Anyway, what would be the justification in ranking the rich, creamy pumpkin ale I enjoyed at the Smokehouse Brewing Company in Columbus in September 2013 relative to the dryer but no less delicious Pumpkin

Ale available in 2014 from Thirsty Dog in Akron? Prefer a thick head that reminds you of the whipped cream atop a slice of pumpkin pie? Visit Smokehouse. Prefer a thinner head atop a brew that you can drink through an afternoon or before dinner? You might want to choose a Thirsty Dog. Make a few visits, drink a few beers, and form your own opinions. If we find ourselves on adjoining bar stools one day, perhaps you will give me your recommendations.

MULTIFACETED VARIETY

In the meantime, you will have a lot to choose from! About three years ago, when work on this book got under way, there were fewer than fifty breweries in Ohio. But the Buckeye State was then on the threshold of an unprecedented growth in craft brewing. As Rick Armon reported in his December 2014 summary for the *Akron Beacon Journal,* "A Year in Beer," at least twenty-five Ohio breweries began operations in 2014 alone! Now, there are more than one hundred breweries in the state, from large producers such Great Lakes Brewing in Cleveland, which distributes its beers across a fourteen-state region, to Kelleys Island Brewing Company, which serves its beers on a lovely lawn overlooking Lake Erie. While the entire brewing system at Kelleys Island would fit comfortably at the base of one of the Great Lakes bright tanks, both breweries make memorable beers and can offer a wonderful experience.

You can enjoy Ohio craft brewing as you sip an amber ale on the front porch of Mt. Carmel in suburban Cincinnati or make your way to the industrial chic and warm camaraderie of Warped Wing in Dayton. You would surely enjoy the historic ambience of Portsmouth, but you can also enjoy tasting exceptional beers in the more utilitarian settings of MadTree in Cincinnati, Actual in Columbus, or Hoppin' Frog in Akron. Then there's Willoughby, where the imaginative can return to the days of interurban travel while enjoying a full menu and creative brews.

Given such a dynamic industry, it is a sure thing that new breweries will have begun operations by the time this book is in your hands. For example, you might check on Fibonacci Brewing in Cincinnati's Mount Healthy neighborhood or on Nine Giant Brewing in Pleasant Ridge. In early 2015, their planning was too tempting to ignore entirely but too tentative for inclusion. It is also possible, perhaps likely, that I may have failed to recognize an embryonic industry leader. Today's nano-brewery may well become tomorrow's Great Lakes or Morlein. Any brewer who believes not enough attention has been paid to her (or his) operation is probably right and should demand a second edition that does!

Two other issues deserve mention. Both could represent important steps forward in making craft beer more broadly accessible, but either might appear in retrospect as a step backwards threatening a possible loss of focus.

In addition to Debonne Vineyards in Madison, which now brews good beer as Cellar Rats Brewery, there are several Ohio wineries that either have started or plan to start their own brewing operations: Georgetown Vineyards (Cambridge), Lil Paws Winery (Lake Milton), Maize Valley Winery (Hartville), Merry Family Winery (Bidwell), Shawnee Springs Winery (Jackson Township), and Valley Vineyards (Morrow). Rick Armon has tracked this phenomenon from a mostly positive perspective. But it might be observed that while there are some affinities between winemaking and brewing and some logistical advantages in operating both under one roof (either literally or figuratively), there are pronounced differences between the two crafts. The concern is that unreflective "expansion" of winemaking to include brewing could result in compromises that would serve neither. So, two cheers for wineries that make a serious commitment to brewing by investing in high-quality systems and by hiring experienced brewers. And a third cheer for those such as Cellar Rats that are proving their mettle.

The other issue is the likelihood over time of some consolidation in the industry. An analysis by business writer Ian Mount (*New York Times,* February 5, 2015) points to two possibilities. The first is that if exuberance fades and prospects for long-term profit margins are examined realistically, opportunities for mergers and buyouts will arise. We can hope that opportunities for growth will attract support that will not compromise creative control of the brewing. But the additional investment required for growth creates debt, and the necessity of paying back that debt may create challenges.

TRYING TO BE CONSISTENT

A final word about the protocols behind this book: I visited as many breweries and brewpubs as I was able to schedule within a sixteen-month period, but my "day job" as a professor and a realistic time limit on research and writing meant that I could not visit as many as I would have wished. Before each visit, I wrote to alert owners and brewers— and to clarify the restrictions that I would observe. I would drink only small samples of a few beers (i.e., no free pints) and accept no free food, mementoes, etc. A couple of times, the generosity of my hosts overcame my resistance, but, by and large, I stuck to my rules.

As mentioned above, I list many beers but write in some detail only about those I was able to taste—those identified in **boldface**. And my glowing reports on menus are just that—a hungry appreciation for what menus promise with no claim that I have evaluated what they deliver. I have come away from this project with a growing list of breweries and brewpubs I look forward to visiting as a paying customer.

One issue that arose regularly during my discussions with brewers concerned International Bitterness Units. In an industry whose "hophead" fans believe that more is better, IBUs have become an effective marketing tool, and I have for the most part listed such information when it has been made available. The problem is that this measure often has very little to do with how a consumer experiences a beer. I heard brewers complain repeatedly about what brewmaster Andy Tveekrem of Market Garden Brewery terms *"Imaginary* Bitterness Units." Yes, IBUs register the level of bitterness-producing acid in a beer. But, according to *The Oxford Companion to Beer,* the measure "is a laboratory construct that was never meant to leave the laboratory." Frankly, anyone who takes beer seriously will tell you that posted IBUs may not come close to indicating how bitter a beer tastes. That depends on the balance between hops and malts and on many other factors as well. Because I badgered breweries for this information, I have decided to leave it where it appears—but without hounding anyone for "missing data." If you find IBUs useful, fine. Otherwise, disregard.

With the completion of this book, it will be a pleasure to reclaim my "amateur" status and to find a seat at the bar without checking for my reporter's notebook. But I would not have missed this opportunity to become acquainted with those responsible for craft brewing in Ohio. Principled, strategic thinkers, they share important values described in Chapter 1. What they have in common above all is an abiding love for what they do. Through their affinities with brewers of hundreds and thousands of years ago, they affirm both a sense of mission and a sense of purpose. They are not "in the entertainment industry." They have reclaimed and are pursuing a sacred trust.

THE COMMUNITY OF BEER

In his engaging book, *At Home: A Short History of Private Life,* Bill Bryson quotes Felipe Fernández-Armesto (author of *Civilizations: Culture, Ambition, and the Transformation of Nature*) in attempting to understand "why people took to living in communities." Climate change may be one reason, as may a wish to remain near the graves of loved ones who have passed on. But people may just as well have been motivated by "a powerful desire to brew and drink beer." By this perspective, brewers required communities—and vice versa. That is still the case. Just drop by Warped Wing or Rhinegeist or Great Lakes or Hoppin' Frog or Yellow Springs or Weasel Boy or any of the taprooms and brewpubs profiled or mentioned here. You will be welcome. You will probably learn something about brewing. You will enjoy the company. And you will enjoy the beer.

[1]

CRAFT BREWING IN OHIO
A PROUD LEGACY RECLAIMED—AND REDEFINED

Before the Eighteenth Amendment took effect in 1920, Ohio could boast one of the nation's great brewing traditions. Most cities of any size supported at least one local brewery—often more. Cleveland was home to twenty-six! Some of Ohio's brands were distributed throughout the Midwest.

One prominent nineteenth-century success was the Hoster Brewing Company of Columbus. Founded in 1836 by Louis Hoster, a native of Germany, the brewery on South Front Street grew from a rudimentary facility producing a few hundred barrels to a plant at the turn of the century capable of more than 300,000 barrels annually. Accounts of many Ohio breweries follow a similar trajectory: impressive growth in the nineteenth century, consolidation and expansion in the early twentieth century, and an abrupt, often fatal hiatus in 1920.

OHIO BREWING AND PROHIBITION

During its brewing heyday Ohio—perhaps not coincidentally—was home also to the movement that led to Prohibition. The Anti-Saloon League, which would grow by the turn of the century into a powerful national lobby, was founded in 1893 in Oberlin and soon opened its first office in Columbus. Twenty years later, the League celebrated its anniversary with a national convention in Columbus. From the heart of Ohio came a message chilling to brewers and their customers: the League would campaign for an amendment to the Constitution to prohibit the manufacture, transportation, and sale of alcohol.

The League was aptly named. Brewing—and the saloon culture it supported—prompted criticisms that helped to make the Eighteenth Amendment possible. After 1890, when beer drinking became the most popular form of alcoholic consumption in the United States, the saloon became the most popular venue for such consumption. And saloons—often unkempt nuisances offering clients gambling and other illicit pleasures in addition to beer—provided those opposed to alcohol in any form with an easy target.

Following the end of the Great Experiment in 1933, there was a modest resurgence in Ohio brewing, as some of the larger local breweries resumed operation, but the best days of the industry lay in the past—or so it seemed until recently.

A CONTINUING DECLINE

Local and regional brewing suffered a further decline beginning in the 1950s, as mass marketing, television, and industry consolidation reduced market share and profits for smaller breweries. Between 1950 and 1980, most Ohio breweries either went out of business or agreed to consolidation with one of the large national breweries. By 1985, brewing in Ohio had become the exclusive province of a few corporations.

From an economic perspective, the story is regrettable in some respects. Local and regional breweries had employed local workers, bought local materials, and inspired a certain sense of place. The loss of many evocative brand names is itself cause for regret. But someone devoted to good lagers and ales in their remarkable range of styles might argue that there was no great loss. Nearly all the beer brewed in Ohio's local breweries had been pilsner-style lager—thirst quenching on a warm day, but hardly distinctive. Minor variations in taste and ingredients—a little more rice in one recipe, a determined effort at "dryness" in another—could encourage partisan local debates and inspire some measure of loyalty. But the competition that existed was based primarily on marketing, price, distribution, and package design, not on the taste of the beer.

THE RESURGENCE

If the story of Ohio brewing became at one point one of decline, so far as local pilsner brewers are concerned, it is more recently one of a remarkable resurgence. Beginning in 1988, with the founding of the Great Lakes Brewing Company in Cleveland, the most interesting development in the industry has been craft brewing, from small operations serving fresh beers and ales to patrons who drop by, to multifaceted operations distributing a broad range of canned and bottled lagers and ales throughout the Midwest, to the many breweries that serve food through a category that did not exist in 1980—the brewery-restaurant and the "brewpub."

As a result of this resurgence, Ohio has regained its place on the map of American brewing. Once again, local breweries, from Athens to Cincinnati to Toledo, are employing local people, buying local products, and giving their products local names. What's the difference between the present and the past? Much less quantity, so far as the craft brewers are concerned. Much more quality. In short, much better beer. Even the mass producers—and Ohio is home to three of their large plants—have attempted to follow suit by offering beers in a wider range of styles with names that are calculatedly whimsical.

Yes, it is a pity that Prohibition led to closings of many local brewers and that afterwards the brewing giants eventually forced most of the survivors out of business. But few beer lovers would sacrifice the range of craft styles available now in order to bring back hundreds of local brewers all brewing more or less the same beer. From the selection of ingredients, through the refinement of the brewing process, to the design of labels, the creation of advertising strategies, and the monitoring of financial health, the story of craft brewing in Ohio offers reason for optimism—not to mention an excellent justification for a road trip.

A NEW KIND OF BREW

As a college student, I enjoyed drinking beer as much as anyone—perhaps more than some. I had a few favorites. For instance, I preferred Schlitz to Falstaff, Budweiser to Miller High Life. But the differences between American mass-produced beers were, to make the point as positively as possible, exceedingly subtle. As they are today. Before Coors expanded to nationwide distribution, self-appointed connoisseurs would drive west to Texas, then the brand's boundary, in order to fill the trunk with "Banquet" beer. You might hear dormitory debates comparing regional favorites, such as Dixie (New Orleans), Stroh's (Detroit), or Schmidt's (Philadelphia). But there wasn't that much to say about the beer itself. They were mostly variations on German pilsner, lagers light in color and, even before "light" beer, light in taste. The variables resulted largely from ways in which American brewers were violating the German purity law, the Rhineheitsgebost, which restricts ingredients to barley, yeast, hops, and water. By brewing with corn, rice, and other adjuncts, many American brewers—I'm not naming names—saved money and found at least some sense of identity. But bars promoting such beers often emphasized not their taste but their temperature—how cold the beer is when served in frosty mugs.

I discovered authentic beer when a grant from the English Speaking Union enabled me to conduct my dissertation research in England. There I found beer pleasantly cool, comparatively light in carbonation, and rich in flavor. There were many different styles. The Pale Ale uniformly referred to as "bitter" was ubiquitous. Stouts, by no means limited to Guinness, differed in dryness, in their dark opacity, and in the smokiness they had absorbed from the dark roast of the barley. A "mild" might be ordered in half-pint servings. There were porters, brown ales, Scottish ales. And there were lagers, of all British beers, the most similar to the American standby.

I returned to the United States as a disaffected beer drinker. When possible, I would order a Bass Pale Ale, a Newcastle Brown Ale, or a Guinness, but these lacked the appeal of a pint pulled in a neighborhood British pub. Many of the imported beers had been carbonated more highly than their British counterparts so as to appeal to U.S. preferences. Also, by the time bottled beers reached the shelves in the corner grocery, many were well past their prime. Other beers were available occasionally as well—Heineken from Holland, St. Pauli Girl and Beck's from Germany, Ichiro from Japan, Red Stripe from Jamaica, and Corona from Mexico— to name just a few. But most of these might as well have been brewed in Milwaukee or St. Louis. They were (and are) mostly straightforward lagers, notable more for their packaging and their advertising than for their taste.

A glimmer of a possible new direction for U.S. brewing broke through the fog of San Francisco in 1965, when Fritz Maytag, a scion of the Iowa appliance manufacturers, invested "a few thousand dollars" to save the foundering Anchor Steam brewery from bankruptcy. Six years later, a century after the founding of the brewery, the bottling of Anchor Steam (a lager brewed with yeast that prefers temperatures warmer than most lager yeasts require) began in earnest. The result was a revelation. Instead of the crisp transparency of mass-produced American lagers, Anchor Steam offered the appearance and taste of craftsmanship. A rich, deep amber when poured from the bottle, Anchor Steam promised a complex acquaintance with malt. Then there was a hint of fruit. Finally, there was a bracing bitterness to encourage the next sip. But I should not be using the past tense. Anchor Steam still satisfies.

Within a few more years, Anchor would be bottling a porter, an ale, a barley wine, and a Christmas Ale. As the Anchor Web site notes, while "the terms 'microbrewing' and 'craft brewing' had yet to be coined . . . it was clear that Anchor was leading a brewing revolution." Indeed, many of the values we now associate with craft brewing appear in the early years of the resuscitated Anchor Steam. There was (and is) a commitment to traditional ingredients—malt, yeast, hops, water—and a refusal to use cost-cutting adjuncts such as rice or corn. To flavor its various styles, Anchor Steam uses a variety of whole-cone hops rather than processed pellets or extracts. And for some styles Anchor revived what was then a neglected tradition, dry hopping, in which bagged hops (think tea bags) are added to beer in process to enhance aroma (mostly) and taste (somewhat). This is not a book about Anchor Steam, but credit should be paid. Contemporary craft brewing, both the revival of an industry and a journey into a new industry with a distinctive culture, widely shared values, and unprecedented product variety, began in San Francisco in 1965.

The next chapter opened in 1977 in Sonoma, California, with the launch of the New Albion Brewery, now regarded as the first "microbrewery" in the United States. While this particular experiment proved unsuccessful, the precedent set there would prove broadly influential. (A side note: the daughter of New Albion's founder, Jack McAuliffe, now lives in the Cleveland area and has worked with Platform Brewing to brew according to her father's recipes.) The following year, on the other side of the bar, there was even more important news, the legalization of home brewing. Why more important? In my sixteen-month tour of Ohio's breweries and brewpubs, I asked many brewers the same question: What inspired you to become a professional brewer? And I heard for the most part the same answer: home brewing.

The train was out of the station. In 1981, what was to become the largest and most highly respected craft brewing competition in the United States opened in Denver, the Great American Beer Festival. In 1982, the first brewpub opened in Yakima, Washington, thanks to new legislation allowing a brewery to serve food on its premises. By 1995, the number of craft brewers in the United States had climbed to nearly five hundred. Today, the number is roughly six times that. By the end of the twentieth century, the United States could claim more breweries than any other country. Now, there's no other country that is comparable. Notwithstanding a couple of "market corrections," the total continues to rise. Perhaps even more to the point, craft beer accounts for an increasing percentage of the volume of beer consumed. That is, more and more people who drink beer are choosing craft beer. In 2015, according to the Brewers Association, there were in the United States more than 4,000 breweries for the first time since the 1870s.

As suggested earlier, to speak of the "restoration" of American brewing is really to miss the point. When every city worth the name could boast several breweries prior to Prohibition, there was on the whole a sameness about the beers, most falling within the fairly narrow spectrum we still enjoy in our major national brands: bottom-fermented lagers brewed more or less in the style of Pilsen, Germany. By contrast, craft brewers have introduced to the American palate an unprecedented spectrum. I have a T-shirt that displays a "beeriodic table" of fifty-seven "ale-e-ments," from lagers such as Maibock and Rauchbier to ales such as lambics, extra-special bitters, oatmeal stouts, and bitters. Given the choice, I doubt that many beer drinkers would trade the current craft brewing scene for the industrial brewing of the nineteenth century.

THE CULTURE(S) OF CRAFT BREWING

I hope one day before long to write a book with the above subhead as its title. It would consider every element of craft brewing other than beer. While that might prove a hard sell, beer being the point of craft brewing, such a book could draw attention to a remarkable social, commercial, ethical, and moral phenomenon. In the meantime, the following paragraphs will have to do.

The more you learn about craft brewing in Ohio, the more you will begin to appreciate its diversity. You scan a brewery's list of beers, some familiar, some not. Some lists, such as those at Fat Head's or Moerlein's Lager House, are impressive in their length and complexity. Others reveal a more limited focus. If you are at a brewpub, such as Maumee Bay in Toledo or a brewery-restaurant such as Wolf's Ridge in Columbus, you may find on the menu some creative and locally sourced dishes that you would not have expected.

Visiting several breweries and brewpubs, however, may begin to teach another lesson—that within this remarkable diversity there are important values represented with remarkable consistency throughout the profession. Perhaps over time craft brewing will suffer a hardening of its still-supple arteries. It may begin to focus more directly on the bottom line as competition prompts acquisitions and mergers and closures. Craft brewing may become less of a calling, more of a pure enterprise. Maybe. But that possibility means above all that we should not take for granted how fortunate we are in this second decade of the twenty-first century to have access to breweries and brewpubs that really do represent a different standard of doing business. So while there are many reasons to celebrate the values that help to define a golden age in craft brewing, let's do so.

First, there's *collaboration within competition*. Like any business, craft brewing must turn a profit through competing successfully. If there is a taproom, it must attract enough customers to drink and pay for the beer that has been brewed. The brewer that bottles or cans must obtain sufficient space for the product in grocery store coolers. Good locations for breweries and brewpubs are not available on every block or in every part of town. So there is no lack of competition.

But there is also a strong collaborative spirit. The Ohio Craft Brewers Association, which might have become just another trade association, is animated by a strong sense of common purpose. Its business meetings turn into collegial gatherings of brewers eager to share observations and advice while drinking beer. Indeed, Ohio's professional brewers are often once novice brewers who have been resourceful enough to seek good advice from more experienced peers. For instance, Jay Wince (Weasel Boy, Zanesville) recounts appreciatively the counsel he received from Eric Bean (Columbus Brewing) and Scott Francis (then at Barley's) prior to his opening. And brewer Jim Lieb (Rocky River Brewing Company, Cleveland) is one of several highly capable brewers who express appreciation for the tutelage of Andy Tveekrem, now at Market Garden.

This spirit appears vividly in Ohio's many collaborative beers, ales, and lagers crafted through ad-hoc partnerships of two or more craft brewers. Yet another interesting kind of collaboration appears in the Brewers' Brunches mounted by Fifty West in eastern Cincinnati. The brewpub works with another brewery and another local restaurant to offer a three-course meal on Sunday mornings. And in late October, Fifty West partners with Cleveland's Great Lakes Brewing to serve beer and barbecue on their ample grounds. But even on the most basic level, there's cooperation. Reporting in the March 2015 issue of *Columbus CEO*, T. C. Brown quotes Sideswipe Brewing's Craig O'Herron: "I've loaned equipment to Land-Grant Brewery and I use their key washer."

The Samuel Adams Brewing the American Dream program offers an especially notable example of this value. Initiated by Sam Adams founder and Cincinnati native Jim Koch (see more in Chapter 4), brewers can consult with Sam Adams professionals about any facet of the brewing industry and receive advice and perhaps even consideration for small loans. A July 2015 "speed coaching event" at Findlay Market covered topics such as e-commerce, packaging, and distribution.

Then there's *architectural restoration and preservation*. From one corner of Ohio to the other—literally, from Bryan to Portsmouth and from Willoughby to Cincinnati, many brewers have invested in the architectural distinction and commercial potential of structurally sound older buildings. Beer drinkers have benefited, but so have neighborhoods and cities. The list is extraordinary—and continues to grow longer. Check out the sidebar, but also consider this five-point flyover. In Toledo, there's Maumee Bay, which manages no fewer than four distinct attractions in the massive Oliver House, said to be the city's oldest commercial building. But in the far northwest, in Bryan, you'll find one of at least three former churches repurposed as a brewpub. In northeast Ohio, there are Great Lakes Brewing and Market Garden. Their continuing restoration and repurposing of venerable brick buildings has helped to trigger the rebound of the dynamic Ohio City neighborhood, and Willoughby Brewing Company, whose

FIFTEEN GREAT ARCHITECTURAL EXPERIENCES

Much good beer in Ohio is being brewed in industrial parks. Indeed, the sight of an industrial park may make you thirsty—just in case. But there is a special pleasure in visiting breweries that have brought timeless buildings back to life. Ohio craft brewing is restoring the state's reputation as a home for good beers. How appropriate that craft brewing is also a leader in restoring Ohio's buildings!

- Cincinnatians once drove west out of town along the Little Miami, through charming Mariemont, to the historic Heritage restaurant. Alas, it closed. But now it lives again—as **Fifty West Brewing**. The Heritage, to speak truth, had become a bit seedy. The building was 180 years old, after all. But there's nothing seedy about this brewpub, thanks in part to new mechanical, plumbing, and electrical systems. Oh, right. You go there also for creative brewing and good food.
- **JAFB** in Wooster is a terrific place to settle down for an afternoon or evening—and feel free to bring the kids along. The comfortable but historic building is one reason. It has in its lifetime housed an internationally renowned horse-drawn carriage factory, a community electric company, and an auto parts dealer. A Wooster landmark, it had fallen on hard times until JAFB undertook its restoration.
- **Star City Brewing** in Miamisburg has renovated an early nineteenth-century sawmill that had later become a local landmark restaurant. The large, rambling buildings are lovely, with original hand-hewn beams and paneling. There's the same story in Garrettsville, where **Main Street Brewing** thrives beside the river in the city's former mill.
- In their renovation of a former Ford dealership in Columbus, **North High** owners Gavin Meyers and Tim Ward decided to create a home for architectural elements salvaged, restored, and repurposed from throughout the state. You'll see doors recovered from building demolitions at Ohio State, mailboxes from a closed post office, and tracks laid beneath the bar to provide a foot rail.
- To quote **Maumee Bay's** Web site: "We transfer the same strength, creativeness, size, uniqueness and complexity of the architecture of the Oliver House to the artistry of our craft beer. No other brewery in the country brews under such history." The oldest working commercial building in Toledo is worth a visit. Go for the architecture. Stay for the beer and the food.
- Look at the brewhouse at **Seventh Son** in Columbus and you'll say, yes, this was once a garage. Turn to look at the tasting room and you'll say, no way! On the bones of an eighty-year-old commercial building, the architects have created an unusually hospitable space for enjoying craft beer and (thanks to visiting vendors) craft food.
- **Moerlein's Malt House** in Over-the-Rhine (Cincinnati) restores to its original function an impressive, multilevel brewery in what was once a neighborhood known nationally for brewing. OTR is now well on the way to reclaiming that status.
- You could fit a small cathedral in to the main hall at **Rhinegeist,** also in Over-the-Rhine. On second thought, perhaps Rhinegeist *is* a small cathedral, one where well-brewed beer inspires the liturgy.

- Working to restore and repurpose one adjoining building after another in its Ohio City block, **Great Lakes** has somehow managed to respect the architectural integrity of each while creating for the first time an overall impression of integration and shared purpose.
- There's little to suggest that a pawnshop once occupied the congenial rooms that **Toxic Brew** has restored in Dayton's historic Oregon District. The brick walls and the sturdy L-shaped bar define and make memorable a space that was once (to put it kindly) nondescript.
- The pews, stained glass, and cruciform bar add a further ecclesiastical ambience to the decommissioned and repurposed Methodist Church that is now the home of **Father John's Brewing Company** in Bryan, Ohio. An even more ambitious repurposing appears in the restored church that is now **Taft's Ale House** in (again) Over-the-Rhine, Cincinnati.
- In order to convert a 1925 grocery story (and, later, an antique shop) into the **Millersburg Brewing Company**, Bill Baker and partner Duane Yoder (to quote Shane Hoover in the *Canton Repository*) had to "strip the walls to bare brick, build a bar from salvaged wood, and shoe-horn the stainless steel and copper brewing equipment into a basement that was once a pool hall."

restored interurban repair facility recalls the days of proud regional transit systems. In the Southeast, you can visit Portsmouth Brewing—again. The charming riverside building that once housed a local brewery does so now. In Cincinnati, there's an embarrassment of architectural riches, from the terrific brewery projects in Over-the-Rhine (Moerlein, Rhinegeist, Taft) to the conversion of the former St. Pius X Church by Urban Artifact to the revival by Fifty West of a noble inn that was once a destination restaurant. Complete the tour in Dayton with Toxic Brew, Warped Wing, Dayton Beer, and Star City or in Columbus with Wolf's Ridge or Elevator or North High or . . . This is a very selective list.

Writing in early 2015, Jason Brewer, a spokesperson for Listermann Brewing in Cincinnati, observed, "We only make three year round beers. Always something new and interesting on tap!" Many of his colleagues throughout Ohio would echo that sentiment, as there is among craft brewers a widely shared emphasis on *creative product development*. Notwithstanding the concern expressed in Lenny Kolada's foreword about some craft brewers falling into ruts, I did not meet one craft brewer in Ohio who regards his job as one of producing endlessly without variation two or three standard styles. While most breweries develop a portfolio of year-round beers in the interest of meeting customer expectations, almost all devote at least some of their taps to experiments. The result is an unusually vigorous industry and an unusually interested and committed clientele. There are several Web sites that share one purpose—to record the responses, often detailed ones, of beer fans who seek out and report on the new beers they have found.

Interestingly, creative product development in craft brewing often has a counterintuitive dimension in a return to traditional techniques, a revival of nearly forgotten styles, and a respect for classic ingredients. The values involved? *Integrity and a respect for history.* Cincinnati brewer (and beer baron) Greg Hardman adopted Christian Moerlein as the symbol of his city's brewing renaissance in part because the brand's earlier brewers had chosen to observe the German purity law: no ingredients other than water, malt, hops, and yeast. Dan Cochran named his Columbus brewery Four String because he plays the bass and because of the four "strings" of beer, beginning with water and malt. "Brewing for commodity won't get you there," he says. "You have to make it art every day." Hoppin' Frog in Akron has brewed a unique German style, Gose, that once exploited the salinity of the only water that was available for brewing in its locality. There are many examples of this value in the pages that follow but, in sum, craft brewers have discovered that there is exciting creativity to be found in discovering, implementing, and, sometimes, reinterpreting singular moments in the history of brewing. No phenomenon reflects this discovery more directly than the current fascination with Belgian beers based on the use of wild yeasts—either captured locally or, more likely, ordered from a supplier. From Jackie O's in Athens to Rivertown in Cincinnati, brewers are investigating what nature will provide, and the results, while they may be to an extent unpredictable, can be remarkable.

Implicit in a commitment to exploration within the context of integrity is the assumption that customers will follow where brewers lead. That appears to be the case, at least so far. Hence craft brewers tend to share both a commitment to *consumer education* and a related *confidence in their customers.* Observe how many breweries offer instructive tours of their breweries. Great Lakes periodically registers "students" for Beer School, a thorough introduction to the brewing and packaging processes. On the other end of the pedagogical spectrum, most craft brewers brew at least one "entry-level" beer, a light lager or ale that invites, then intrigues the beer drinker who has been lulled by the saturation advertising of mass-market lagers.

Jackie O's founder Art Oestrike describes a familiar phenomenon. Having attained his twenty-first birthday, a hypothetical Ohio University junior wanders in and orders a [fill in the brand] light. The bartender says, "How about a taste of Ja Bitte Kölsch? It's similar—just more interesting." A few semesters later, the graduating senior may approach to ask whether the Bourbon Barrel Skipping Stone is available. Once you start, you never stop learning about beer. For many, craft brewing has offered the beginning of an exciting journey of discovery, and brewers are almost always happy to support the journey.

Breweries and brewpubs seek an *engagement with their communities* in one of two ways: they bring the community into the brewery or they take the brewery to the community. For instance, Weasel Boy Brewing in Zanesville sponsors "Beer for Boobs" with proceeds directed to the prevention and treatment of breast cancer. Market Garden and Great Lakes in Cleveland helped to found the Ohio City Farm, one of the largest urban farms in the United States, and they buy produce from the farm for their menus. On a very different plane, breweries as different as Warped Wing in Dayton and Temperance Row in Westerville use cleverly named beers to teach their customers local history. Without the beer named Corbin's Revenge, who would remember the twice-bombed Westerville saloon owner? Without the brewery named Warped Wing, how many would recall the Wright Brothers' aeronautical innovation that enabled them to pilot their planes? In a different kind of collaboration, Akron's Aqueduct Brewing worked with a home brewer who is also a keeper at the local zoo. Proceeds from the sale of the hobbyist's IPA (called EF5 after the scale used to describe the strength of a tornado) were directed largely to Wildlife SOS. These instances only begin to suggest the range of examples. Community engagement is a consistent and multifaceted value of craft brewing. And there are the events—lots of them, only some of them focused on beer. One favorite: Brews + Prose, a monthly event sponsored by Market Garden that features writers and promotes discussion. Beer helps.

A closely related value—that of *local sourcing*—will also recur repeatedly in the pages that follow. Although brewers must usually depend on distant suppliers for the essential ingredients of their beers, they often turn to local suppliers when they can. Actual Brewing buys Cascade hops from Ohio growers, for instance, and Maumee Bay brews its Total Eclipse Breakfast Stout through collaboration with a local espresso roaster. Local sourcing becomes even more conspicuous as brewpubs turn to local farms for their greens, spices, pork, beef, etc. Or to local bakers. Smokehouse has pointed to its patronage of a baker in its Columbus neighborhood. Jackie O's cites its own farm as well as "Laurel Valley Creamery, Starline Organics, Dexter Run Farm, Gillogly Orchard, Faller Foods, Athens Own, Integration Acres, Shew's Orchard, Sticky Pete's Maple Syrup, Snowville Creamery, Shagbark Mill, Casa Nueva & Cantina, Brite Farms, [and] Shade River Farm." And Wolf's Ridge goes one step further by listing not only local food and flower purveyors but the manufacturers of the furniture, soap, and aprons they purchase! I quote: "By focusing on craft and locally sourced products and services as much as possible, we are staying true to our primary goal of supporting and emulating the community in which we reside."

You might expect breweries as principled as these to demonstrate a high degree of *ecological responsibility*. You will not be disappointed by the examples in the pages that follow. Enabling local farmers to use spent grains as fodder, using collected kitchen grease to fuel the brewery's van, building and remodeling in ways that are energy efficient—craft brewers are an exemplary industry in many ways. "Sustainably crafted with purpose" is a good motto for Jackie O's, which in July 2015 received a grant from the USDA Rural Energy for America Program to install solar panels. But the motto serves for craft brewing in general.

Great Lakes has taken a prominent leadership role, not only within craft brewing, but within Ohio industry more broadly. The brewery's annual Burning River Fest on the banks of the nearby Cuyahoga reaches out to those who share its commitment to "improving, maintaining and celebrating the vitality of our regional freshwater resources." Since 2007, the related Burning River Foundation has sponsored efforts to position Northeast Ohio at the forefront of environmental leadership. Eric Wobser, formerly a spokesperson for the Ohio City neighborhood in Cleveland, memorably observed that Great Lakes is "constantly piloting new environmental technologies and putting them to work." In July 2015, cofounder Pat Conway spoke at the tenth annual Ohio Brew Week. Cleveland.com reported: "To have a throwaway economy just doesn't make sense. We'd like to change the paradigm. We'd like to have people think about 'take-make-remake' instead of 'take-make-waste.'" There's good beer at Great Lakes, with a chaser of ecological vision.

Make no mistake. The cultures of craft brewing would fall into disarray if the focus on brewing consistently good, consistently interesting beer were to be compromised. But the ancillary values of the craft brewing culture do not distract from its priority on beer. They are synergistic with that priority. That is one of the reasons why the experience of drinking a craft beer can be so rewarding. As you enjoy the good taste of the beer, you are also demonstrating your good taste—in more ways than one.

2

WHAT'S AT STAKE NEAR THE LAKE
CLEVELAND, AKRON, AND THE WESTERN RESERVE

A Connecticut lawyer and surveyor, Moses Cleaveland became a pioneer when he accepted a commission to map his state's "Western Reserve." His assignment brought him to what is today Northeast Ohio and gave him the opportunity to found the city that bears his name. Two centuries later, beer fans may sense some of his pioneering spirit in the rebirth of brewing in Cleveland. The more recent pioneer? Great Lakes Brewing Company, an enterprise that began with clearly defined values and has since grown steadily both in quantitative and qualitative terms—rather like the Western Reserve. It has grown above all in influence, as the breweries described in the following pages will suggest. According to a January 2015 story by Amy Plitt on the Condé Nast Traveler Web site, Cleveland now ranks as one of America's "best beer cities."

Akron's contribution to brewing history is hardly less striking. A fall 2007 article by Rob Musson in *The Keg* tells a story that began around 1865 with the Burkhardt brewery. When the original wooden brewery burned to the ground, a larger plant arose from the ashes, this time built of brick. In 1904, a six-story brewhouse was added. Restarting production following Prohibition, Burkhardt made beer until 1956, when Burger Brewing bought the plant and brewed beer there for eight years before shutting the doors. Thirsty Dog opened them again, first purchasing the front building on Grant Street to begin production and in 2014 obtaining much of the remainder of the plant. Grant Street has become once again a contributor to the history of brewing in the Akron area—a history still being made from Medina to Wooster.

One measure of success in the northeast lies in the enormous growth and diversity of its craft brewers. The profiles below describe a wide spectrum, from nano-breweries making just enough beer to keep up with the demand of those who walk through the doors to large enterprises that distribute beer across a multistate area. Another measure of success lies in the continuing expansion of production capacity and in range of distribution. Established brewers now market to areas once far beyond their reach. And within just the last couple of years, several brewpubs

TEN GREAT UP-CLOSE BREWERIES

Most breweries and brewpubs separate the brewing equipment from the tasting experience. However, there are a few that make it possible to drink a beer among the sights, sounds, and aromas of the brewing process. It's a bit like sitting at the chef's table at a fine restaurant. You may see (and smell) the steam rising from the boiling wort, watch the process of dry hopping, or feel grateful that someone else has the job of shoveling spent grain from the bottom of the tun. In any case, you will be enjoying a pint that has emerged from the tanks around you.

- The expanding brewing and bottling system stands close to the indoor beer garden and bar at the **Fat Head's** production facility in Middleburg Heights. You will enjoy all the aromas, all the noise, and all the pleasure in watching others work while you enjoy drinking the results of their labor.
- At **Rhinegeist** in Over-the-Rhine, Cincinnati, the brewing system, impressive at the outset and now even more imposing, stands at one end of the brewery's cathedral space. The stainless-steel tanks command respect and inspire confidence.
- At **Weasel Boy** in Zanesville, you cannot enter the comfortable bar and seating area without passing the brewing system. If there's beer being brewed, the brewers will be happy to explain what's going on.
- The taproom at **Four String Brewing** in Columbus was described by one patron as "raw, but fun." Sitting at the bar puts you close to the brewing action and in all likelihood will lead to a conversation with the brewers. That should continue even as the brewery shifts much of its production to an off-site facility.
- **Warped Wing** in Dayton offers beer drinkers the ambience of a restored industrial plant divided roughly between a spacious bar and seating area at the front end and an impressive thirty-barrel brewery at the back end.
- In Dayton's Carillon Historical Park, the **Carillon Brewing Company** offers visitors a glimpse of what it was like to brew beer in the 1850s. "Watch steam billow from copper kettles, feel the heat of charcoal fires, and smell the malt wafting through the air as each hand-stirred batch of brew is crafted in front of you."
- The growing popularity of **MadTree's** (Cincinatti) canned beers may force a separation of the production facility and the taproom. But there has been a great pleasure in hearing the clank of the grain shovel and smelling the wort on the boil. Somehow that gives an even greater sense of purpose to tasting the beer.
- It is not very large, but the brewing system at **Nano Brew** (Cleveland) is right at your elbow as you sample what the brewers have crafted. A larger system is inevitable, given the popularity of Nano's house beers, but it will probably be not that far from your elbow either.
- At **Thirsty Dog** in Akron, the taproom lies at the heart of the operation, the brewery on one side, packaging and storage on the other. There's constant traffic between the two, and nothing gets in the way of the sights, sounds, and smell of the brewing.
- **Rock Bottom's** brewery (Cincinatti) may be separated from the bar area and dining rooms by plate glass, but nevertheless stands at center stage. The architects knew what they were doing in placing the brewing system at the heart of the matter.

have opened production facilities separate from their brewpub locations, with the result that their beer in bottles and cans has become increasingly prominent on shelves in and beyond the region.

It would be difficult to predict just how much further craft brewing in Northeast Ohio can expand. As recently as five years ago, no one would have predicted the growth that has already occurred. But if the hardy pioneering spirit that led to the settlement of the region continues to direct the region's craft brewers, there's no reason not to be optimistic.

BREWPUBS

THE BREW KETTLE

8377 Pearl Road, Strongsville, Ohio 44136
440-239-8788 • http://www.thebrewkettle.com/index.htm

Two paths have led to the multifaceted and remarkably synergistic operation that is today's Brew Kettle. One leads from the small Strongsville craft brewhouse founded in the mid-1990s as Ringneck Brewing. The other leads from the mats at Indiana University, where Chris Russo attracted international attention as a collegiate wrestler. Following his graduation from IU, he moved to Northeast Ohio to help coach the wrestling program at Cleveland State and began working in the hospitality industry to make ends meet. Ends met—and Russo's entrepreneurial flair led him to own and manage several successful franchise restaurants. But there was still something missing, the opportunity to put his stamp on an emerging and inviting trend, the rise of craft brewing. In the varied enterprises of the Brew Kettle, he has done just that.

There is so much that is distinctive about the Brew Kettle: the longevity of its staff in an industry prone to frequent turnover, the strategic approach to growth that has supported a methodical expansion of brewing capacity, the in-house graphics professionals who produce the memorable menus and labels, and the offering of an impressive food menu through the

Owner Chris Russo enjoys the Brew Kettle's Black Rajah IPA.

coordination of prep and service kitchens. But that's all behind the scene. For the visitor, what stands out above all is this: there's a lot that's good going on at the Brew Kettle.

First, there are the Brew Kettle beers, crafted by "TBK Production Works" in a dedicated brewing facility about ten minutes south of the brewpub. In brewing for its taproom and smokehouse and for distribution throughout Ohio, the Brew Kettle draws on more than twenty years of experience, from an original three-barrel brewhouse to the current twenty-barrel system. Because of the range of styles, the beer drinker who takes hops seriously will find the Brew Kettle ideal for educating the palate. Second, there is the restaurant. Third, there is Ohio's "first and finest" do-it-yourself brewery, offering "home" brewing under the best possible circumstances, with supplies, expert advice ("brew coaches"), and gleaming equipment close to hand. Finally, there is the adjacent wine cellar where you can sample a range of wines or make your own. This range of missions might suggest a possible lack of focus in one area or another. That does not appear to be the case. The production works brews good beer, the restaurant serves good food, and the do-it-yourself wine and beer facilities hum with activity. And there's more "hum" on the way, thanks to plans for a 40,000 square foot building that will include *all* of these enterprises.

The Beers

From a wide range of ales and lagers produced by its brewery, the Brew Kettle offers a changing selection at its smokehouse. In September 2014, for instance, there were seven TBK offerings. **White Rajah** (ABV 6.8 percent, IBUs 70), one of TBK's signatures, is an unusually fragrant IPA. At first taste, it hints enticingly at bitter lemon, but the finish, round and floral, is as gratifying as a San Diego sunset bouquet. **Black Rajah** (ABV 6.8 percent, IBUs 70) has a strong family connection. Like its brother, this IPA has lots of fruit, especially in the aroma, and offers the pleasing bite of Citra hops, which, as the trademarked name suggests, evoke a wide range of fruit associations, from melon to lychee. But there is also more than an echo of toasted malt. If White Rajah evokes a summer day in San Diego, Black Rajah offers fall in San Francisco. And the color! Black? Not really, not like a stout. Hold it to the light, and you'll see a clear, dark red—a ruby in a glass.

4C's (ABV 5.0 percent, IBUs 55), an American Pale Ale, takes its name from the familiar 3C American hops (Cascade, Centennial, Columbus) with the addition of piney Chinook. You will thus find unexpected overtones of cedar along with the expected bitterness and citrus. While 4C's will remind you of some IPAs you have known, a whiff of its fresh outdoors aroma will invite you to a beer that diplomatically straddles the boundary between Pale Ale and its Indian cousin. **Old 21** (ABV 9.0 percent IBUs 90) deploys Simcoe hops in quantity in an imperial IPA that carries the Simcoe signature: a lovely aroma yielding to an earthy balance of pine and fruit. Although no one will (or should) regard Old 21 as a session beer, its deft balance between malt and hops creates an impact that depends far more on flavor than on alcohol. Memorable.

Ryan Corp smokes the Brew Kettle's barbecue chicken.

Big Woody (ABV 5.0 percent, IBUs 18) is described by TBK as a "malty lager brewed in the Munich style and tradition." OK. But this beer offers more complexity and depth than you'll find in Bavaria. You can pair it with the Brew Kettle's bratwurst for an ideal meal, but the beer will hold your interest all by itself from first sip to last. Then there is the **El Lupulo Libré** (ABV 8.8 percent, IBUs 88), which, despite its take-notice ABV, is far more about the hops than the alcohol. The standout hop here is Mosaic, which takes the stage set by Vienna malt and flaked corn. (Though a common adjunct in mass-produced American lagers, flaked corn has long been used in British bitters and milds to create a beer lighter in color and body without distorting its flavor.)

You will be happy with any of these beers, but you should also consider **Imperial Red Eye** (ABV 7.0 percent, IBUs 65), their "robust porter" known as **One-Eyed Jack** (ABV 6.2 percent, IBUs 50), or, for that matter, any of the beers they have on tap, including the wide range of guest beers available.

For especially serious fans, the Brew Kettle taps a cask ale every Thursday. There's only one variety at the time, and the firkin holds only 10.8 gallons, so it doesn't last long. But as a rule of thumb, if you like a particular style, you will *really* like that style on cask. In between visits, you can find a wide range of TBK bottled beers throughout Ohio and Kentucky.

The Food

The Brew Kettle menu is colorful, detailed, and inviting. There's lots of barbecue available—including barbecue spaghetti, a "backyard sampler" (ribs, pulled pork, wings), and the Triple Pig (a sandwich stuffed with sliced pork loin, pulled pork, and bacon). But there is much else, including several unexpected offerings. For instance, there's a grilled meatloaf grinder, perch tacos, and a highly original take on six-way chili (here it's mac and cheese topped with Amber Ale chili, shredded cheese, peppers, sour cream, and scallions). A variety of burgers is available also, including a lamb burger served with a goat cheese yogurt dressing and cucumber slices. There are daily specials: e.g., burgers on Monday, wings on Tuesday, and a chef's special on Friday.

Other Stuff

There's *lots* of other stuff! • You can arrange for catering, order large-quantity take-out items from the restaurant, buy a cycling shirt, or order tickets to special events. • There's live music from time to time. • Check out everything that's happening on the Brew Kettle Facebook page or pick up a monthly calendar.

Newsworthy

The Brew Kettle attacks the winter doldrums with an annual Ogrefest, a celebration of high-ABV beers brewed on the premises as well as ones brewed by selected Ohio and national breweries. • In early 2015 the brewery announced the purchase of a three-barrel system for brewing experimental, innovative beers. • The Brew Kettle has collaborated with the Cleveland Cavaliers to brew "All for One," a session IPA (ABV 4.75 percent, IBUs 35) available at the brewpub, at the downtown arena, and at some Northeast Ohio grocery stores. • In January 2015, TBK announced plans for a July opening of a second location in Amherst (owner Chris Russo's hometown) at 300 Church Street. And in September came the announcement of a new facility that will replace the present one. • Paste, the entertainment Web site, ranked 119 American IPAs from all over the country in 2015. Number one: TBK's White Rajah. Jim Vorel, who wrote the story describing the competition: "It's an absolutely incredible beer." TBK earned a bronze medal in the highly competitive IPA division at the 2015 GABF.

THE SKINNY

LOCATION	Take the Pearl Road exit off I-71. The Brew Kettle is about five miles south of the Cleveland airport. But stay alert for the new location!
HOURS	Mon–Thu 11:30 A.M.–12 midnight • Fri–Sat 11:30 A.M.–1:00 A.M. • Sun 11:30 A.M.–9:00 P.M.
PARKING	There is a large lot surrounding the Brew Kettle and there is additional parking available next door in a lot behind the BW3 restaurant.
KIDS	Yes, there are special menu items aimed at "little brewers."
TAKEOUT	Growlers, to be sure, as well as bottled beer. But they also sell half-barrel and six-barrel kegs.
DISTRIBUTION	Several varieties are available in four-packs and six-packs throughout Ohio and Kentucky.

CORNERSTONE BREWING COMPANY

58 Front Street, Berea, Ohio 44017

440-239-9820 • http://www.cornerstonebrewing.com/index.html

This brewery really *is* a cornerstone of its community, Berea, the lovely Cleveland suburb known for cornerstones. Founded in 1836 as a quarry town, Berea soon gave its name to a particularly durable form of sandstone still marketed as "Berea Stone." You will not have a rocky experience at this comfortable brewpub, however. Since 2005, Cornerstone has been serving pub food as well as some imaginative entrées in Berea while brewing some very satisfying ales in its diminutive on-site brewery. Although this entry focuses on the Berea location, there's a second Cornerstone location in Madison, the heart of Ohio's wine country. This downtown pub offers a comparable but distinctive menu of food and beer. The address is 74-70 West Main Street, Madison, Ohio 44057, and the phone is 440-983-4520. Driving directions are given below.

The Beers

Brewer Jonathan Cox brews for both Cornerstone locations. If he has a favorite style, it's the "session IPA" (ABV 5.5 percent and under). Through his annual production of roughly six hundred barrels, he manages to offer a considerable variety. Check the on-tap listings for the location you plan

Cornerstone's brewer Jonathan Cox opens the doors on a summer morning in Berea.

to visit. A few worth mentioning are the **Grindstone Gold** (ABV 5.5 percent, IBUs 11), popular with visitors unfamiliar with craft beer but, for that matter, with anyone who enjoys a good, smooth Kölsch. Another beer inspired by Germany (and by Berea's quarries) is **Sandstone** (ABV 4.5 percent, IBUs N/A). This interesting Märzen combines Pilsner, Vienna, and Munich malts. Cox describes the flagship IPA, **Seven** (ABV 7 percent, IBUs 90), as "hopped like a West Coast IPA, but flavored like an East Coast IPA." I'll let you figure that out. Your on-tap list may also include **Rowan** (a Scottish wee-heavy ale), **Rusty Pheasant** (a rye lager brewed with different rye varieties), a porter, an Irish ale, and an Irish stout.

The Food

Cornerstone's kitchen offers a traditional brewpub menu with several imaginative variations. For instance, in addition to the expected range of burgers, there's the Californian, with avocado, hummus, and provolone. Pizzas feature a Buffalo chicken variation that includes a grilled chicken breast, Buffalo sauce, and blue cheese dressing on the side. The Cornerstone, an eight-ounce sirloin served on grilled Italian bread with mushrooms and provolone, leads the sandwich list. The potato skin eggrolls are memorable: all the charms of a loaded baked potato are

Jody Balogas serves a Rusty Pheasant at Cornerstone Brewing.

wrapped in a house-made spring roll. There's even a side of sour cream. You can learn about the weekly specials for both Berea and Madison by glancing at Cornerstone's Facebook page.

Newsworthy

Cornerstone is in some ways rather like a British pub. The news that matters most is community news, and its contribution to that news takes the form of craft beers and the food to accompany it. Hence the announcement in June 2014 that Cornerstone would be canning its IPA made news.

Other Stuff

Cornerstone often participates in local and regional beer festivals.

Cornerstone Brewing's Rusty Pheasant.

THE SKINNY

LOCATIONS	Berea lies about twelve miles south of Cleveland and two miles south of the Cleveland airport. Take I-71 to Bagley Road and head west to Front Street. Turn left (south) on Front and drive to the brewery at the corner of Church. It is (ahem) on the corner. To reach the Madison location, take I-90 east from Cleveland to the clearly marked Madison exit, Route 528, also known as River Street. Drive north on 528 to the first major intersection, with Main Street. You'll find the brewery one block to the east.
HOURS	Berea kitchen open Sun noon–9:00 P.M. • Mon–Thu 11:30 A.M.–10:00 P.M. • Fri–Sat 11:30 A.M.–11 P.M., with the bar open later. Madison kitchen open Sun 8:00 A.M.–8:00 P.M. • Mon–Thu 11:30 A.M.–9:00 P.M. • Fri–Sat 8:00 A.M.–10:00 P.M.
PARKING	There is some on-street parking for the Berea location as well as nearby lots. Check with the Madison location before visiting.
KIDS	At mealtimes, surely.
TAKEOUT	Growlers are available.
DISTRIBUTION	See the above reference to plans to can the IPA.

FAT HEAD'S BREWERY

24581 Lorain Road, North Olmsted, Ohio 44070

440-801-1001 • whttp://fatheadscleveland.com/

It's true that the concept originated in Pittsburgh, where there's still a Fat Head's restaurant—but not a brewery. Also true that there's now a Fat Head's in the heart of Portland's beer scene. No matter. Cleveland's Fat Head's is all Cleveland, all the time. There are really two experiences on offer, each enjoyable in its own way. There's the location on Lorain Road, a comfortable, sprawling restaurant with a large bar, a compact brewing system, and a *really* large dining room. It's a convenient, welcoming place for just about any meal, anytime. There really is something on the menu for, well, just about everyone. But there's also a tasting room

Michael Zoscak checks the boil at Fat Head's.
At Fat Head's Middleburg Heights, Janet enjoys a Rye Saison.

on Sheldon Road in Middleburg Heights, where you can sample the output of the Fat Head's production facility on the spot. Yes, the look is "industrial park modern," but the growing plant is fascinating, and there is a "limited menu of pub grub" to keep you from going hungry. While this article focuses on the brewpub and restaurant, it casts a vote for the Middleburg Heights experience as well.

The Beers

Fat Head's welcomes *serious* beer fans. Like some seafood restaurants that print a new menu every day, head brewer Matt Cole greets you with a *daily beer list*. Yes, the impressive Web site lists nearly 140 styles brewed at Fat Head's since 2006. But the daily list is even more impressive in offering a range of beers that includes both the regularly reliable and the seasonally adventurous.

My sampler began with a **Rye Saison** (ABV 7.1 percent, IBUs 30), which offers unexpected complexity and depth. Brewed in the style of a Belgian farmhouse ale, there's the expected twist of citrus but also a malty warmth arising from the spiciness that rye adds to the grist. (See the Word List.) **Jack Straw Kölsch** (ABV 4.8 percent, IBUs 28), ideal if you're settling down to watch a game or match on one of Fat Head's big screens, does capture the distinctive balance of Cologne–German hops and malt in seemingly perfect balance. The clear golden color invites you to a familiar but bracing opening and to a crisp aftertaste that calls for another sip.

Bottles soon to be filled with beer roll on the Fat Head's line.

The **Head Hunter IPA** (ABV 7.5 percent, IBUs 87), perhaps most familiar as a colorful, widely available six-pack, is worth tasting at the source. To experience the "savage amounts of Simcoe, Columbus, and Cascade hops" at their freshest is memorable—and really not as intimidating as you might think. Similarly, while it is appropriate to approach the **Hippy Sippy Imperial Stout** (ABV 10.0 percent, IBUs 70) with respect, you will not find it overwhelming. The intense flavors—coffee, cocoa, malt—claim the spotlight from the brew's considerable strength. A superb beer!

The **Ancho Mama Imperial Smoked Porter** (ABV 8.9 percent, IBUs 47) also demands respect. Cole's description: "A robust imperial porter brewed with malted barley that was smoked over alder wood by our brewers on site and infused with Ancho and chili peppers." Although I might prefer a snifter of this "robust" beer to a full pint, it would be difficult to imagine a better platform for these variations than the Fat Head's porter. Imagine drinking a good porter as you are seated by a fragrant campfire and you'll get the idea.

While it never hurts to check out the list of current drafts before visiting, the wide range available at any time at Fat Head's virtually guarantees that even the most particular beer drinkers are likely to find something they'll enjoy. If there are any gaps in the Fat Head's repertoire, there will be well-chosen guest beers to fill them.

The Food

Although the menu doesn't threaten to become esoteric, the variety it offers suggests a kitchen prepared to work interesting variations on all of the staples. Like wings? Fat Head's offers twenty-five "classic" and "smokehouse" styles. Hungry for local fare? Try the Parma Karma: kielbasa, brats, and bangers with sautéed pierogies and Stadium Mustard. Sandwiches carry on the local theme. There's Danny's Cleveland Club for which only Browns fans are eligible, the Full Cleveland (sausages, sauerkraut, Stadium Mustard), and the thermonuclear Beauty and the Beasty (pulled pork, coleslaw, and the restaurant's hottest barbecue sauce).

The Cuyahoga Burger on the other side of the menu is a close relation. "This one is on fire!" By contrast, the Euclid Beach Burger, with only the traditional accompaniments, is meant to recall summer days at Cleveland's iconic amusement park in Collinwood. (It closed in 1969.) Subs such as The Dawg (Pounder) offer yet more puns, while the name of one of the Big Fat Melts provides its own warning: "Artery Clogger."

Pizzas, made by hand and baked in a stone oven, cover the lakefront— or you can create your own from a list of twenty-six ingredients. Chef's specials appear on the Fat Head's Facebook page.

Newsworthy

As mentioned above, Fat Head's has entered the craft brewing scene in Beervana—Portland, Oregon. The location is good: three blocks from Powell's Book Store and a block from Whole Foods. They have arrived with considerable cred—many of their beers have won awards. • Among the most recent? The Alpenglow

Fat Head's displays some of its awards.

Weizenbock won gold at the 2014 GABF, the Battle Axe Baltic Porter won silver and the Black Knight Schwarzbier won gold at the 2014 Denver competition, the Bone Head imperial red ale won silver at the 2014 World Beer Cup, and Hop JuJu imperial IPA won gold at the GABF 2013. Fat heads are wearing many medals, including four new ones from the 2015 GABF for Hop JuJu, Bonehead Imperial Red, Black Knight, and Midnight Moonlight. Three are gold!

Other Stuff

There's a collaborative Heavyweight Brewers Brawl in the spring that features strong beers. Fall brings the Pumpkin Harvest Fest and Celebration of the Hop IPA Fest. • The "events" page on the Facebook site will keep you up to date. • Quick tours of the ten-barrel brewing system at the saloon can sometimes be arranged. • Saturday afternoon tours at the expanding twenty-five-barrel facility are becoming a regular thing at 1:00, 2:00, and 3:00 P.M. • At both locations, there's an ample selection of "headgear" for purchase: shirts, glasses, gift cards, and a distinctive racing shirt for cyclists.

THE SKINNY

LOCATIONS	The North Olmsted brewery and saloon on Lorain Road, just northwest of Hopkins airport, can be reached from I-480, but a GPS will help with some counterintuitive turns. Or you can take the Valley Parkway to Brookpark Road for an easy connection to Columbia Road (north) and Lorain (east). You can reach the Middleburg Heights brewery by exiting I-71 and driving west on Bagley Road for just a couple of blocks. Turn right on Engle Road, then take a left on Sheldon to 18741.
HOURS	North Olmsted: Mon–Thu 11:00 A.M.–midnight • Fri–Sat 11:00 A.M.–1:00 A.M. • Sun 11:00 A.M.–11:00 P.M. Middleburg Heights: Wed–Thu 4:00–9:00 P.M. • Fri 4:00–10:00 P.M. • Sat noon–10:00 P.M. • Sun noon–7:00 P.M.
PARKING	There's ample free parking at both the North Olmsted saloon and the Middleburg Heights tap house.
KIDS	The North Olmsted brewery and saloon are "family friendly." The kids' menu arrives with crayons. Middleburg Heights is more of an adult scene.
TAKEOUT	Fat Head's drafts are available in growlers. Most of the beers may be purchased in six-packs.
DISTRIBUTION	There are plans to distribute beyond northeast Ohio and western Pennsylvania to parts of Indiana and Florida.

Great Lakes anchors the revitalization of Ohio City.

GREAT LAKES BREWING COMPANY

2516 Market Avenue, Cleveland, Ohio 44113

216-771-4404 • https://www.greatlakesbrewing.com

One could write a book solely about Great Lakes Brewing Company, the oldest and largest of Ohio's craft brewers. To a considerable extent, the spring from which Ohio craft brewing has flowed can be located in Ohio City, just across the Cuyahoga from downtown Cleveland. In 1988, brothers Patrick and Daniel Conway, working with experienced brewers and engineers, invested their ideas, their values, and their capital to found the brewery.

The precedents they have set have been influential. In fact, virtually every element in the "cultures of craft brewing" I discuss in the introduction can be traced to the Great Lakes model of product purity and differentiation, of ecological sensitivity and innovation, of local sourcing and collaboration, of architectural attentiveness, of civic responsibility, of sustainability, and of focus on consumer education and satisfaction. But because this book must consider a few other Ohio breweries as well, just a few instances of the Great Lakes example must suffice:

- A preference for time-honored ingredients and methods. "Great Lakes Brewing Company avoids preservatives, synthetic chemicals, and pasteurization, which ultimately compromise flavor."

- While a respect for architectural integrity was apparent when the brewery opened its iconic bar for business, the more impressive measure may be found in its expansion. What you will find now is the tasteful amalgamation of three Victorian buildings: a former hotel and saloon, a feed and seed company, and a tavern once frequented by crack lawyers such as Eliot Ness. Even as impressive additional investments in state-of-the-art equipment have followed, Great Lakes has remained a good neighbor, its architectural footprint not just compatible with but an enhancement of its community.
- The ecology? Consider the Fatty Wagon, a van fueled by kitchen grease as it ferries fans to Cleveland sports events. According to Eric Wobser, formerly executive director of Ohio City, Inc., Great Lakes is "constantly piloting new environmental technologies and putting them to work" (YouTube: GLBC Company Video).
- Great Lakes has created enviable regional collaborations. It makes the spent grain produced through the brewing process available as nutritious food for animals while relying on local farmers to provide much of the food served in its restaurant and at its celebrated brewmaster dinners. Luke Purcell, brewer and quality specialist, affirms that sustainability is more than a slogan for Great Lakes. In brewing, he observes, "everything's kind of reusable."
- The brewery is a principal sponsor for the nearby Ohio City Farm, one of the largest urban farms in the country. The farm "exists to provide fresh, local and healthy food to Cleveland's underserved residents, boost the local food economy, and educate the community about the importance of a complete food system" (http://www.ohiocity.org/ohio-city-farm). GLBC also raises farm-to-table crops on a small plot at Hale Farm and Village.
- The brewery's annual Burning River Fest on the banks of the nearby Cuyahoga reaches out to those who share its commitment to "improving, maintaining and celebrating the vitality of our regional freshwater resources." Since 2007, the related Burning River Foundation has sponsored efforts to position Northeast Ohio at the forefront of environmental leadership (http://www.greatlakesbrewing.com/sustainability/burning-river-foundation).

The Beers

The GLBC beers, firmly grounded on traditional brewing practice and a commitment to traditional ingredients, are by now so familiar and well established that they represent standards for the industry. The labels have changed (see Chapter 7: Work in Progress) but not much else. That

Luke Purcell (*far right*) and Great Lakes colleagues enjoy the first pints from a new conditioning tank.

does not mean these beers are in any way bland or predictable. Having purchased and enjoyed GLBC beers for fifteen years, I could offer tasting notes for many, but will confine myself to a few.

What many regard as the brewery's flagship beer, **Dortmunder Gold** (ABV 5.8 percent, IBUs 30), began life as The Heisman, named for the iconic football player who lived in the neighborhood. Its present name reflects its rich color and its gold-medal success at the 1990 Great American Beer Festival. This lager offers a good introduction to GLBC beers by the reliable balance it strikes between hops and malt. But it has character and depth as well, thanks in part to GLBC's avoidance of adjuncts (e.g., rice, corn) and of nontraditional additives (preservatives) and methods (pasteurization).

Eliot Ness Amber Lager (ABV 6.2 percent, IBUs 27) is named for the famous "untouchable" enforcer of Prohibition, of course. But, more to the point, in the mid-1930s Ness took on the challenge of reforming the Cleveland bureaucracy by firing corrupt police officers and indicting public officials for criminal activity. There's no reform needed in this amber lager, which relies on noble hops (see the Word List) to give point to the rich malt experience it offers.

Burning River Pale Ale (ABV 6.0 percent, IBUs 45) and **Commodore Perry IPA** (ABV 7.5 percent, IBUs 70) might be compared to fraternal twins with different personalities. There's a strong family resemblance, in that

Everything must compute to create Great Lakes Burning River Pale Ale.

both honor the GLBC commitment to traditional methods and ingredients, but the IPA is the extroverted cousin with the stronger personality—a formidable hops presence offering both bitterness and fruitiness. The Pale Ale refuses a backseat, however. As "hoppy" as some IPAs, Burning River was offering the citrus and evergreen tastes of the popular Cascade hops before "West Coast" became a sought-after style. The **Edmund Fitzgerald Porter,** named for the tragic Great Lakes freighter, hits all the right notes (coffee, chocolate, malt), a surprise chord (a more pronounced hops presence than in many porters), and no wrong notes. Departing from the original plebian style, as so many craft porters now do, this is not a beer to slake a laborer's thirst, but a complex beverage demanding and repaying attention.

There's no room to write about all of the GLBC seasonal beers, which offer a very pleasant incentive for turning calendar pages, but I must mention two favorites. **Conway's Irish Ale** (ABV 6.5 percent, IBUs 25) is named for the grandfather of the Conway brothers, GLBC's founders. Like a stout, this red ale uses roasted malt. But, as it is clearly not a stout, its malt is but *lightly* roasted to create a flavor that evokes roasted nuts more than dark toast or peat. An interesting combination of hops—the expected Northern Brewer, the unexpected Willamette and Mt. Hood—beautifully complements a malt presence in which UK's Crystal 77 brings its impression of caramel and raisin.

The trend-setting **Christmas Ale** (ABV 7.5 percent, IBUs 30) may vary in subtle ways from one year to the next, but it is a consistently successful and satisfying seasonal brew—as its six silver and gold medals will attest. Like some artful cocktails, which carefully balance ingredients so as to avoid any one of them becoming dominant, GLBC blends honey, fresh ginger, and cinnamon so that none overpowers. The hops (Mt. Hood, Cascade) and a creative blend of malts (Harrington 2-Row Base Malt, Crystal 45, some wheat, and a bit of roasted barley) confirm that this is good beer to enjoy often during the holidays, not fruitcake in a glass. Other seasonals include a rye IPA, an imperial IPA,

When Great Lakes Christmas Ale arrives, the holiday season can begin.

an Oktoberfest, a Russian imperial stout, an imperial red ale, and, most recently, Sharpshooter Session Wheat IPA, a "hoppy wheat beer with orange peel and Jarrylo hops, named to honor Ohio's Annie Oakley."

The result of consistent quality within an expanding range of beers has been consistent growth. In 2013, its silver anniversary year, GLBC reported a 22 percent increase in beer shipments to more than 140,000 barrels and pledged to "elevate expansion opportunities."

The Food

The menu reveals a concerted effort to remind diners that they're in a brewery. For instance, the Stilton Cheddar Ale Soup features the brewery's Dortmunder Gold Lager. Then there are the Brewer's Barley Pretzels, Pub Bites (cod deep fried in Edmund Fitzgerald Porter batter), and chicken wings with barbecue sauce based on the porter. And there's a salad that combines Commodore Perry IPA blue cheese and Eliot Ness Amber Lager vinaigrette!

The other theme that runs through the menu is that of GLBC's strong commitment to local sourcing. The burgers are made from GLBC spent grain-fed beef that is ground daily at the West Side Market. The butternut squash ravioli comes from nearby Ohio City Pasta. And the Porter Chocolate Chunk ice cream is made by Mitchell's Homemade (just around the corner) using Edmund Fitzgerald Porter. According to brewery spokesperson Marissa DeSantis, the brewery's owners and managers undertook "a significant menu overhaul" in late 2014. "We recommitted ourselves to finding creative uses for local, seasonal ingredients." The menu is not so extensive as to create availability issues. Nor is it so inventive as to challenge diners seeking traditional fare. Food at GLBC occupies a welcome zone: familiar enough to be easily enjoyed, innovative enough to be interesting.

Newsworthy

It's an unusual week when GLBC is *not* making news of some kind! Hence any summary can but suggest the range of initiatives, releases, and events that deserve the headlines they receive. In addition to those mentioned elsewhere I'll limit myself to three. (1) In spring 2014, the brewery released a new seasonal, Spacewalker, an ale brewed with Belgian yeast and American hops as a tribute to "the 25 courageous astronauts who have called Ohio their terrestrial home" (GLBR press release). (2) In summer 2015, the brewery offered a contest challenging fans of its beers to submit photos showing folks "responsibly enjoying GLBC beer" in far-flung locations. The grand prizes (a tent, kayak, etc.) all expressed an outdoor theme. (3) In April 2014, the brewery hosted an Earth Day tour featuring service projects in thirteen cities (Washington, D.C., Chicago, Raleigh, etc.) within their distribution area. The brewery collaborated with nonprofit environmental organizations. Following the projects, local retailers thanked volunteer participants with parties offering GLBC beer and free food.

Other Stuff

The expanded (as of spring 2015) GLBC gift shop is worth a visit for the merchandise—a wide variety of brewery-related products such as beer, clothing, glassware, posters for hanging at your home bar, etc. But the values it embodies are also worth noticing. "We've made great strides in responsibly sourcing the majority of our merchandise." DeSantis reports

Just one course in a Great Lakes brewmaster's dinner.

that the brewery's "Responsible Purchasing Team" surveyed suppliers, found areas where improvements could be made, and made them. "We're very proud to say that the majority of our gift shop items reflect our standards for environmental conservation, human rights, and local sourcing & community building." When you visit, you'll be likely to find as well some "limited edition" gifts and foods created by local artisans.

Every month brings a full roster of pub events, including brewery tours, firkin (keg) tappings, trivia nights, and "Beer School"—an informative, instructive introduction to the brewing, packaging, and tasting of beer. There are also occasional brewmaster's dinners, offering pairings of food and GLBC beer. Private tastings and live music presentations convene in the cellar. Except on Fridays and Saturdays, the Rockefeller Room and the Beer Cellar can be rented for private events.

THE SKINNY

LOCATION	Given its contribution to the revival of Ohio City, now a thriving neighborhood of restaurants, condos, and breweries, Great Lakes enjoys a well-justified reputation as a civic catalyst and anchor. Drive across the Carnegie Avenue Bridge, turn right on West 25th, then make a left on Market. You're there.
HOURS	Brewpub hours are Mon–Thu 11:30 A.M.–10:30 P.M. • Fri–Sat 11:30 A.M.–11:30 P.M. • The bar is open until midnight Mon–Thu and until 1:00 A.M. Fri–Sat. CLOSED SUNDAY.
PARKING	On weekend nights, parking can be a challenge. There is a small lot just to the west of the brewery on West 26th and a couple of large lots just to the north and to the northeast of the nearby West End Market. Another option? Take the RTA Red Line (Airport) to the Ohio City Station, and you're just a couple of blocks away.
KIDS	A menu for children twelve and under offers favorite foods (a Vienna-style hot dog, chicken strips, a kid's pizza) and kid-friendly drinks (Peggy's Punch, Cranberry Lemonade).
TAKEOUT	Beer is available for purchase in the gift shop.
DISTRIBUTION	Great Lakes distributes its beers over a fourteen-state area. Of all Ohio craft brewers, this is the one you're most likely to locate in Chicago, Washington, D.C., or Louisville, Kentucky.

HOPPIN' FROG BREWERY

1680 East Waterloo Road, Akron, OH 44306

330-352-4578 • http://www.hoppinfrog.com/

If you were to suspect that this brewery with the memorable name might boast of its IBUs, you would be right. Award-winning owner and brewmaster Fred Karm exercises a generous hand with hops. If there were a Cy Young award for pitching hops, he would win. The result since the brewery's founding in 2006? Multiple awards from the Great American Beer Festival (GABF) and the World Beer Cup and ardent customers in twenty states and fifteen countries. In 2013, the brewery was ranked among the world's top twenty by RateBeer. com. With the opening of a tasting room in June 2013, the brewery's draw has grown even stronger. Like the changing lineup of beers—both Hoppin' Frog and an inspired selection of guest beers—the dishes turned out by the tasting room's small but creative kitchen change with the season, draw on local ingredients, and offer no more variety than is consistent with high quality.

Flanked by brewers Zachary Bastin (*left*) and Lee Gidley (*right*), Hoppin' Frog's Fred Karm raises a Hoppin' to Heaven IPA.

The Beers

"Our pride and joy," the brewery proclaims of its beers. There are nine year-round brews listed on the brewery's Web site. Not all are aimed at hopheads, but most are as assertive within their styles as their lengthy labels and detailed descriptions suggest. The most well known may be **Hoppin' to Heaven India Pale Ale** (ABV 6.8 percent, IBUs 68). Not particularly challenging within its category, this ale nevertheless pleases by balancing a range of American hops well grounded in a full malt presence. If you want challenge, try instead the **Mean Manalishi Double India Pale Ale** (ABV 8.2 percent, IBUs 168). Although IBUs should be interpreted with caution, that figure is not a misprint. "Explore the extremes of hops," the brewery invites. Perhaps surprisingly, the astonishing hoppy edge finds a match of sorts in the caramelized malts that are used to smooth what could otherwise be a rough ride.

As its name suggests, **Café Silk Porter** (ABV 6.2 percent, IBUs 26) specializes in smoothness. The style once created to slake the thirst of laborers proves an ideal vehicle for a blend of chocolate and coffee flavors and aromas. If you like porters but have found execution inconsistent from brewery to brewery, you will enjoy this one especially. A less complex but no less enjoyable version? There's **Silk Porter** (ABV 6.2 percent, IBUs 26), where the emphasis falls more directly on the malts selected and roasted to honor the British tradition. In their review for the July 2015 issue of *Beer Advocate*, Jason and Todd Alström observe that "the silkiness of this beer rounds out its brashness."

Why not jump at this point to the imperial stouts? There are three served year-round, and any one of them will justify your visit: **Barrel Aged D.O.R.I.S.**

Silhouetted against the afternoon sun, beer fans cool off with Hoppin' Frogs' brews.

[Double Oatmeal Russian Imperial Stout] **the Destroyer** (ABV 10.5 percent, IBUs 70), **B.O.R.I.S.** [Bodacious Oatmeal Russian Imperial Stout] **the Crusher** (ABV 9.4 percent, IBUs 60), and the **Barrel Aged B.O.R.I.S. the Crusher** (ABV 9.4 percent, IBUs 60). Hoppin' Frog's descriptions offer fair warning: "The Crusher" will "crush you like no other," while "The Destroyer" will "overwhelm, satisfy, and destroy your taste buds like no other." But you don't have to be a masochist to enjoy these trend-setting beers. You simply need the patience to cool (not chill!) the beer properly, to pour it with care, and to sip it slowly.

One of the most memorable beers in my sixteen-month beer pilgrimage was **King Gose Home** (ABV 6.0 percent, IBUs 9), a sharp departure from the Frog's heavily hopped beers in favor of a unique German style. Gose beer, associated with Saxony in eastern Germany, is distinctive for its yellow translucence, its avoidance of bitterness, and, above all, an odd but appealing tang recalling the salinity of the local water first used to brew the beer. A rough analogy for its sweet/sour/salty balance? Perhaps a margarita. Of course, the name offers another of the Frog's puns by celebrating the return to Northeast Ohio of, shall we say, a prominent basketball player.

Seasonals include the Frosted Frog Christmas Ale (ABV 8.6 percent, IBUs 12), which also comes in a barrel-aged version, two varieties of pumpkin ale (one barrel aged), a fresh and straightforward take on summery shandy, and an Oktoberfest lager. Specialty ales include experiments with cherries, vanilla beans, a rye IPA, a Belgian ale, and a wet-hopped imperial Pale Ale. Frogs can be slippery. There one moment, gone the next. So check out the Web pages (year-round, seasonals, specialty, vintage specialty) that describe Hoppin' Frog's many beers (http://www.hoppinfrog.com/brewery/beers) and catch them when you can.

The Food

"Small but effective"—thus Hoppin' Frog describes its kitchen. And distinctive, the Frog might add. For one thing, there are no fried or grilled foods. That means the predictable list of burgers is nowhere to be found. Instead, as one seasonal menu suggests, there may be rosemary and roasted pine nut hummus, a candied pecan berry salad, an original version of a Cuban sandwich with house-made mustard, brisket sliders with barbecue sauce made from B.O.R.I.S. (see above), and a "Crusher Ice Cream Cake." As is the case with many brewery restaurants, the Tasting Room aims to appeal by using local ingredients as much as possible. One note: Hoppin' Frog does not sell food for takeout.

Newsworthy

Since its founding, Hoppin' Frog has won awards consistently. The influential Web site RateBeer.com, which reflects the preferences of customers rather than the reviews of critics, has shown a particular interest in what's going on in southeast Akron. In 2014, the Frog took the top lily pad: top brewer, top brewery, and top taproom in Ohio. And D.O.R.I.S. (see above) was picked as Ohio's top beer. • In late 2014 Fred Karm indicated that he would brew five-gallon test batches for the evaluation of his tasting room patrons. • In early 2015, RateBeer included Hoppin' Frog among the top one hundred brewers in the world and pronounced B.O.R.I.S. (see above) Ohio's top beer. • The GABF has offered recognition as well: gold medals for B.O.R.I.S. the Crusher in 2008 and 2011 and a bronze medal in 2013. Barrel-aged B.O.R.I.S. earned a gold medal at the 2012 World Beer Cup and a bronze medal at the 2013 GABF. A highly decorated brewer!

Other Stuff

See the dedicated tasting room Web site (http://www.hoppinfrog.com/tasting-room) for special events. There are many—including, recently, Live Music Mondays. On the one night of the week when most music venues are dark (and if there's no private party scheduled), HF invites local or regional bands to play a couple of sets starting around 7:30. • There's a daily "hoppy" hour (3:00 P.M.–7:00 P.M. weekdays, noon–3:00 P.M. Saturdays), and weeknights are special: "Tower" Tuesdays (featuring innovative beer infusions), $5 pint Wednesdays, "Vinyl" Thursdays (for spinning oldies), Feature Fridays (focused on selected guest beers), and New Release Saturdays (introducing new guest beers). • The Tasting Room is available for private parties on Mondays. • There is a broad range of Hoppin' Frog merchandise available at the gift shop, from wall signs to dog collars. Frame your license plate with a frog!

THE SKINNY

LOCATION	Located in southeast Akron just off U.S. 224 within view of the gigantic blimp hanger. The hanger is one of the largest structures without interior braces or columns in North America.
HOURS	Tue–Wed 3:00–10:00 P.M. • Thu–Fri 3:00–11:00 P.M. • Sat noon–11:00 P.M. CLOSED SUNDAY.
PARKING	Could hardly be easier. Plenty of space outside. But watch your footing if it's dark.
KIDS	The Tasting Room restricts admission to customers twenty-one and over.
TAKEOUT	There is a selection of Hoppin' Frog beers in twenty-two-ounce bottles. No growlers.
DISTRIBUTION	You will find the Frog's distinctive twenty-two-ounce bottles through a twenty-state region.

LAGER HEADS SMOKEHOUSE & BREWERY

2832 Abbeyville Road and 325 West Smith Road, Medina, Ohio 44256

330–725–1947 • http://www.info@lagerheads.us/

First there was barbecue—meats smoked on the premises over hickory and served with a secret sauce. That was in 2004. But we cannot live by barbecue alone. There must be beer! The owners, two brothers, Matt and Jon Kiene, had become serious home brewers by that time. So they decided to open the Lager Heads Smokehouse & Brewery. They sought and received good advice on starting up a brewery and were able to locate and purchase a good used brewing system in California. Its first pints in 2010 prompted a difficult question. Should you go to Abbeyville (rural Medina) for the barbecue or for the beer? The answer: both! Now there's an even more difficult question: Lunch or dinner at the Abbeyville Road location or taste a few beers in downtown Medina?

The environment at the Abbeyville Road location is "down home," a comfortable building with original beams harkening back to the nineteenth century. There is a long bar, tables, and a separate dining room. Even the parking lot is inviting because of the good smells of the hickory smoking that's going on. The downtown location may not be as venerable, but it offers a comfortable space to sample the Lager Heads' brews.

Lager Heads owner Matt Kiene (center) and brewers Tom Robbins (left) and Joseph Andrea enjoy wet-hopped Harvest Ale.

The Beers

As its name suggests, even with its once-limited (and now expanded) brewing capacity Lager Heads has not limited its brewing to ales. While not all of its beers are available on tap at any one time, there is usually a good balance of lagers and ales.

One of the staples, **Barnburner Lager** (ABV 6 percent, IBUs 27), should please anyone making the climb from mass-produced to craft beers. While it in no way challenges a beginner's palate, it will interest even a veteran. Even more than ales, lagers must be brewed with great care. Because a false note that might pass unnoticed in a big, hoppy ale will rise to the surface in an inexpert lager, Lager Heads' expertise and care are especially welcome. The same attention to detail informs their **Bed Head Red** (ABV 5.9 percent, IBUs 28), a smooth brew with lustrous color.

Their **Oktoberfest** (ABV 6.0 percent, IBUs 28) is well worth an afternoon's serious commitment. Many Oktoberfest beers are enjoyable in the context of fall weather and harvest celebrations. This is one that could be enjoyed all year long. Perhaps Lager Heads should make it available under a different name the rest of the year. The **High Five IPA** (ABV 7.5 percent, IBUs 100) is described by the brewery as "a very citrusy West Coast style."

Two Lager Heads beers available in fall 2014 were astonishing. The first, a **Harvest Ale** (ABV 5.5 percent, IBUs 35), had been brewed with fresh hops picked from vines that grow on the brewery's western wall. The word is that wet-hopped ales are an acquired taste. Nonsense. This

A couple of guests join the Lager Heads house taps.

fresh-tasting ale offers sunshine in a glass. Lovely. The other was an **Imperial Stout** (ABV 10 percent, IBUs 54) that had been aged for five months in bourbon barrels. This is a magical beer. Some ales aged in barrels emerge tasting like a poorly mixed whiskey and soda. Not this one. This is above all a well-brewed stout, with plenty of weight. The bourbon aging adds nuance without dominating. There may be other varieties available when you visit. As always, check the Web site.

The Food

Lager Heads *Smokehouse* is above all a barbecue restaurant—a serious one. "All pulled pork and beef brisket is hand rubbed and slowly cooked in our smoker for up to 14 hours." But that does not mean a limited menu. There are creative appetizers such as abbey cakes (similar to crab cakes but made with pulled pork mixed with peppers, onions, and cheese, breaded and fried) and boar tales (rolled tortillas stuffed with beef brisket and cheese, then fried). Wings can be ordered with a choice among thirteen sauces. Sandwiches feature barbecue, of course, but there are also burgers, a BLT, a tuna wrap, a fish sandwich, and the like. Dinner portions feature St. Louis-style ribs, pork loin, steaks, smoked chicken, and a Southern-style brisket with onion rings and gravy.

Ribs, greens, and cornbread demand a Lager Heads beer.

Newsworthy

In early 2014 Lager Heads announced plans to move much of its production to a separate site in downtown Medina and to open a tasting room at that site. About a year later, the move was complete. Although the brewery was doing considerable bottling and distribution before the move, the expansion allows for as much as a doubling of volume (from two thousand barrels a year to four thousand) and for expanded public access in the tasting room. Many more beer drinkers will be able to become "lager heads." • Lager Heads won its first GABF medal in 2015, a bronze for Smokie Robbins, a smoke beer.

Other Stuff

There were no scheduled tours of the Abbeyville brewing facility, but the relocation of much of Lager Heads' brewing to downtown Medina may change that. • Lager Heads will cater your party with its pulled pork, beef brisket, wings, ribs, and side items. • There are specials every day, from wings on Monday, to hickory-smoked prime rib on Saturday. Sundays will get you two bucks off on the full-slab rib dinner. • Their secret barbecue sauce is available in bottles.

LOCATIONS	Abbeyville: Near the intersection of Hamilton Road and Abbeyville Road in Medina, about five miles west of I-71, not far from Rocky River. Downtown Medina: 325 West Smith Road, three blocks southwest of the square, two blocks west of U.S. 42 and Smith.
HOURS	Abbeyville: Mon–Thu 11 A.M.–10 P.M. • Fri–Sat 11 A.M.–12 midnight • Sun 11 A.M.–9 P.M. Downtown: Wed–Sat 4 –10 P.M.
PARKING	Abbeyville: Easy, usually plentiful, but sometimes crowded at peak hours. You may get a whiff of hickory smoke as you park. Downtown: There is a large adjacent lot, but check to be sure.
KIDS	Abbeyville: Yes, no problem. There are special menu items for kids ten and under. Downtown: TBA, but probably not as much their scene.
TAKEOUT	Abbeyville and downtown: Growlers are available.
DISTRIBUTION	Available in bottles throughout much of Ohio north of Columbus and on tap in selected restaurants and bars.

MAIN STREET GRILLE & BREWING COMPANY

8148 Main Street, Garrettsville, Ohio 44231

330-527-3663 • http://www.msg-brew.com/

Garrettsville is not close to an interstate exit, and any route you take will be a bit indirect. "Not to worry," as a British barman might say, because Garrettsville is well worth visiting. The lovely Headwaters Trail for hiking and biking, a "rails to trails" conversion from the former Cleveland-Mahoning Railroad, links the town with Mantua to the west. There's a picturesque boardwalk that follows Silver Creek (or Eagle Creek, depending on your map) through the town. You will find also a small, well-stocked bookstore, antique shops, and a marker indicating the birthplace of American poet Hart Crane. Do you recall how much James A. Garfield accomplished during just two hundred days in office? I thought not. So you should visit the Historical Society dedicated to the nation's twentieth president. Oh, yes! Thanks to Pete and Peggy Kepish, founders and owners, there is also a superb brewpub at the heart of Garrettsville. The town formed around a grist mill powered by the creek, and that mill, now restored, houses the Main Street Grille & Brewing Company.

Garrettsville's mill on the creek lives again—this time as a brewery.

The Beers

Working with a small (but highly polished!) brewing system, Main Street offers a generous selection of house brews. I enjoyed the sampler, which appears in the accompanying photo. (Main Street in turn enjoyed my photo and has used it on their Web page to my delight.)

The **Edelweiss Hefeweizen** (ABV 5.2 percent, IBUs 26), which is made with local honey, offers a pleasing variation on what are often fairly "yeasty" wheat beers. It is appealingly crisp and fruity—a lithe fräulein, not a sturdy *Hausmädchen*. **Garrett's Gold Kölsch** (ABV 3.9 percent, IBUs 9), inspired by Köln's signature brew, offers eastern Germany's answer to southern Germany's wheat beer. While either might appeal to a visitor

Main Street's sampler arrives as a big wheel—or part of one.

unfamiliar with craft brewing, both have enough personality to interest an afficianado. Indeed, this Kölsch is one of Ohio's most appealing interpretations of this tradition.

River Rat Irish Red (ABV 5.2 percent, IBUs 22) offers a reminder that the line between "amber ale" and "red ale" may be indistinct. Who cares? This delicious beer draws on a broad palette of malts, roasted and crystal(izing), and of hops, German and U.S., to achieve a delicate balance. The **Progress Porter** (ABV 5.0 percent, IBUs N/A) I tasted had won a medal at the 2010 World Beer Championships, and I could understand why. Collaborating at the time with a Northeast Ohio coffeehouse, Main Street relied on crushed espresso beans used during the aging process to add rich coffee flavor and aroma to its light porter.

Depending on when you visit, the brewery may also be offering a double oatmeal stout, an IPA, a birch beer (better than the root beer you remember), or, often, a seasonal ale. The one I tried was a Belgian ale brewed with raspberries. What I most liked about **Razzle Dazz-Ale** (ABV 6.0 percent, IBUs N/A) was the subtlety of the fruit. There was a pleasing Belgian edge, just a hint of sourness, informed by—not overwhelmed by—the berries. I wanted to try their WBC medal-winning Scotch ale and a hefty Belgian Trippel (ABV 8.5 percent) brewed with juniper berries and rose hips but reserved that experience for another day.

The Food

Both the lunch and dinner menus have more variety and depth than you might expect. At lunch, you might begin with the nicely seasoned turkey and white bean chili, then enjoy the pot roast sandwich with mashed potatoes and home-style gravy. The pretzel-encrusted chicken and the veal Parmesan also look good. The dinner menu repeats many of the luncheon offerings but adds, for instance, three flatbreads, an interesting High Street Salad, and several entrées, including a ten-ounce sirloin with Asian scallion glaze, pappardelle with crab and corn, a pork osso buco, Main Street Ribs, and a vegetable risotto. Desserts? There's a panna cotta with roasted peaches, a tiramisu with a reduction of porter, and a Real Beer Float. The menu suggests particular beers to accompany your foods, but I suggest that you begin with a beer sampler, then make your own decisions.

Main Street's brewing system reflects why some brewers call tuns "coppers."

Newsworthy

As of early 2015, there were plans afoot for an event that would invite competition from home brewers and celebrate craft beer.

Other Stuff

You will find a special offer just about every day of the week, from a $10 bottle of house wine on Tuesday and all-you-can-eat pasta on Wednesday, to Thursday's burger-and-beer night with $2 house pints and Friday's seafood night. There's an impressive steak at market price on Saturdays, and the dinner menu is available all day on Sundays. There is also a nice selection of memorabilia available at the gift shop.

THE SKINNY

LOCATION	Exit I-80 (Ohio Turnpike) at OH-44. Drive north and turn right on OH-82. In Hiram, follow OH-82 signs with care as route turns south before continuing east to Garrettsville, where it becomes Main Street.
HOURS	Tue–Thu 11:30 A.M.–9:00 P.M. • Fri–Sat 11:30 A.M.–10:00 P.M. • Sun noon–8:00 P.M.
PARKING	Easy parking on the streets of Garrettsville.
KIDS	Yes, indeed.
TAKEOUT	Growler fills are available.
DISTRIBUTION	The brewery did not respond to request for current information.

Laura Isaacs pulls a pint at Market Garden's front bar.

MARKET GARDEN BREWERY

1947 West 25th Street, Cleveland, Ohio 44113

216-621-4000 • http://market-gardenbrewery.com/

NANO BREW CLEVELAND

1859 West 25th Street, Cleveland, Ohio 44113

216-862-6631 • http://nanobrew-cleveland.com

Market Garden's name suggests its distinctive mission: since 2011, this brewery and restaurant, adjacent to Cleveland's celebrated West Side Market, has offered Northeast Ohio its first American Beer Garden. If summers in the garden can be memorable, there's a warm ambience during Cleveland's chilly falls and winters as well. What the name *does not* suggest is the variety of Market Garden operations. It's not easy to summarize a craft brewery that operates four closely adjacent but highly individualized venues that can serve upwards of five thousand patrons on a busy day. There's the principal location (my focus) with an all-season garden, several bars and dining rooms, and the primary (for the moment) craft brewing system. But across the street there's Bar Cento (an Italian bistro), McNulty's Bier Markt (a Belgian beer bar), and an appropriately clandestine downstairs Speakeasy. Just up West 25th from Market Garden you'll find the recently expanded Nano Brew Cleveland, a "neighborhood brewpub" serving food from a distinctive menu and cutting-edge beers from an on-premises one-barrel brewing system. Nano Brew has its own vibe: a warm dining room, a summer roof garden, a discount on beer for helmeted bicycle riders, and a cycle tune-up pad with basic tools. By the time this book is published, MGB's multimillion-dollar production facility—a chilly, drafty hulk of a building when I walked through the construction site in November 2014—should be brewing and packaging beer just a couple of blocks to the east. Although I must concentrate on the two breweries, visitors to Ohio City should take advantage of the opportunity to observe in operation a remarkably multifaceted enterprise.

Brewmaster Andy Tveekrem offers a welcome to Market Garden's Nano Brew.

The Beers

With the exception of Bar Cento (which offers beer but emphasizes a selection of Italian wines), the Market Garden venues emphasize beer. That's not surprising. Brewmaster Andy Tveekrem enjoys a strong reputation not only among Market Garden's customers, but also among the many in the craft brewing community that he has mentored. Andy's "all time beer list" of more than sixty reveals an impressive commitment to innovation and exploration. There are interpretations of nearly every major style, and more than a few have carried a local message. The **7-Day Lager,** for instance, offers a subtle hint that Cleveland's newspaper of record,

Andy Tveekrem enjoys a winter day in the beer garden.

the *Plain Dealer*, should consider resuming *daily* publication and delivery. The **Cleveland Illuminator Doppelbock** celebrates the city's early introduction of street lights, while **St. Emeric's Stout** points to a neighborhood church.

Even more impressive is the broad variety of brews available at any given time, typically twelve to fourteen styles that offer a balance between year-round favorites and seasonal offerings—all unfiltered, all unpasteurized. Sampling a broad range, I found in every Market Garden beer a memorable poise between faithfulness to a style and imagination in its execution. With thanks to MGB founder Sam McNulty for his unerring choices, I will highlight six.

With the snow swirling outside on the occasion of my visit, it might have seemed counterintuitive to begin my sampling with **Pearl Street Wheat** (ABV 5.5 percent, IBUs N/A). (Pearl Street was the original name for what is now West 25th, where Market Garden is located.) But this Hefeweizen is not just for summer anymore. Its pale straw color offers little hint of the complexity to follow. Yes, there is banana on the nose and a hint of citrus as well, but the wheat beer yeast lifts up the taste of the malt. This is a beer that piques your interest while it satisfies your thirst. Move next to a stout? What? Nitro-delivered **St. Emeric Stout** (ABV 4.5 percent, IBUs N/A) will resolve any doubts at first taste. Yes, roasted malts give the beer its darkness and its delicious dry warmth on the back of the tongue, but this silky smooth stout, graced by hints of coffee and chocolate, presents no rough edges anywhere.

Boss Amber Lager (ABV 5.0 percent, IBUs N/A) is yet another MGB beer that a beer fan might suggest to a novice—simple enough to gratify the inexperienced guest, complex enough to interest the host. Like the prize-winning pilsner (see below) this Vienna-style lager honors its model: malt makes a profound impact, but noble hops lift the palate to a nice balance. The **Fall Porter** (ABV 7.0 percent, IBUs N/A) offers consolation for days growing shorter—not by any particular innovation but by hewing to the best characteristics of this workingman's pick-me-up. Some might ask about the ABV in a style ordinarily brewed to an ABV more in the neighborhood of 5.0, but in this instance the alcohol allows an attractive but not overbearing taste of well-browned toast to prevail in a beer that resolutely avoids heaviness. **Old School American Lager** (ABV 4.5 percent, IBUs N/A) honors a pre-Prohibition recipe. So how does MGB's lightest beer differ from post-Prohibition mass-marketed lagers? The floral hops offer an initial impression of quality—and of restraint—while a subtle bitterness exceeds what might be expected. Even if this beer stands in the shade of its MGB colleagues, it clearly is worth the effort. Such beers are a part of our heritage and deserve faithful execution from time to time.

It is not difficult to understand why **Progress Pilsner** (ABV 5.0 percent, IBUs N/A) won a medal at the 2013 GABF. At that competition the international judging panels consider above all a beer's faithfulness to its style, and this careful balancing of German noble hops with a solid malt base should have pleased them. It pleased me. The beer's name is yet another of MGB's nods to a sense of place. Cleveland's slogan, "progress and prosperity," might just as well describe MGB's strategic plan.

Several other beers deserve brief mention: **Cluster Fuggle IPA, Viking Pale Ale** (a shout-out to Cleveland State but also a reminder that Andy Tveekrem impresses new acquaintances as the "striking Viking"), and **Hop Drive,** a session IPA at ABV 5.4 percent.

Nano Brew is above all an inviting beer bar with a well-chosen list of guest beers and a few house styles brewed using the small resident system. So

Market Garden founder Sam McNulty sets out an array of samples.

there are two kinds of excitement. One is to be found in discovering among the guest taps a remarkable beer that you have not experienced. The other arises from exploring with the brewers the opportunities for innovation and experimentation a small system offers. The experience of Market Garden is one of enjoying masters at work. That of the expanding Nano Brew is one of tasting history (perhaps) being made.

Finally, I want to acknowledge the assistance of brewmaster Tveekren in my effort to create a Word List entry for IBUs. His memorable phrase, "*imaginary* bitterness units," offers a reminder that such figures are often misleading if not meaningless. For the sake of consistency, the N/A abbreviation used in all other profiles to indicate information not available appears above. But in this instance N/A doesn't mean "not available" or "not applicable." It means "never ask."

The Food

The beer menu has the starring role at Market Garden, but executive chef Andrew Bower makes sure that the kitchen qualifies as a strong supporting actor. Like many other brewpubs (MGB prefers "gastropub"), this one pursues an emphasis on local sourcing whenever possible and on the judicious integration of brewing ingredients in food preparation. In fact, during the growing season some of the produce comes from just down the street at the Ohio City Farm. Sponsored in part by MGB, it is among the largest urban farms in the United States. The MGB menu is not the broadest among Ohio's brewpubs, but it is one of the more interesting. There's a local favorite, for instance, cheddar and potato pierogies, but there's also the classic staple of British pub lunches, a Scotch egg. Beer cheese soup features the brewery's Hop Drive Session IPA and is served with barbecue popcorn. Brunch, served from 10 A.M. to 3 P.M. on Sundays, nicely straddles morning and midday with fried chicken waffles, pastrami hash, and, with a view northward across Lake Erie, breakfast poutine.

With its recent expansion, the kitchen at Nano Brew can offer a wider menu. But faithful patrons may be excused for hoping that the creative buzz of the kitchen's early period will continue. There's the Acid Trip burger given its zing by pickled onions and a balsamic reduction, for instance, or a veggie burger based on the Southern favorite, Hoppin' John (black-eyed peas). There's a refreshing lack of formality, but if you're looking here for good food, you will not be hungry when you leave.

Newsworthy

The contributions MGB's different enterprises are making to Cleveland and its Ohio City neighborhood are the stuff of headlines, but the building of a production brewery on West 24th (the former Culinary Market Building) represents a significant leap forward. • Collaborations with other breweries on beers and events also deserve and receive notice. • On the other end of the spectrum, Nano Brew's expansion is always good for an oxymoron: "mega nano" (a coinage attributed to brewmaster Tveekrem), "macro micro," etc. • MGB's hosting a craft beer and home-brewing course offered by Cuyahoga Community College has to be good copy, and a certificate program on brewing and fermentation science is in the works with Cleveland State.

Other Stuff

Located just across the Carnegie Avenue Bridge from downtown Cleveland, Progressive Field, and the Quicken Loans Arena, Market Garden rarely misses an opportunity to respond to an event or throw a party. When there's a fresh beer to release, a season opener to celebrate, or a collaboration to roll out, there's an event. By the way, "collaboration" refers not only to Market Garden's partnering with other breweries—though it is a leader in this regard. You can enlist MGB in planning and hosting your event or party.

THE SKINNY FOR MARKET GARDEN

LOCATION	Follow the signs to Progressive Field, then turn onto the Carnegie Avenue Bridge. Once across the bridge, look for the West Side Market. Turn right on West 25th Street at the corner of the market and you will be in front of the brewery.
HOURS	11:00 A.M.–2:30 A.M. every day.
PARKING	There is a sizable municipal lot just to the east (toward the downtown skyline) of the brewery and a commercial lot just down the street at West 26th. The city lot is not available on a game day. You can avoid having to park by riding RTA's Red Line to the West 25th/Ohio City station.
KIDS	For lunch or an early dinner, why not? Later on in the evening, why?
TAKEOUT	Fill a growler.
DISTRIBUTION	With the opening of MGB's new "Palace of Fermentation" (the working name for the production brewery under construction) distribution will begin in earnest.

THE SKINNY FOR NANO BREW

LOCATION	First locate Market Garden, as suggested above. Then drive or walk one block north (moving away from the West Side Market). You have found it.
HOURS	Mon–Thu 4:30 P.M.–2:30 A.M. • Fri–Sat 11:00 A.M.–2:30 A.M. • Sun 10:00 A.M.–2:30 A.M.
PARKING	See above. There are several lots adjacent to Nano Brew. Ask about accessibility.
KIDS	The same questions apply as at MGB, but there is a giant jenga (stackable blocks) setup that kids love.
TAKEOUT	Growlers.
DISTRIBUTION	See above.

ROCKY RIVER BREWING COMPANY

21290 Center Ridge Road, Cleveland, Ohio 44116

440-895-2739 • http://rockyriverbrewco.com/

The idea for an exceptional neighborhood restaurant came first. Then, before the opening, co-owner Gary Cintron had another idea. Having found inspiration in a visit to Cincinnati's Main Street Brewery, he decided to make the restaurant really special by incorporating a brewery. His brother and coinvestor, Bob, agreed. Main Street Brewery closed in 1999, sad to say, but its spirit lives on at Rocky River Brewing Company. Founded in 1998, well before the onset of the more recent proliferation of breweries, Rocky River soon won over a loyal local clientele, which has enabled it to weather the ups and downs of the industry and to experience sustained growth in quality and reputation. More recently, it has won its share of national and international medals. But the beer is only part of the story. As a glance at the Rocky River menu will suggest, the restaurant is no less aspirational—and no less worth a visit. Though "synergy" is a word often overused these days, there's no other that better describes the comfortable, enjoyable experience Rocky River offers its visitors.

The Beers

Because Rocky River's small brewing plant limits the range of brews available at any one time, the usual caveat—check the Web site before you go—is important. But there's always something good to drink, and there's never any question about freshness: once brewed, the beer moves to serving vessels visible just behind the bar, ready to be poured.

A leisurely afternoon at Rocky River.

Examples of what you might find on your visit include American blond ale **Pirate Light** (ABV 4.6 percent, IBUs 21). It could offer an "entry-level" beer to a prisoner of industrial brewing looking for an escape route. **Cooper's Gold Kolsch** (ABV 5.0 percent, IBUs 27), an alt-style German ale, uses German hops to provide an interesting edge to its layers of malt taste.

There must be a railroad fan in the brewery, because two of Rocky River's most distinctive beers have names that summon up the Nickel Plate Road, a line that once connected Cleveland to Buffalo and Chicago and that took its name from an offhand comment in a Norwalk, Ohio, newspaper. The **Nickel Plate Porter** (ABV 5.0 percent, IBUs 50) is outstanding. It offers medium-roast coffee to the nose and a characteristic rich sweetness at first taste, but finishes with a lingering, highly satisfying bitterness thanks to Northern Brewer and Crystal hops. The other Nickel Plate beer, **Loco #765** (ABV 7.5 percent, IBUs 55), runs through the English countryside. Brewed with Kent Golding hops, it's an IPA that impresses more through its lovely floral aroma than through its bitterness. It *is* an IPA, but a particularly amiable one.

The Nickel Plate beers find their contrast in **Hop Goblin** (ABV 7.6 percent, IBUs 67.5), an IPA that takes its inspiration (and its hops) from the U.S. West Coast. As you detect Centennial and Simcoe, ask head brewer Jim Lieb to give you the full rundown. Finally, there's the threatening sound of **Punch in the Nuts** (ABV 5.3 percent, IBUs 20.8). But this amber ale brewed with peanut butter could not be less threatening.

Every day is special at Rocky River.

The peanuts appeal mostly to the nose. The overtones of peanut taste, while enjoyable, do not get in the way of the beer's drinkability.

The Food

The kitchen will never attract notice for its pretension. You won't be presented an amuse-bouche. But you will find an ample menu with familiar pub favorites—and a few special dishes as well. Among the appetizers, to choose one example, you find not the usual chips, but potato chips laced with fresh rosemary and other seasonings. The customary nachos? Rocky River's transnational fusion is its biggest seller: chicken marinated in Thai spices, mozzarella cheese, and wasabi sour cream. The Cobb Salad, which usually features chicken, here combines blackened tuna with the familiar blue cheese, hard-boiled eggs, and bacon.

Sandwiches reveal the same balance of the familiar and the creative. Consider ale-battered grouper, or chicken topped with bacon, Gouda, and fresh arugula, or the Ricky Ricardo, Rocky River's interpretation of a Cuban sandwich, with sliced pork loin, ham, and melted cheese on focaccia. Burgers? Again, the usual and the unusual. Among the latter? A Chorizo burger built on ground beef mixed with house-made sausage and served with cheddar, avocado, and remoulade sauce.

Entrées display corresponding cross-cultural inspirations. Lake Effect Chili (turkey chili with pasta and cheddar) offers an interesting variation on the classic Cincinnati theme, while Louisiana Jambalaya blends andouille, chicken, and shrimp. You can visit Thailand (Pad Thai), Jamaica (Calypso Chicken), and St. Louis (Baby Back Ribs) without leaving the dining room.

Newsworthy

Rocky River has been a regular—and a very successful—entrant in the Great American Beer Festival, the World Beer Cup, and other competitions. Among its most notable awards are a 2006 GABF gold medal for its Mexicali Smoke and a 2004 gold medal for its Kohlminator Bock at the World Beer Cup in San Diego.

Other Stuff

Rocky River offers special events on holidays such as Halloween, New Year's Eve, and St. Patrick's Day. • There are electronic games in a couple of corners. • The brewery and restaurant caters special events in its large dining room and, when the weather permits, on its patio. In the summer, the patio sometimes offers a steel drummer. • A small beer truck called the Micro Woodie—well, let RRBC offer the invitation: "Select your beers and we will deliver the Woodie to you, ready to party. We park it and you pour it! And when your party is over, we will come back and pick it up."

THE SKINNY

LOCATION	Center Ridge Road (U.S. 20) runs parallel to and south of I-90, just to the west of Rocky River and the Valley Parkway. You can reach the brewery in less than fifteen minutes from downtown Cleveland.
HOURS	Open every day from 11:30 A.M. to "at least 11:00 P.M.," depending on what's happening.
PARKING	There's plenty on the right side of the building (as you face north) and in the back.
KIDS	Yes, there's a menu for kids—and a welcoming family atmosphere.
TAKEOUT	Growler fills and kegs are available. Principally a brewer for its own premises, Rocky River recently has begun limited canning.
DISTRIBUTION	The brewery is considering keg distribution to key local areas.

WILLOUGHBY BREWING COMPANY
4057 Erie Street, Willoughby, Ohio 44094
440-975-0202 • http://willoughbybrewing.com/

In 1926, Willoughby's role as a prominent interurban station and service depot ended when the last car of the Cleveland, Painesville & Eastern rolled to a stop. Employees of the line later collaborated on a nostalgic song:

> Let us all turn back to the bull pen,
> And dream of Willoughby,
> The yarns they told, they could never grow old,
> With the days of the C, P & E.

As the lyric suggests, Willoughby was an important station for passengers traveling east from Cleveland. They could ride as far as Painesville on the C, P & E, then on to Ashtabula on the Cleveland, Painesville & Ashtabula.

The Willoughby Brewing Company remains a prominent station stop for thirsty (and hungry) travelers. Located on Erie Street, where the tracks of the C, P & E remain beneath the pavement, the brewpub operates in the rail line's restored maintenance facility. The cranes that lifted the interurban cars are still visible overhead. Craft brewer Rick Seibt, who signed on in 2011 as this train's conductor, brings to his leadership both the passion of craft brewing and the savvy of many years' experience as an IT project manager. He thus began his engagement with the brewery by developing the twenty-eight-page strategic plan

that continues to guide its growth. He is both the driving force behind Willoughby and its public face. He enjoys representing the brewery in the community as much as planning for its even more vigorous future, which is likely to include, he says, a production brewery located apart from the mainline station.

The Beers
Within the past three years, Willoughby has reassembled its extensive manifest of house beers in favor of a more traditional and consistent lineup. Seibt describes himself as "a fan of

Willoughby's Rick Seibt offers a Willoughby Wheat in the hops garden.

Willoughby offers two spaces for outdoor dining (and drinking).

drinkable beer." From the thirty-five beers that may appear from time to time, Willoughby generally makes eight to ten available on draft.

At the top of the list—alphabetic order or no—stands the brewery's most widely known product, the **Peanut Butter Cup Coffee Porter** (ABV 5.5 percent, IBUs 30). Conceived as an interesting experiment, this remarkable beer soon established itself as a prizewinner, a customer favorite, and a go-to beer for special occasions. It has evolved into an in-demand staple on the brewpub's list that you have to try at least once. Built in stages, the beer begins life as a forthright porter that provides a platform for surprisingly compatible infusions. The first is coffee, "roasted locally." The second is "peanut butter and chocolate." Here's the pitch: "Some people say they taste more coffee than peanut butter, others say the opposite. Which is it you taste?" To find out, you will want to go to the brewpub, because the beer is not (yet) bottled or canned—other than in the thirty-two-ounce cans mentioned below. No beer will appeal to every drinker, but it is difficult to argue with the success of the 2014 World Beer Cup gold award winner for specialty beer. (*Men's Journal* includes the beer in a list of the 100 Best Beers in the World!)

The other cars on this train show a wide variety of styles, including blonde ales, German lagers, Belgian brews, and a range of IPAs, brown and red ales, stouts, and Scottish ales. I sampled six during my visit. The **Downtown Willoughby Brown** (ABV 5.4 percent, IBUs 22), a classic U.K. style, offers a lighter, more versatile approach to the familiar oatmeal stout. The version aged on Cacao nibs adds an interesting dimension to an otherwise straightforward (but satisfying) beer. **Rosana Red Rye Ale** (ABV 5.8 percent, IBUs 26) is indeed *red*, a beer that makes its first impression by its color and clarity. The taste confirms that impression. Through the pleasing balance of base malt and hops the interesting bite of the rye malt emerges. A snapshot from early 2015 would also include **Snowbelt** (a Helles Weizenbock), **Kaiserhof** (a beautifully nuanced Kölsch), **Cosmic IPA** (bracingly bitter but not incapacitating at 6.5 percent, IBUs 58), and **Gutterpup,** which the brewery labels a "robust porter." As the list changes often, be sure to review the current lineup at the brewpub's Web site.

The Food

The dining car on this brew train doubtless surpasses anything that might have been available on the C, P & E. "Shareables" include "brew-wings," brewery pretzels, and, in a nod to the Belgian brewing tradition, "waffle pomme frites." "Handhelds" feature a Lake Erie perch po-boy (properly spelled for once), a prime rib French dip, and veggie burger sliders that a carnivore would enjoy. A "build your own" mac and cheese option anchors the menu with seven meat options and an equal number of veggie choices. At the even more ambitious end of the menu there are, for instance, a twelve-ounce Angus sirloin, citrus-glazed salmon, and a splendid local take on fish and chips, Crispy Perch Bite Baskets with waffle fries. Pizzas, salads, sides, and "chef's creations" such as empanadas and bratwurst corndogs round out the menu.

Newsworthy

In summer 2014, Willoughby took home the boxing glove from the Heavyweight Brewers' Brawl sponsored by Fat Head's. The winner? Nut Smasher, a peanut butter imperial stout that clocks in north of 11 percent ABV. • In early 2015, Willoughby attracted notice as the first craft brewer in Northeast Ohio to package beer in thirty-two-ounce cans, the so-called "Crowler." • In 2014 Willoughby marketed a spring 2015 brewery-sponsored tour of Germany pitched specifically to beer drinkers. • Stay tuned for plans to open a production brewery off-site.

Other Stuff

Willoughby maintains an active calendar that includes special meals, bottle releases, and other events. You can rent either the lounge or the banquet room and choose a menu for your occasion.

LOCATION	On I-271N approaching its intersection with I-90E, stay in the right lane and exit to SOM Center Road. Turn right to go north on SOM Center and turn right on Euclid (U.S. 20), which becomes Erie Avenue. In downtown Willoughby, turn right on Glenn and look for Willoughby at the end of a large lot on your left.
HOURS	Mon–Thu 11:00 A.M.–10:00 P.M. (kitchen) midnight (bar) • Fri–Sat 11:00 A.M.–11:00 P.M. (kitchen) 2:00 A.M. (bar) • Sun noon–9:00 P.M. (kitchen) midnight (bar)
PARKING	There is limited parking in a large shared lot in front of the brewpub, additional parking in nearby lots, and valet service—which may be your best option on a busy weekend evening.
KIDS	Absolutely! Kids will love the train rolling along overhead. And there's a kids' menu.
TAKEOUT	Growler fills are available—as well as the above-mentioned "crowlers."
DISTRIBUTION	In addition to the thirty-two-ounce cans mentioned above and occasional other cannings, Willoughby sometimes sells on site twenty-two-ounce bottles of specialty beers. Because the problem has been one of capacity, an expanded off-site brewing system should encourage expanded distribution.

TAPROOMS

JAFB BREWERY

120 Beall Avenue, Wooster, Ohio 44691

330-601-1827 • http://www.jafbwooster.com/

Wooster? Yes, it's the home of a highly regarded private college, but it's in the hinterlands—roughly equidistant from the metropolises of Mansfield and Massillon. No matter. A good brewery requires someone who loves beer, takes beer making seriously, does the homework, pays the dues,

Laura, Autumn Rose, and Adriane (*left to right*) enjoy JAFB brews.

discovers a location, and finds the backing. That would be Paul Fryman. The love of beer came easily during Paul's undergraduate years, which included a semester in Lancaster, England, and a senior thesis on U.S. microbrewing. Paul then paid his dues at Great Divide (Denver), Great Adirondack Brewing (New York), and Snake River Brewing (Jackson Hole, Wyoming) before returning to Great Adirondack as head brewer. From there in 2011 he returned to his hometown, Wooster, to open a brewery in partnership with his father and brother.

Its location is a landmark building that once served as the home of a manufacturer of high-end horse-drawn carriages. JAFB has restored the handsome structure by sandblasting the brick walls, removing the dropped ceiling, and repairing the large industrial windows. The result is a large, comfortable taproom with family-style tables hand-hewn by the brewmaster's father, Jerry Fryman. In fact, with the exception of the windows, the Fryman family members (Paul, brother Tony, father Jerry) did just about all of the restoration work themselves.

Jerry had a vision: "a different style of lifestyle in a bar." In an increasingly fragmented society, a good brewpub can offer an enjoyable environment in which people can enjoy one another's company, he explains. "Every small community deserves a craft brewery," he says.

The Beers

In keeping with its comfortable space, which invites customers to linger awhile, most of JAFB's beers post modest ABV percentages. But there's nothing modest about the spectrum of their beers, from the "everyday" (JAFB's chosen adjective) **Wayne Country Cream Ale** (ABV 5.0 percent,

Paul, Laura, and Jerry Fryman toast JAFB's brews and Jerry's wood carving.

IBUs 19) to the singularly assertive **Barrel Aged MFC Abbey Quad** (ABV 10 percent, IBUs 15). One welcomes the newcomer to craft beers and the thirsty traveler on a hot summer day. The other, a Belgian-style beer brewed with Oregon cherries and aged in bourbon barrels for ten months, requires a serious beer fan's full attention.

Other offerings fall somewhere in between. I tasted five. The **Wooster New Stout** (ABV 6.8 percent, IBUs 50) deserves its GABF silver medal. This is a beer with great integrity: its components—roast and chocolate malts with a discernable but unobtrusive hops presence—coalesce gracefully to create a rare balance in this demanding style. Dark and dry, with just enough fruitiness on the margins to be interesting, Wooster New Stout attests to JAFB's craftsmanship. The **New Stunt IPA** (ABV 7.7 percent, IBUs 75+) represents the best kind of controlled brewing experiment: maintain the same barley malts as a control, then modify the hops—New Zealand and Australian as well as American—so as to offer an interesting range, in Paul Fryman's words, of "New World flavors." The New Zealand hops, offering a fresh, verdant impression, were up front when I tasted a sample, offering an inviting aroma when poured and an aggressive but not discouraging bitterness when tasted.

The **Coffee Porter** (ABV 5.8 percent, IBUs 25), which was on nitro when I tasted it, draws its coffee overtones from whole beans (rather than brewed coffee), and the result is a delectable smoothness. Not all beers improve when served through the nitro tap, but this one clearly does. The **Red Ale** (ABV 5.9 percent, IBUs 20) might easily become your steady friend for an afternoon of the NFL or the Premier League. A good partner for food, this traditional German standby (not to be confused with Irish

Bartender K. C. Bockmiller pulls a JAFB Red Ale.

red ale) offers considerably more character than its lighter neighbors without much more alcohol.

The **Roggenbier** (ABV 5.6 percent, IBUs 15) further attests to the brewery's overall orientation toward Europe. One of several rye-based beers now in production in Ohio, JAFB's version begins with balanced rye and pilsner malts and uses Weizen yeast. While some versions lean more toward the simplicity of a Bock, this one may remind Continental beer fans rather of a Doppelbock, a weightier beer with a more pronounced malt presence just right for chilly winter evenings.

The Food

JAFB encourages beer lovers to bring food with them or order food from nearby restaurants that deliver.

Newsworthy

Recent awards include five medals from the GABF: a silver medal for Wooster New Stout (2014), a silver for Great Adirondack Kölsch (2011), a silver for Whiteface Stout (2010), a bronze for Belgian Summer Ale (2010), and a silver for Rain Delay IPA (2015). JAFB is a formidable competitor in this oldest and most authoritative of festivals. JABF also proved a strong competitor in a 2014 judging to choose the best IPA in Ohio. • JAFB's planned expansion into West Salem attracted notice in 2015.

Other Stuff

The name? For the record, let's say the abbreviation signifies "Just Another Friendly Brewery." And JAF IPA? That must mean "Just Another Fine IPA." Right?

THE SKINNY

LOCATION	In the heart of downtown Wooster, about six blocks south of the college.
HOURS	Tue–Thu 4:00–9:00 P.M. (or later, if there's a crowd) • Fri 3:00 P.M.–midnight • Sat 1:00 P.M.–midnight • Sun noon–8:00 P.M.
PARKING	It's easy—and it's free. There are a few spaces just to the right of JAFB along the fence of the power substation, but there are many more in nearby lots. Look for the signs.
KIDS	No reason not to bring them. In a summer 2015 article inspired by a visit to JAFB, Rick Armon observes: "It's not unusual nowadays to see kids, often several of them, hanging out in brewery tasting rooms, as many craft brewers are welcoming babies and toddlers and even encouraging parents to bring them along."
TAKEOUT	Growlers.
DISTRIBUTION	Some of Wooster's watering holes offer JAFB beers on tap. There are no plans at the moment to expand distribution.

THIRSTY DOG BREWING COMPANY

529 Grant St., Akron, Ohio 44311

330-252-2739 • http://http://thirstydog.com

Founder John Najeway (a cofounder of the Ohio Craft Brewers Association) had his tasting epiphany in 1993 at northern Kentucky's Oldenberg Brewery—an early (and, sadly, overambitious for that decade) outpost of the growing craft brewing movement. Having enjoyed home brewing and having observed at Oldenberg the commercial potential in his hobby, he decided to make beer his business. Four years later, he opened the original Thirsty Dog in Canton. Other brewpubs followed. But in 2003 Najeway decided on a different path, production brewing. His new site was Akron's former Burkhardt Brewery—the story mentioned in the introduction to this chapter. (Thirsty Dog can provide a more thorough history of the renovations that began in 2006.) The story ever since has been one of methodical, systematic growth.

In the summer of 2014, Thirsty Dog announced that it might have to move in order to undertake a needed expansion. But good news followed.

John Najeway recalls the historic foundation for today's Thirsty Dog.

Cask ales enjoying secondary fermentation at Thirsty Dog.

Najeway was able to secure adjoining structures that had belonged to the original brewery, historic spaces that now allow Thirsty Dog to grow in several directions. For instance, a dedicated "sours" chamber enables isolated barrel aging of the medieval Belgian ales that are not always good neighbors to more contemporary brews. With the spring 2015 addition of a new bottling line, production capacity has expanded from hundreds of bottles an hour to eight thousand. And there's room for more aging rooms, labs, and storage, and a space for customers.

Now that Thirsty Dog approaches its twentieth birthday, it can boast a history of many beers in many styles, national and international awards, discriminating fans, and a broadening distribution base. Even as the brewery expands in terms of product diversity and distribution, it continues to offer a welcoming ambience and a broad range of changing styles, including some available only on draft.

The Beers

Thirsty Dog advertises "an infinitely complex and thoroughly enjoyable experience." The beers deliver just that—with recipes as distinctive and as inventive as the labels—through a wide variety of styles that continues to develop. With more than sixty beers to consider in Thirsty Dog's brewing history and a current list that may include upwards of twenty varieties available at the taproom and in bottles, you're likely to find several that meet your expectations as well as many that expand your awareness of what brewers can achieve.

As always, my describing a few of the brewery's beers is no guarantee of their availability at any given time in the taproom—or of their place in your grocery's cooler. Be sure to check the brewery's online list before

Citra Dog offers one of Ohio's most striking label designs.

visiting the taproom and keep an eye on the cooler where you shop. My longtime Thirsty Dog favorites are widely available in bottles.

Citra Dog (ABV 6.5 percent, IBUs 95) is an IPA that provides a bracing bitterness made more interesting and accessible by the edgy fruitiness of its iconic hops. Neither exactly British nor exactly West Coast in its lineage, this beer, now Thirsty Dog's most popular, finds a middle ground. Perhaps we should call it "Akron style." **Labrador Lager** (ABV 6 percent, IBUs 22) invites the faint of heart to craft beer while still offering enough interest to please the seasoned beer drinker. A German (rather than American) lager, this is the beer to have on hand for the World Series. Or the World Cup.

The label of **Old Leghumper** (ABV 6.7 percent, IBUs 24) shows a black Lab looking wistfully at a table occupied by three young women: "So many legs . . . So little time." You should make the time for this widely available robust porter. Malts impart character and depth, but hops, not entirely out of the picture, bring discipline to the porter's characteristic sweetness. **Rail Dog Smoked Black Lager** (ABV 6.7 percent, IBUs 24) deserves mention for several reasons. For one thing, the thundering locomotive on the cover of the bottle offers a reminder that Thirsty Dog is a major supporter of the nearby Cuyahoga Valley National Park, home to the Cuyahoga Valley Scenic Railroad. For another, the beer begins with grain roasted in the brewery's own ovens. Grain to be used for the production of an ancillary malt is smoked using apples from the brewer's farm. Most important is the taste. Unlike some German Rauchbiers, which may call to mind a dash of Liquid Smoke™, there is but a wisp of authentic smoke and a hint of chocolate in this smooth lager.

Also available in bottles is Thirsty Dog's **Pumpkin Ale** (ABV 5 percent, IBUs 13.5). This seasonal challenges a popular category by offering above all the taste of good beer, albeit good beer informed by (but not overwhelmed by) flavors of pumpkin, squash, honey, and ginger. Unlike those that may remind you of a slice of pumpkin pie in a glass (not that there's anything wrong with that), this seasonal brew lets you know that fall has arrived without offering you dessert. (As noted below, the pumpkins come from the proprietor's garden.) The **Cerasus Dog Flanders Style Red Ale** (ABV 5 percent, IBUs N/A) may be one of the most flavorful beers on tap anywhere. The wild yeast takes center stage in a beer that lives in oak barrels with Michigan cherries for two years. Interesting and engaging rather than intimidating, this unfiltered brew is a memorable mouthful! Are there some hops on the fringe of the neighborhood? Perhaps.

If space permitted, I would write also of **Twisted Kilt** (ABV 5.3 percent, IBUs 13.5), Thirsty Dog's version of Irish Export Ale, of **Siberian Night** (ABV 9.7 percent, IBUs 58), a huge imperial stout best served in a brandy snifter, or of **Brooklyn Dog** (ABV 4.2 percent, 35 IBUs), a Saison brewed collaboratively with Brooklyn Brewery. But, as the black Lab might say, so many beers, so little space! Finally, there is the annual gift of **12 Dogs of Christmas Ale** (ABV 8.3 percent, IBUs 18.5), distinctive within its popular category for its mix of spices (nutmeg as well as the more familiar cinnamon, ginger, and honey) and for an intriguing aftertaste that suggests a mysterious slant. Perhaps you will be able to solve the mystery.

The Food

Thirsty Dog does not serve food, but it invites patrons to bring food along with them to enjoy with their beer. There are occasionally food trucks parked outside.

Newsworthy

There are too many awards to list them all. Since 1997, Thirsty Dog has won more medals than any other Ohio brewery. And it has done so in the most competitive of venues. The most notable recognition may be that of the 2014 New York International Beer Competition as "USA Brewery of the Year." The brewery also won awards for its Bernese Barley Wine

Mejan and David enjoy the Thirsty Dog ambience.

Ale (double gold), its Wulver (bronze), and its Citra Dog (bronze). • There have been awards also in the World Beer Cup, including a gold medal in 2002 for Old Leghumper and a bronze in 2014 for Siberian Night Imperial Stout. (That beer earned a gold medal from the 2005 GABF.) • In January 2015, RateBeer.com ranked Thirsty Dog among the world's best one hundred breweries. • The New York International Beer Competition named Thirsty Dog its 2015 "Ohio Brewery of the Year" and awarded *five* medals. • A major Washington, D.C., summer festival, "SAVOR," picked Thirsty Dog as Ohio's only representative among the seventy-three breweries served in 2015. This is a hot ticket in the District! • A colorful page on the brewery's Web site provides a continuing update on awards, festivals, and the like.

Other Stuff

Where to begin? Thirsty Dog is the "resident brew" at the Akron Art Museum, perhaps the first relationship of its kind in the nation. • The brewery makes its space available for after-hours rentals. • Committed to being as "green" a brewery as possible, Thirsty Dog reserves its spent grain for the camels, zebras, and other inhabitants of Wagontrails Animal Park in Vienna, Ohio. "We recycle everything," Najeway says. • Najeway grows, harvests, and roasts the pumpkins and other squash that help to flavor the pumpkin ale described above. You get the picture. • Thirsty Dog's Web site list of upcoming events will suggest the range of competitions, engagements, and outreach events this very active brewery pursues. Beer festivals, benefits, beer dinners—you will likely to find an event that interests you. • A gift shop, available both on the premises and via the Web, offers glassware, apparel, and other canine ware.

THE SKINNY

LOCATION	Located in downtown Akron not far from the University of Akron.
HOURS	Wed–Thu, 4:00–8:00 P.M. • Fri 12 noon–8:00 P.M. • Sat 2:00–6:00 P.M.
PARKING	Parallel parking immediately on either side of the Thirsty Dog building and in a lot across the street. Note the signs forbidding parking next to adjacent buildings.
KIDS	Thirsty Dog welcomes kids with root beer brewed on the premises.
TAKEOUT	Growler fills available.
DISTRIBUTION	Through a fourteen-state region, from Illinois and Michigan to New York and South Carolina.

CONSIDER ALSO

THE TAPROOM AT AQUEDUCT BREWING (529 Grant Street, Akron, Ohio 44311) is open every day beginning with the happy hour Monday to Friday and for all afternoon and evening on Saturday and Sunday. The eight or so house beers represent the major varieties, from Honey Whit to Silenus Stout, and they hold to a middle way. While none is really a session beer, none is extreme—even though Silenus, Dionysus's sidekick, is the god of intoxication. ABV levels run from 6.0 percent to 7.5 percent. Don't let the address puzzle you. Aqueduct rents space from Thirsty Dog. The entrance is on the north side of the building. Telephone: 330-606-6583 Web: https://www.facebook.com/AqueductBrewing or https://aqueductbrewing.shutterfly.com/

BLACK BOX BREWING COMPANY (24945 Detroit Road, Westlake, Ohio 44145) distributes its cleverly named beers (My Asis Dragon, a stout; Plumbers Crack, an amber ale, etc.) to restaurants, taverns, and retail outlets throughout Northeast Ohio. The brewery sponsors occasional events, such as the June 2015 Black Box 5K run. Telephone: 440-871-0700 Web: http://bbbrewco.com/

BOTTLEHOUSE BREWERY AND MEADERY (2050 Lee Road, Cleveland Heights, Ohio 44118) is open seven days a week to serve its small-batch beers, a range of house-made meads, and simple fare, including pierogies from Parma and both "classic" and "signature" sandwiches. Telephone: 216-214-2120 Web: http://thebottlehousebrewingcompany.com/

BRICK AND BARREL (1844 Columbus Road, Cleveland, Ohio 44113) shares its focus on quality brewing four days a week, Wednesday to Saturday. The name is mean to signal the brewery's deep engagement with its city, its location within the city, and its affinity "with the gritty, working-man history of our street and neighborhood." The brewer focuses on traditional styles: cask ales, barrel-aged beers, and "Old World" beers." Telephone: 216-331-3308 Web: http://www.brickandbarrelbrewing.com

Having opened as a pizza restaurant, the BRICKOVEN BREWPUB (604 Canton Road, Akron 44312) invited customers to enjoy its craft brews early in 2015. First out of the tap? A cream ale, a witbier, an oatmeal stout, and an IPA. Current information as to what's on tap is posted to Facebook. Telephone: 330-475-7005 Web: http://www.thebrickovenbrewpub.com or https://www.facebook.com/thebrickovenbrewpub

BUCKEYE BEER ENGINE (15315 Madison Avenue, Lakewood, Ohio 44107), a neighborhood restaurant that combines "gourmet burgers" and "gourmet beer," earns this mention for having once been an outlet for the beers of Buckeye Brewing. They're still on tap, but Buckeye Brewing now operates its own tasting room, Tapstack, and the Beer Engine offers a wide range of brews. Note well: there are eighteen different burgers. Eighteen. Telephone: 216-226-BEER Web: http://buckeyebeerengine.com

BUTCHER AND THE BREWER (2043 East Fourth Street, Cleveland, Ohio 44115) offers a popular and thriving neighborhood a distinct Cleveland experience: a menu inspired by the ethnicities and culinary resources of the city paired with brewing grounded in classic techniques but open to innovation. Open Monday through Saturday, the restaurant has plans for a Sunday brunch and the brewer hopes to brew sours. Telephone: 216-331-0805 Web: http://www.butcherandthebrewer.com

CANTON BREWING COMPANY (120 3rd Street NW, Canton, Ohio 44702) was scheduled to open in spring 2015 after debuting some of its beers at a late 2014 tasting. Located a short forward pass from the downtown location where the Pro Football Hall of Fame holds its enshrinement festival, the brewpub in the former McCrory's represents a significant enhancement for its neighborhood: a sizable brewhouse, an open kitchen, a patio on 3rd Street, and a minimuseum recalling when Canton last could boast a brewery. Telephone: N/A Web: http://www.cantonbrewery.com/ and https://www.facebook.com/cantonbrewing

CELLAR RATS (7743 Doty Road, Madison, Ohio 44057) was the first Ohio brewery to open as a scion of a vineyard. Open seven days a week (closed on Mondays in January), the brewery seeks to offer, per its Web site, "fresh, fun and interesting choices." There are many brewing traditions evident in the list, "but we always add our own 'interpretation.'" The location of the brewery close to the heart of Ohio's wine country could inspire an attractive itinerary for a day or weekend. I wonder whether the brewery's name might be meant to echo the German word for "city hall": *Rathaus*. A topic for conversation? Telephone: 440-466-3485 Web: http://ratbrew.com and https://www.facebook.com/pages/Cellar-Rats-Brewery/313055364029

When CHARDON BREW WORKS (200 Center Street, Chardon, Ohio 44024) opened in 2010 it became "the first brewery in Geauga County since Prohibition." A small brewing system turns out five year-round varieties as well as one or two appropriate to the season. For food there's "pub grub" that appears unambitious but inviting. At the corner of Center and Washington. Telephone: 440-286-9001 Web: http://www.chardonbrewworks.com/

The CLEVELAND BREWERY (777 East 185th Street, Cleveland, Ohio 44119) distributes draft beers with resonant local names (Terminal IPA, 185th Street Wheat, Old Stone Black IPA, Lake View Cemetery Pumpkin Ale) to local taverns and restaurants. The brewing system is small but likely to expand and a taproom opened in May 2015. Telephone: 216-534-6992 Web: http://www.theclevelandbrewery.com

GRANITE CITY FOOD & BREWERY (24519 Cedar Road, Lyndhurst, Ohio 44124) offers reliable food and craft beers at this Legacy Village location as part of a thirteen-state franchise. A craft brewer? In a sense. Using a trademarked brewing process called *Fermentus Interruptus*, Granite City creates its worts (see Word List) at a central location for shipment to its restaurants. They complete the brewing process using on-site fermentation tanks. Open seven days. Telephone: 216-297-4495 Web: http://www.gcfb.net/

Part of a growing franchise that "brings Bavaria to you," HOFBRÄUHAUS (1550 Chester Avenue, Cleveland, Ohio 44114) is open seven days a week in the Theater District offering German beer brewed in-house and German food—that is, "an authentic German experience." In May 2015, the brewery opened a spacious Biergarten to complement its large beer hall. Telephone: 216-621-2337 Web: http://www.hofbrauhauscleveland.com/

INDIGO IMP BREWERY, formerly located on Superior Avenue in Cleveland, closed in late summer 2015. A press release announced: "We have determined that the personal effort and investment required to sustain and grow the business is increasingly in conflict with our family life and personal goals." The brewery specialized in ales brewed in open fermenters. This traditional Belgian approach, which encourages wild yeasts to play a role in fermentation, created distinctive flavors. Though the taproom was open only on Fridays, the distinctive bottles had earned a niche on the shelves of upscale grocery stores and other outlets. Any industry as dynamic and as volatile as craft beer will experience closings as well as openings, but this is a loss.

LITTLE MOUNTAIN BREWING COMPANY (7621 Mentor Avenue, Mentor, Ohio 44060) opens Tuesday through Sunday for "classic American pub fare" and hefty house-brewed beers, including a Belgian Tripel at ABV 9 percent and a Russian imperial stout (aptly named KGB) at 10 percent. A brew-on-premises opportunity enables amateurs to use the brewery's professional equipment and recipes as well as guidance. Telephone: 440-256-1645 Web: http://littlemountainbrewing.com

LUCKY OWL (8660 Tamarack Trail, Chagrin Falls, Ohio 44023) brewed its first beer on Christmas Eve 2014. "It's in the fermenter and up to the yeast now," the brewery posted. What better time for a leap of faith? Barrel aging, wild fermentation, and fruit, spice, and herb infusions are all part of the plan. Summer 2015 offerings included a red ale and an IPA. Telephone: 440-836-3440 Web: http://www.luckyowlbrewing.com/

MADCAP BREW COMPANY (883 F Hampshire Road, Stow, Ohio 44221) can no longer describe itself as "the Midwest's newest craft brewery." Hundreds have opened since MadCap began. But MacCap can point to expanded distribution from its tiny brewing system and it draws locals for tappings and festival appearances. Telephone: N/A Web: https://www.facebook.com/MadCapBrewCo/timeline. (Caution: Madcap Brewing [lower case "c"] is in Scotland.)

MENIRU MEADERY & BREWERY LLC (5866/5868 Fulton Drive NW, Canton, Ohio 44718) first declares that it is "part of the Mead and Hard Cider renaissance movement." Next: "Our brewery is up and running." Hours are Monday through Saturday. That Meniru is serious about brewing beer appears in the astonishing range of styles brewed with what is so far a very small system. Perhaps an inveterate beer drinker should make craft mead the priority but sample the beers. Telephone: 330-244-8515 Web: http://www.menirumeadery.com

Look for NUMBERS BREWING COMPANY to add up at 127 North Beaver Street, Lisbon, Ohio 44432, a block away from the intersection of OH-45 and U.S.-30. Rick Armon reports that the name reflects a fraternity protocol two of the owners encountered at their college. Look for the brewery to "incorporate numbers into the names and labels of all our beers." Telephone: 330-383-3983 Web: https://www.facebook.com/pages/Numbers-Brewing-Company/1516484575237827

PHOENIX BREWING COMPANY (131 North Diamond Street, Mansfield, Ohio 44902) may represent new life (as phoenixes do, after all) within Mansfield's Carousel District. Open Thursday to Sunday, the taproom encourages patrons to order food from nearby restaurants. Telephone: 419-522-2552 Web: https://plus.google.com/102761767735269267982/about?gl=us&hl=en

PLATFORM BREWING COMPANY (4125 Lorain Avenue, Cleveland, Ohio 44113) works with local restaurants so that patrons who come for the beer will not go away hungry. Open six days a week (closed Sundays) in what was once a Hungarian social club, the brewery offers eight or nine house-brewed beers and a wide selection of guest beers. Several barrel-aged beers add even more interest to the list. It earned its first GABF medal in 2015, a gold for Black Eagle Gratzero. If you can't make it to Ohio City, you may be able to find Platform's New Cleveland beer in cans at your grocery store. Telephone: 216-202-1386 Web: http://platformbeerco.com/

PORTSIDE BREWERY (983 Front Avenue, Cleveland, Ohio 44113), downtown between West 10th and West 9th streets, is the brewing arm of the colocated Portside Distillery. While you may have some reservations about combining wineries (grapes) with breweries (grain), the synergy between brewing beer and distilling rum may be a good thing. One could even imagine an unprecedented boilermaker! (One *could.*) Reporting in the *Cleveland Plain Dealer*, Marc Bona quotes Portside partner Dan Malz on the brewery's interesting variety of styles: "We want to make beers that you can drink a lot of, and we want to make beers you can't drink many of." Hence, as Bona observes, there are session ales and a 12 percent ABV imperial maple stout—and lots in between. A new tasting room opened in early 2015. Telephone: 216-586-6633 Web: http://portsidedistillery.com

R. SHEA BREWING (1662 Merriman Road, Akron, Ohio 44313), which opened in September in 2015, afforded potential patrons a week-by-week opportunity (http://rsheabrewing.com/the-journey/) to watch a brewery coming together, right down to the details of tiling the walls, setting up the equipment, and remembering to pay the rent. Really! Telephone: N/A Web: http://rsheabrewing.com/

RUST BELT BREWING (112 West Commerce Street, Youngstown, Ohio 44503) opens its downtown taproom six days a week to serve year-round beers that recall the city's storied industrial heyday: Blast Furnace Blonde, Coke Oven Stout, Old Man Hopper IPA, Rusted River Irish Red. Roll up the sleeves of your blue-collar shirt and sample also the seasonal and taproom-only beers. Telephone: 234-855-0609 Web: https://rustbeltbrewing.com

TAPSTACK (9941 Walford Avenue, Cleveland, Ohio 44102) opened in 2015. Finally, a tasting room for Buckeye Brewing! Beers familiar because of the popular twenty-two-ounce bottles are here on Thursday, Friday, and Saturday. For instance, there's the superb Hippie IPA, the Cleveland Porter, and the Martian Marzen Lager. Especially recommended on tap? The Buckeye Warm Fuzzy, a "tropical stout" that blends English pale, crystal, and chocolate malts to create a less dry stout with overtones of naval (very dark) rum. Trouble locating it? "Look for the stack." Telephone: 216-860-1434 Web: http//www.buckeyebrewing.com/tapstack/on-tap

TRAILHEAD BREWERY closed in December 2015, just as this book was going to press. Located on Merriman Road in Akron, the brewery's informal taproom served imaginative beers to thirsty cyclers from the Towpath Trail—and to fans of bartender and brewer Eli Smart. A family relocation to California meant "last pints." Thanks to R. Shea, however, CVNP visitors still have a watering hole on Merriman.

Offering Cleveland cheesesteak sandwiches, bocce, their own Pale Ale (brewed in partnership with Platform Beer Company), and a few well-selected guest beers, WATERLOO BREW (15335 Waterloo Road, Cleveland, Ohio 44110) seeks above all to be indigenous. There's a limited menu of sandwiches and snacks and, on Friday, an invitation to bring along a fish-fry meal purchased from the Slovenian Workmen's Home, which shares Waterloo's address. Telephone: 216-785-9475 Web: http://www.waterloocleveland.com

3

AT THE HEART OF IT ALL
COLUMBUS AND ENVIRONS

Cincinnati and Cleveland can justly claim their respective places in brewing history. So can Columbus, where there was a robust brewing industry prior to Prohibition. Chapter 1 mentions in particular the Hoster Brewing Company, which at the beginning of the twentieth century was brewing more than 300,000 barrels a year. But Columbus was also a center of the temperance movement that led to Prohibition. Hence the growth of craft brewing in the center of the state may be an even greater cause for pride than the history of early accomplishment. The Columbus area now can claim several of the state's most creative and successful breweries, from popular brewpubs serving politicians, college students, and locals, to serious restaurants serving house-brewed beer, to enterprising smaller breweries that welcome the adventurous to newly flourishing Columbus neighborhoods and to the hinterlands as far as Zanesville and Athens.

BREWPUBS

BARLEY'S BREWING COMPANY
467 North High Street, Columbus, Ohio 43215
614-228-2537 • http://www.barleysbrewing.com/

Once upon a time, there were two Barley's brewhouses in Columbus—the downtown brewpub and Barley's Smokehouse & Brewpub out on Dublin Road—both the inspiration of industry leader Lenny Kolada. Following an amicable separation, as Kolada shifted his primary focus to the Smokehouse, both kept the name "Barley's" for a time while operating under separate ownership and management. Now the confusion has ended. There is the Smokehouse Brewing Company (see below) and—an entirely separate enterprise—this fine downtown brewpub. Barley's is a magnet for several different audiences: locals seeking a good meal and a good brew downtown, conventioneers out for a distinctive Columbus experience, hockey fans visiting before and after a game at Nationwide

Barley's beers awaiting sampling.

Arena, and beer fans drawn to Barley's long-standing commitment to creative brewing using traditional methods.

The Beers

During its more than twenty years of operation, Barley's has created a broad variety of innovative beers that share a penchant for fresh approaches and noteworthy ingredients in the context of a dedication to "real ale." Meaning? "Beer that is brewed from traditional ingredients, matured and fermented without the use of external carbon dioxide," and allowed to "continue to ferment due to active yeast left in the beer." Barley's celebrates this tradition every Friday by tapping a firkin (see

Influential, longtime Barley's Brewing brewmaster, Angelo Signorino.

the Word List) of cask-conditioned ale (again, the Word List). I decided not to risk a sidebar listing "ten great Ohio brewmasters." There's just too much talent. But if I were to create a list of, say, three great Ohio brewmasters, Barley's Angelo Signorino Jr. would be on it. He's terrific—modest, unassuming, experienced, marvelously creative, and a living encyclopedia of brewing.

The brewery documents its twenty-year history in an informative time line that provides detailed information for about sixty of the beers it has brewed—an education in itself.

As the brewery's Web site justly claims, "the spirit of inquiry and the pursuit of new and different styles and flavors has inspired many styles over the years." You will not find sixty when you visit, but you will enjoy a considerable range.

I sampled first the **Rye IPA** (ABV 5.9 percent, IBUs 70), which balances a nice bitterness (Simcoe and Nugget hops) with malt taste that is distinctively dry and spicy—there's something there in addition to barley, clearly—without becoming intense. My notes indicate that I would have been happy to set aside my scribbling, order a pint, and relax for the afternoon. The brewery's best-selling **MacLenny's Scottish Ale** (ABV 6.6 percent, IBUs 14) has an interesting edge that suggests a glance across the Irish Sea from Glasgow south to Dublin—by no means threatening confusion with a stout, but interpreting the Scottish ale so as to develop a darker, richer palate. The answer behind this unique taste lies partly in the risky approach of heating the brew kettle before adding the wort with the expectation that some caramelization may occur. (It does.) Another part of the answer may lie in the use of American hops to provide a context for the English base malt. Once again, I was prepared to abandon all so as to make an enduring friend of this ale rather than a mere acquaintance.

Ignoring the traditional sampling order, I next enjoyed the winner of Barley's fourteenth annual Homebrew Competition, **Blood Thirst Wheat** (ABV 5 percent, IBUs 2.9). Home brewer Lloyd Cicetti has every reason to be proud of his creation, a delicious beer brewed with blood oranges. It is unusual in several respects. British malts and German hops together make for what would be a pleasing wheat beer in any event, but the addition of blood orange zest to the brew kettle and of puree to the fermenter creates a memorable all-season brew. (In 2014, for the first time, it was available on draft during the holidays in addition to the Christmas Ale.) Orange is a presence but not an overwhelming one. This is a superb wheat ale, not alcoholic orangeade. Again you will enjoy Barley's notes, which in this instance provide a capsule history of oranges!

There is a definition of "imperial" in the Word List, but Barley's **Alexander's Russian Imperial Stout** (ABV 7.6 percent, IBUs 51) captures the complete story by offering a link to a rich history. True to the style's origins, Barley's brews with a grist of English malts and Fuggle hops—though with American Chinook bittering hops and Slovenian and Polish finishing hops as well. The result is intense: highly flavorful, dense in body, and with great warmth at the finish. Barley's recommends it as an accompaniment to rich desserts. I disagree. This is a beer that merits your undistracted attention.

TEN GREAT "ENTRY-LEVEL" BEERS

Sometimes what you want is a simple, clear, cold brew. Or you may be looking for something more interesting—but your companion is intimidated by the craft-brewing scene. On such occasions, it can be a pleasure to order an entry-level beer.

- At **Market Garden** the **Progress Pilsner** invites you to celebrate Cleveland's commitment to "Progress and Prosperity" (the city's motto), to enjoy a well-made beer in the style of good mass-market lagers, and to toast MGB's winning a medal for this beer at the 2013 GABF.
- Spending the day with a friend who always orders a "light beer"? For two bucks you can treat him or her to a four-ounce taste of the **5th Street Wheat** at **Toxic Brew** in Dayton. There's a bit of character, just enough to persuade your friend that a new day in beer has arrived. Then she or he may order a pint.
- **Cornerstone's Grindstone Gold** (ABV 5.5 percent) is deservedly popular with visitors unfamiliar with craft beer but will appeal to anyone who enjoys a good, smooth Kölsch—or, for that matter, anyone who ordinarily steps up to the bar and says, "Give me a light." (Berea)
- Sip a **Summer Haze** (ABV 4.5 percent) sitting on the lawn at **Kelleys Island Brewery** and enjoy the summer haze on Lake Erie without becoming hazy yourself.
- **Barnburner Lager** (ABV 6 percent) at **Lager Heads** (Medina) will please most palates, experienced or not. As the profile indicates, lagers must be brewed with great care. Any wrong step will be evident. There are no wrong steps here.
- The CM **Helles Lager** (ABV 5.2 percent) at **Moerlein Lager House** interprets the style most typical of German (especially Bavarian) beer by creating a version of "the light one" that you might enjoy at a Munich *bierhaus*. If you have tasted this beer in Munich, you might enjoy CM's version more.
- **Rocky River** will serve you an American blond ale named **Pirate Light** (ABV 4.6 percent), which offers an invitation to reconsider the tired familiarity of mass-produced beer. No? The plank awaits.
- Mt. Carmel's **Blonde Ale** (ABV 5.5 percent) meets you where you are, gives you what you want from a beer, then offers just a bit more. Perhaps enough to interest you in a second pint. Perhaps enough to intrigue you. (Cincinnati)
- Ever have a Genesee Cream Ale in a bright green can? **JAFB** in Wooster won't give you a green can, but you will probably enjoy their **Wayne Country Cream Ale** (ABV 5.0 percent). It offers a gateway to well-made craft beers and refreshment to a thirsty traveler.
- **MacLenny's Scottish Ale** has been continuously brewed at two Columbus breweries for nearly a quarter-century. "Conceived as an accessible, easy-to-drink ale at a time that ales hadn't yet caught on in Columbus," it still welcomes the interested but inexperienced to both **Smokehouse Brewing** and **Barley's**. The great British beer writer, Michael Jackson, gave the beer high marks in his *Beer Companion*. They are still well deserved.

Gretchen Mocker serves a pint of Barley's Blood Thirst Wheat.

Columbus Crew star Frankie Hejduk raises Barley's Scottish ale—and one of his championship rings.

(By the way, a serendipitous aside. The Alexander who gave his name to this beer was one of three czars with that name. Alexander is also the name shared by the first sons of two highly influential Columbus brewers, Scott Francis and Lenny Kolada. According to Kolada, "that sealed the deal" in the naming of the beer. And it seems to have worked out! Alex Francis is brewing at Temperance Row Brewing Company and Alex Kolada is brewing at Smokehouse Brewing Company.)

On my next visit I would like first to taste what's on cask. Then I would compare Barley's F.H.A. IPA made with the "freshest hops available" and Barley's Four Seas IPA, which also makes a priority of using the hops available at the moment of brewing. The pilsner would be well worth a try also, for I imagine that Angelo achieves an interesting interpretation of this most traditional of lagers. And I definitely want to be there for one of the Firkin Fridays!

The Food

Like its beer list, Barley's menu offers some original takes on standard offerings while showing a resourceful use of the brewery's good work. Begin with Pale Ale Chili? Then you can order an IPA-brined pork chop with cheese grits, broccoli, and a bourbon-mustard barbecue sauce. Or you can satisfy your inner Clevelander with an entrée that includes a cheddar potato pierogi, bratwurst, kielbasa, and chorizo sausage. There's also a Clevelander burger that adds kielbasa and pierogies to a steak burger, a Dragonfire burger with Cajun spices, pepperjack, jalapeños, diabla sauce, and guacamole, and a Cali Burger with alfalfa sprouts, guacamole, smoked gouda, roasted red pepper coulis, and cilantro-lime aioli. Other options include sandwiches, wraps, and veggie choices. The dessert list is brief, but its two homemade specialties—a crème brûlée du jour and an Imperial Stout Brownie Bash—appear particularly enticing.

Newsworthy

Barley's invites home brewers once a year to an Afternoon with the Brewers, a competition that evaluates home brews and taps the previous year's winner. As mentioned above, at least one home-brew winner has become a staple offering at Barley's. • Tappings and tastings regularly make the news. • A collaboration of the brewery with a Columbus cinema/drafthouse in summer 2014 created an interesting pairing between a movie (Spaceballs) and Barley's beers. • In March 2015, just in time for St. Patrick's Day, Barley's introduced a highly literate "reboot" of its Irish ale. "It's fruity, toasty, with a hint of butterscotch and an abundance of warming alcohol."

Other Stuff

Menu specials and beers on tap appear on the Barley's Facebook page. • Rent the brewery's atmospheric Underground for a special event, and Barley's will take care of the details. • In October 2015, Barley's announced plans for an upstairs arcade and bar.

THE SKINNY

LOCATION	In the heart of downtown Columbus (between the Short North and Arena districts in the North Market Historic District) across the street from the Convention Center and in easy walking distance of the Nationwide Arena.
HOURS	Mon–Thu 11:00 A.M.–midnight • Fri–Sat 11:00 A.M.–2:00 A.M. • Sun 12:00 A.M.–11:00 P.M.
PARKING	There's ample parking because the brewery is across the street from the convention center. But there can be competition if there is a convention at the center or a game at the arena.
KIDS	Kids are welcome with a special kids' menu.
TAKEOUT	Beer is not bottled or canned but may be taken out in growlers.

ELEVATOR BREWERY & DRAUGHT HAUS

161 North High Street, Columbus, Ohio 43215

614-228-0500 • http://www.elevatorbrewing.com/

Which Elevator to take? The restaurant or the brewery? They're both going up. The ascent began more than fifteen years ago in Marysville, Ohio, when Dick and Ryan Stevens, father and son, began brewing in a grain elevator (hence the name). In March 2000, the Stevens family opened the Elevator Brewery & Draught Haus on North High to introduce their brews to Columbus. Then in January 2009, they moved the brewery's production facility from Marysville to just two blocks from the restaurant—once the location of the General Tire building at 165 North Fourth. Since that time the brewery has added sixty-barrel fermenters, an industrial-scale bottling line, and a simple but comfortable 13th Floor taproom.

Elevator founder Dick Stevens serves one at the "13th Floor" taproom of Elevator.

Because of the emphasis of this book, we'll focus primarily on the North High location, which offers a full menu and an unmatchable historic ambience. Also, it's open six days a week. But beer aficionados should not overlook the production brewery, where Elevator brews most of its beer. (The restaurant houses a nano-brewing system.) You should visit the 13th Floor to drink Elevator beer where it's made, bottled, and canned. If that's not enough, you can catch a game on the large television or play a vintage Nintendo game. Either way, Elevator will take you to a new level.

The Beers

Brewmaster Vic Schiltz and his crew brew the Elevator beers in three categories: flagships, seasonals, and special editions. While all may be available regularly or periodically at the Draught Haus, many of the flagships—Bleeding Buckeye Red Ale, Dark Force Lager, Three Frogs IPA, and Big Vic Imperial IPA—may be familiar also through their broad distribution.

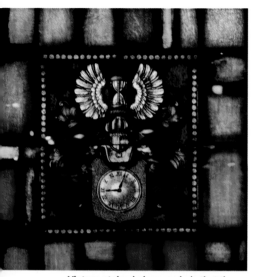

Vintage stained glass reminds that time flies when you're enjoying Elevator beers.

I enjoyed sampling three of the four flagship beers. Ohio State fans should find **Bleeding Buckeye Red Ale** (ABV 5.7 percent, IBUs 34) perfect for an afternoon watching football. Similar to popular amber ales such as Fat Tire or Bell's Amber, Bleeding Buckeye draws attention above all to the malts but offers hints of citrus and cedar. The pronounced hops presence ensures a satisfying finish. As the name suggests, **Dark Force Lager** (ABV 5.9 percent, IBUs 22) pours as a deep copper-colored beer. Hops stand in the background. Look for the horse on the label—perhaps a reference to the beer's bronze medal recognition at the 2007 GABF when it was named Dark Horse. The field was crowded, and the betting was heavy on the gray and the mare, but those who bet on Dark Force to show were rewarded by the taste: caramel, pepper, and perhaps potato?

Among Ohio IPAs, **Three Frogs** (ABV 7.6 percent, IBUs 45) shows particular attention to detail. Here, hops rule. In addition to the bittering hops added to the wort during the boiling process, Elevator dry hops the beer twice. The result is a floral aroma that offers an appealing context for the bitterness. I did not taste the fourth flagship, which Dick Stevens says is a favorite of many of his customers, the Big Vic Imperial IPA (ABV 8.6 percent, IBUs 80). Named for the brewmaster, this IPA is described as "medium-to-full bodied, dry hopped with Citra to achieve its bold, hoppy taste, with aromas and flavors of grapefruit, pineapple, peach and pine."

Elevator beers available only on draft (at the brewery or at local bars) include Procrastinator Doppelbock (ABV 7 percent, IBUs 25), Dirty Dick's Nut Brown Ale (ABV 5 percent, IBUs 15), Xtra American Light Lager (ABV 5 percent, IBUs N/A), and Fly'n Hydrant Light (ABV 4 percent, IBUs N/A).

The seasonal beers have their own flagship, the popular **Winter Warmer Ale** (ABV 8.6 percent, IBUs 33). A bit spicier than some, this beer will please especially those for whom nutmeg and ginger, which stand out in the rich mix of flavors, are essential tastes of the season. Other seasonal selections are Horny Goat (ABV 7.5 percent, IBUs N/A), Heiferweizen (ABV 5.5 percent, IBUs N/A), and Oktoberfest (ABV 5.7 percent, IBUs N/A).

Special Edition beers have included Bar-Bar (ABV 12 percent, IBUs

N/A), a barley wine aged in bourbon barrels for six months! According to the brewery, "aromas and flavors of toffee, caramel, vanilla, toasty oak and whiskey" develop through the aging and can be enjoyed years after bottling. Another is Ghost Scorpion (ABV 5 percent, IBUs N/A), quite possibly the "world's hottest beer." Using the Ghost Chile and Trinidad Scorpion Chile peppers, this classic German-style lager dares "Can you handle it?" (According to the brewery, these peppers clock in at well over 1 MILLION Scoville Heat Units!) Finally, there is Horus Limited Release Imperial Red Ale (ABV 10 percent, IBUs N/A), brewed in small batches as the brewery's anniversary, celebratory beer!

The Food

The restaurant's lunch and dinner menus offer imaginative entrées as well as familiar pub fare. You can choose to cook your own tenderloin filet or tuna steak on a "tulikivi firestone" brought to your table piping hot. Or you can order the short rib mac and cheese and let the kitchen do the work. For starters, the sauerkraut balls are popular, as are the pot stickers. On a cold winter's day, the Aztec Chicken Chowder is a reliable warmer. Ingredients? "Chicken, great northern white beans, poblanos, garlic, thyme, cream, tortilla strips." The dinner menu adds a New York strip, halibut, a grilled pork chop, and other more ambitious fare. Although I rarely "save room for dessert," as servers encourage, there's reason to keep that course in mind, if only because of the Buckeye Brownie and the ice-cream float made with house-brewed root beer.

Elevator Brewery's Winter Warmer Ale en route to be capped.

Elevator's "Degree Programs" require completion of all requirements.

Newsworthy

In blind taste testings conducted by *All About Beer* magazine, Elevator has won a platinum award, nine golds, a silver, and a bronze. Brewery representative Jay Taylor explains that the magazine's ratings, which depend on the judgments of experienced tasters at the Beverage Tasting Institute, are particularly worthwhile. • Elevator also took a bronze medal at the 2015 GABF for Mogabi, a wheat beer.

Other Stuff

The beautiful nineteenth-century building on North High is on the national registry of historic landmarks. While admiring the original saloon bar and some interesting stained glass, look down at the mosaic tile floor. Then glance up at the ceiling. When you have finished exploring, you can try your hand at darts or accept a billiards match. There are three dartboards and two antique billiards tables in the rear. • There are two "degree programs"—the Masters of Beer Appreciation (MBA) and the Professor of Hearty Drinking (PHD). Complete the requirements (enjoy the listed beers) and win an impressive certificate. The 2014 PhD program featured twelve herbal beers! • You can make a reservation for a tour of the production brewery on the third Saturday of every month at 4:00 P.M., but groups of twelve or more may be able to schedule tours by calling or e-mailing (see above) the brewery. • Occasional events such as seasonal celebrations and fundraisers are announced on the Web site.

THE SKINNY

LOCATION	The brewpub is downtown, three blocks from the Nationwide Arena.
HOURS	Mon–Thu 11:00 A.M.–midnight • Fri 11:00 A.M.– 2:00 A.M. • Sat 5:00 P.M.–2:00 A.M. (The kitchen closes at 10:00 P.M. Mon–Thu and at 11:00 P.M. Fri and Sat.) CLOSED SUNDAY.
PARKING	Well, this is downtown Columbus, but free parking is available next to the taproom on Saturdays, and there are nearby street-level lots and parking garages for restaurant patrons. You may want to develop a strategy for evenings when there are events at the nearby arena. Public transportation, perhaps?
KIDS	Kids are welcome at the restaurant on North High. The North Fourth production brewery may not be their scene.
TAKEOUT	Growlers and six-packs in cans and bottles can be purchased at the brewery.
DISTRIBUTION	Elevator products are available throughout Ohio in many bars and restaurants and on grocery shelves.

GORDON BIERSCH

401 North Front Street, Suite 120, Columbus, Ohio 43215
614-246-2900 • http://www.gordonbiersch.com/locations/
columbus?action=view

Yes, Gordon Biersch belongs to a chain. In fact, Gordon Biersch is owned by the same corporation that owns the Rock Bottom and Old Chicago franchises, namely, CraftWorks Restaurants & Breweries, Inc. But who cares? The question is whether guests walking through the doors in downtown Columbus have a good experience. And there's plenty of evidence that they do. There's much about GB that will impress you: its location adjacent to the Nationwide Arena; its scale, with accommodations for more than four hundred—not counting the outside patio; its diverse menu; and beers crafted by brewmaster Keith Jackson in a gleaming twenty-barrel brewing system. But above all you are likely to be impressed by the commitment to quality. Whether you are hoping for a quick bite before the face-off or a leisurely beer on a summer afternoon, GB is likely to have what you're looking for.

Brewmaster Keith Jackson of Gordon Biersch.

The Beers

As the name suggests, GB honors fairly closely the German brewing tradition. "Purity. Precision. Perfection." Those are the GB hallmarks. Yes, in the past there may have been a trade-off so far as creativity is concerned. Not surprisingly, breweries honoring the Reinheitsgebot are less well known for surprising, cutting-edge brews. Their ingredients for the most part have been those you would find in any German brewery: Weyermann Malt from Bamberg ("malting competence since 1879") and Bavarian Hersbrucker hops, known for both floral character and a balance of spiciness and fruitiness. The benefit in terms of consistency and quality is considerable. But lately there has been more good news. In Jackson's words: "More variety—yet still with the commitment to quality and German hallmarks of Märzen and Export."

GB's five standard beers are all authentic, all enjoyable, and all compatible with good food and good times. **Golden Export** (ABV 5 percent, IBUs 17) recalls the early days of lager. Light, crisp, and delicate, it can be enjoyed cold. Take a pint outside on a warm summer day and you'll understand why nineteenth-century Europe and the United States celebrated the new style. However, the **Hefeweizen** (ABV 5.5 percent, IBUs 12) may be even better suited to summer weather. Unlike Widmer's trendsetting West Coast beer, this unfiltered wheat beer gives an impression of spices and banana and will encourage you to skip the orange slice.

Not obviously Germanic—but a delicious burger at Gordon Biersch.

Joseph Harder tosses a pizza in the works at Gordon Biersch.

The **Schwarzbier** (ABV 4.3 percent, IBUs 21) offers a reminder that dark beers are not necessarily dense or strong. (See the sidebar "Ten Not-So-Great Craft Beer Myths.") Yes, there's a delicious evocation of coffee and chocolate, but the body is light and the finish is dry. The **Märzen** (ABV 5.7 percent, IBUs 18) echoes the mild sweetness of many Bavarian beers. The GB Web site says this is their most popular beer, and it is not difficult to see why. Neither so bright as a light lager nor so rich as the Schwartzbier, this lager with a focus on malt spans styles and seasons. Finally, the **Czech Pilsner** (ABV 5.6 percent, IBUs 36), GB's most complex and interesting beer, honors its style by using lots of Czech Saaz hops, a "noble" variety known more for its floral aroma than its bitter taste. In addition to these standards, Jackson offers rotating brewmaster's specials. On one visit, these included an ESB and an American brown ale.

TEN NOT-SO-GREAT CRAFT BEER MYTHS

The server at a fine restaurant in Indianapolis who cautioned me against ordering an IPA because "they have to come all the way from India" was wrong, of course. Unfortunately, as A Beer Fan's Word List explains, the supposedly correct account—that IPA was created to survive the long ocean voyage to troops *in* India—is also misleading. But no matter. That waiter's combination of inadequate knowledge and bluster is not uncommon. Restaurants that train their staff with regard to the wine list should devote comparable training to the beer list. Some do. One restaurant I visited recently in Boulder, Colorado, offered both a "certified cicerone®" and a sommelier. But too often, enthusiasm for craft beer has outstripped the necessary commitment to appropriate stocking, storing, describing, and serving. Into the resulting vacuum have rushed myths—fallacies or near-truths—that, if pronounced with sufficient confidence, may persuade the unwary. Don't be unwary! The next time you hear one of these myths, be tactful but suggest, "You know, there's a book called *Ohio's Craft Beers* that includes a list of ten myths . . . ."

- **Dark beers taste dark.** Sometimes, yes, because the darkness of the beer expresses that of dark roast grain. Often, no, because the darkness arises from other factors that have nothing to do with flavor. Lenny Kolada, of Smokehouse Brewing Company (Columbus), makes the point: "Don't judge a book by its cover."
- **Dark beers are higher in calories.** Dark beers on average tend to be lower in calories than lighter craft beers. In a sampler, the stout may be the beer that is lowest in both calories and alcohol.
- **Craft beers are all heavy and filling.** People who complain about craft beers cannot be acquainted with the range of varieties. For every beer drinker, there's an appealing craft beer. Or several. Or many.
- **Craft beers tend to be stronger than mass-produced beers.** Although craft brewing has gained some attention for experimenting with strong beers, most brewers offer beers that span the spectrum—and they are usually up-front so far as alcohol (ABV) is concerned. (See A Beer Fan's Word List.) There is just as much buzz these days about good *low*-alcohol craft beers.
- **No one cans real craft beer.** Wrong. In fact, cans have some advantages over bottles. They keep out oxygen and block light, both of which can afflict a beer. It is true, however, that a craft beer lover does not drink beer *from* a can. Find a good glass, pour, and enjoy.
- **Pour a craft beer down the side of the glass to minimize the head.** Wrong—for two reasons. First, a decent head, by presenting you with the beer's aroma, enables you to anticipate the pleasure of drinking the beer. Second, because many beers in the United States are too heavily carbonated, pouring directly into the bottom of glass, waiting a minute or two for the head to subside, then pouring again will give you a less fizzy and more flavorful beer.
- **If it looks like a craft beer, it probably is.** Look again—carefully. Losing market share to craft brewers, some mass producers are now retaliating by offering what may appear at first to be craft brews. But their colorful labels camouflage corporate recipes. Here are two hints. First, if the beer appears on the wave of a major marketing effort, it is probably not a craft beer. Second: a label has no effect on the taste of a beer.

- IPAs were originally created for shipment to British troops in India. Higher alcohol content and higher levels of hops served as preservatives to prevent the beer from spoiling during the long ocean voyage. According to *The Oxford Companion to Beer,* virtually every element of this charming story is wrong. I will not repeat the four-page article (pp. 482–86 if you're interested) but, in short: (1) strong, heavily hopped ales long predated the India trade; (2) the sea journey usually helped to condition rather than threaten the beer; and (3) the troops preferred porter to the far more expensive Pale Ale.
- IBUs (International Bitterness Units) tell a beer drinker how bitter the beer under consideration will taste. Perhaps—but perhaps not. IBUs measure the proportion in a brew of the alpha acid associated with bitterness, but how bitter a beer tastes depends on many factors, e.g., which malts are used and how they are prepared, what other ingredients may be added, how carbonated the beer is when served, and how strong the beer is.
- Drinking craft beer will make you more sensitive, more attractive, and more interesting. This is not a myth!

The Food

No hasenpfeffer, no sauerbraten, no spaetzle, no Kartoffelsalat—if you go to Gordon Biersch expecting a menu focused on German foods, you will be disappointed. The list of "chef's favorites" visits Louisiana (jambalaya, Cajun pasta, Creole chicken), Hawaii (seared Ahi tuna), Italy (Tuscan chicken pasta, chocolate budino cake), Mexico (house-made tacos), and Maine (lobster and jumbo lump crab cakes) but unless you count mini bratwurst sliders, Germany is not in the picture. Try to find sauerkraut! (You won't.) That said, the menu offers an inviting variety of small plates, salads, the favorites mentioned above, and a GB exclusive, Woodford Reserve Bourbon entrées. Choose one of these and your salmon, Gulf shrimp, or chicken breast will be seasoned, grilled, and "glazed with signature sauce." As an accompanying photo indicates, GB fires its pizzas and flatbreads in an authentic oven. The goat cheese and artichoke flatbread looked particularly tempting. Desserts are house-made.

Newsworthy

Given their consistent commitment to high standards for brewing traditional German styles, Gordon Biersch should be able to earn recognition in its chosen categories—and it has. There are GABF gold medals for the Czech Pilsner (2004, 2007), for the Schwarzbier (2007), and for the Weizenbock (2006). There are also four silver medals, but the bronze medals are particularly interesting in that they point to some of GB's more creative products, albeit ones still securely within the German tradition. There's a 2011 medal for a Gose, a sour ale with a bit of salinity, and a 2010 medal for a Rauchbier made with smoked malt. GB has also earned recognition at the World Beer Cup, with a 2014 gold medal for its Winter Bock and a bronze for a rauch (smoked) Märzen.

Other Stuff
GB's size enables it to host private parties of up to five hundred. There is a group sales menu you can consult. • A loyalty program called the Stein Club offers prizes to faithful GB customers.

THE SKINNY

LOCATION	It anchors the Arena District.
HOURS	Mon–Sat 11:00 A.M.–11:00 P.M. • Sun 11:00 A.M.–9:00 P.M.
PARKING	There are a few street-level lots within easy walking distance as well as the large garage that serves the Arena. Caution: Charges for "event parking" may apply if there's something scheduled at the arena.
KIDS	Kids are welcome with a special kids' menu.
TAKEOUT	Beer is not bottled or canned but may be taken out in growlers.
DISTRIBUTION	Kegs and bottles. To the dismay of many Northeast Ohio travelers, GB's popular satellite location in Terminal D at Cleveland Hopkins airport closed when United Airlines discontinued its Cleveland hub and shuttered its regional jet terminal.

JACKIE O'S PUB AND BREWERY
22–24 West Union Street, Athens, Ohio 45701
740-592-9686 • http://jackieos.com/
Production Facility
25 Campbell Street, Athens, Ohio 45701

Assuming that a visit to one of Ohio's most innovative and influential breweries at the outset would be a good strategy, I made Jackie O's the second brewery I visited in preparation for this book. I was right. My discussion with owner, guiding spirit, and industry leader Art Oestrike and my tour of their brewing system—which has since been greatly expanded—persuaded me that craft brewing deserves all the attention it is receiving, not only because of the beer, but also because of the distinct values Art and his colleagues represent.

Jackie O's holds a well-deserved reputation for innovation by defining and exploring fresh arenas such as barrel-aged beers and sours. As Oestrike told me, "It's about creativity, giving folks the opportunity to invent, to take ideas further. Everything else is boring." Jackie O's excels also in the pursuit of a closely related value: customer education. (Oestrike is also a professor at Ohio University, by the way.) Close proximity to the university affords the brewery an opportunity to guide new patrons from their first legal beers to more sophisticated and challenging styles.

Commitment to architectural preservation is evident in Jackie O's restoration and repurposing of its space, which formerly belonged to a bar named O'Hooley's. That commitment was made more conspicuous in the brewery's response to the November 2014 fire on its downtown Athens block that destroyed their Public House kitchen and stalled normal operations for several months. Brewpub doors opened three days after the blaze. Jackie O's has since made long-term improvements to both of its uptown facilities while expanding its mission through a taproom on the other side of town. There you'll find unique art crafted from their cans and bottles as well as clothing, glasses, and other merchandise.

Sustainability and local sourcing? They have both. At its twenty-acre Barrel Ridge farm, Jackie O's grows vegetables, herbs, and flowers. Its

The rough-hewn Jackie O's sign advertises carefully crafted, complex beers.

Chris, Hank, and Ashley (*left to right*) enjoy a "session" at Jackie O's in Athens.

commitment to "Farm to Table, Jackie O's Style" enables it to supply its own kitchen and to operate a Community Locavore Club as a supplier of fresh produce and baked goods to contract customers. "Sustainably crafted with purpose" is a good motto for Jackie O's.

This brewpub and its new production brewery fill so many roles well: They offer comfortable, family-friendly hangouts for town and gown, a testing laboratory for new styles, a community magnet for beer tourists, an informal but creative restaurant, a training ground for brewing talent—you get the picture. One disclaimer: Having visited Jackie O's early in my statewide survey, I have not yet seen the production facility and taproom. That is why Jackie O's is prominent in the sidebar listing of breweries I most want to visit following this book's publication.

The Beers

For most other breweries, I report on beers I have tasted and list a few others. For Jackie O's, that approach would be woefully inadequate. Every style I sampled struck me as a complete yet creative embodiment of its style. My notes include phrases such as "incredibly complex" and "a watershed beer." Speaking of the **Raccoon Dubbel** (ABV 7.0 percent, IBUs N/A), I describe its maple overtones as "a quality, not a quantity." While this particular beer is no longer on the Jackie O's list, that perception applies to many of brewer Brad Clark's products. They move toward the edge, many of them, but with subtlety and grace.

Rather than detail my other tastes, I'll simply suggest the range of beers from which you might choose. You might begin with a beer favored by many first-time visitors, the **Razz Wheat** (ABV 5.0 percent, IBUs

Art Oestrike, one of Ohio's craft-brewing pioneers, produced sublime beers with a compact basement system before opening Jackie O's new production brewery.

N/A), a mild American ale brewed with Oregon raspberries. (In a candid aside, Oestrike conceded the beer to be a "favorite of the patrons, not of the brewers.") Canning has since made it a favorite of patrons statewide. You might just as easily edge into craft brewing with the **Pilsazz** (ABV 5.0 percent, IBUs N/A), a European-style pilsner. There's also **Ja Bitte Kölsch** (ABV 4.9 percent, IBUs N/A) and **Berliner Weisse** (ABV 4.0 percent, IBUs N/A). With a bit more experience, you may become interested in the **CSAison Reserve** (ABV 6.0 percent, IBUs N/A), a farmhouse ale "with herbs fermented on house sour culture," or (my favorite) the **Mystic Mama IPA** (ABV 7.0 percent, IBUs N/A), which leverages five different hops to create a bitter, fragrant interpretation of this popular style.

Intent on a graduate degree? You may be ready for the **Bourbon Barrel Skipping Stone** (ABV 11 percent, IBUs N/A), an imperial stout, **Oro Negro** (ABV 10.0 percent, IBUs N/A), or a beer brewed collaboratively with Fat Head's (Olmsted Falls), an American-style barley wine named **Liquid Courage** (ABV 10.5 percent, IBUs N/A). This list, as broad at it may seem, does not describe the full range of beers available at Jackie O's.

Jackie O's is well worth a trip to Athens, as some of the special brews are available nowhere else. Their bottle releases (see Newsworthy) are also Athens-only events. But if you can't make it to the brewery, you should be able to find some of their production beers nearby, on draft or in bottles and cans. Their interactive Web site can point you to the nearest source. Beers available year-round in many locations include Firefly Amber Ale, Mystic Mama IPA, Chomolungma (a honey nut-brown ale), and the Hop Ryot IPA. Their seasonal and imperial beers may be a bit harder to find, but they are also well worth the effort.

The Food

As mentioned above, the Jackie O's Public House was extensively damaged by a downtown Athens fire in November 2014, but has bounced back since then. At the time this book went to publication, Jackie O's was again serving much of their classic menu at the brewpub. Their specialties include spent-grain pizzas, imaginative burgers, unusual sandwiches, fish and chips, and cheese curds—all locally sourced as much as possible. There is also food available at the taproom on weekends thanks to a visiting cart.

Newsworthy

Jackie O's is one of the two or three most newsworthy craft brewers in Ohio. Its periodic releases of bottled beer draw devoted fans. Visitors drive in from over ten states to attend these events, some going as far as to sleep in their cars to be at the front of the line when the very rare craft beers go on sale in the early morning. • Best brewpub in Ohio? This one, according to rankings released by RateBeer in early 2015. • BeerAdvocate gave highly favorable reviews to three of Jackie O's barrel-aged beers in early 2015. • In June 2015, Jackie O's collaborated with three other breweries—Yellow Springs and Fat Head's from Ohio, Crooked Stave from Denver—to brew interesting partnership releases.

Other Stuff

Jackie O's Barrel Ridge Farm supports a club that supplies its members with harvested produce, freshly baked bread, and desserts. The Jackie O's bakeshop, a separate entity, provides the pub with its bread and serves Athenians through the local farmers' market and in delis, diners, and food carts.

THE SKINNY

LOCATION	The Brewpub and Public House are located in downtown Athens. From U.S. 50N take Exit 17 to OH-682. Turn right on Richland and drive through the OU campus. Take a slight left on South Congress for a long block to West Union. You're there. To reach the production brewery and taproom at 25 Campbell Street from the downtown location, go north on North Congress for about three blocks, turn right on Stimson for about six blocks, and then turn right on Grant and right on Campbell. Easy.
HOURS	Check Web site. Brewpub: Mon–Sun 11:00 A.M.–2:00 A.M. Taproom: Tue–Fri 4:00–9:00 P.M. or later • Sat noon–9:00 P.M. or later
PARKING	For the Brewpub and Public House, the nearby Athens Parking Garage (West Washington and North Court) will often be your best bet. Parking at the production facility and taproom may be a bit easier. There are several lots in the vicinity, but check on accessibility.
KIDS	All facilities are kid-friendly! The taproom even offers a vintage video game machine (free!), as well as board games to entertain little ones.
TAKEOUT	Kegs, 12.7-ounce bottles, canned beer, and growler fills are available.
DISTRIBUTION	Long before the opening of its production facility, Jackie O's was bottling experimental beers for connoisseurs at its cramped Union Street location. Nothing wrong with that! But its new production facility has enabled the brewery to can its most popular beers and to contract with a distributor so as to "get Jackie O's beers into more hands across Ohio."

SMOKEHOUSE BREWING COMPANY

1130 Dublin Road, Columbus, Ohio 43215

614-485-0227 • http://www.smokehousebrewing.com/

Once known as Barley's Smokehouse, this attractive and inviting brew-pub started life as a sibling of the downtown Barley's Brewing Company (see above). Smokehouse founder Lenny Kolada started that enterprise in 1992 as only the second brewpub in Columbus. Then in 1997 he created what is now the Smokehouse. To oversimplify a complicated story, Lenny has concluded his association with downtown Barley's so as to concentrate on the more simply named Smokehouse. The one remaining link between the two locations—their sharing the services of one of Ohio's most creative and enterprising brewers, Angelo Signorino Jr.—ended in late 2014 when Signorino left the Smokehouse to brew at Barley's full time. Now the enterprises are completely separate. As its name might suggest, Smokehouse Brewing offers an experience quite a bit different from what you'll find downtown. Avoid downtown congestion in favor of easy parking, informal dining with an emphasis on barbecue, and a tradition of brewing great beers—these are the selling points.

The Beers

The Smokehouse's new head brewer is Sam Hickey, formerly a brewer at Mystic Brewing Company near Boston. Among his accomplishments? He was part of the team at Mystic that won a gold medal at GABF for Vinland II, an experimental beer brewed using a yeast strain isolated

From the Smokehouse Brewing Company cask, Katie Simon pumps an IPA with vanilla.

from a Maine blueberry. At Smoke-house, he should be in his element. In a clear signal to craft beer devotees, the brewer taps a firkin every Friday, pulls two cask-conditioned ales at all times, keeps another on nitro, pours six or seven house-made beers, and schedules a broad range of guest drafts to address any gaps.

I began with the **Pale Ale** (ABV 5.6 percent, IBUs 27), a faithful rendering of British bitter. Because the deep amber of this style might seem at odds with its name, Smokehouse offers the reminder that the British chose the name because this ale is pale in comparison with porters and stouts. This is a relatively uncomplicated but deeply reassuring "pint of bitter," the "comfort food" of beers, and it would pair perfectly with a

Smokehouse pumpkin ale offers a slice of pumpkin pie in a glass.

mild curry and a telecast of Chelsea vs. Manchester United. The **Centennial IPA** (ABV 7.6 percent, IBUs 71) takes the Pale Ale up a notch. While the brewery describes it as a British (rather than American) IPA, one might think of it instead as a "transatlantic" IPA, with the smooth, rich base of British malts in détente with the aromas of citrus and resin arising from U.S. Centennial and Columbus hops. I have not tried this beer on cask but would enjoy doing so.

The **Punkt Imperial Pumpkin Porter** (ABV 6.8 percent, IBUs N/A) was on nitro during my visit—one memorable beer. The chalkboard description—"like whipped cream on your pie"—was not far off. The photo will give you an idea of what the beer looks like but cannot convey just how creamy and delicious it really is. If you prefer a pumpkin ale that simulates the experience of a slice of pie, this one is for you. The pumpkin and squash tastes are in the foreground. Everything else plays second fiddle. A pint might be too much, but a half-pint served as dessert could be the perfect ending to a holiday meal.

Other house beers available in December 2014 included an imperial IPA, a cask-conditioned Christmas Ale, St. Nick's Winter Warmer (ABV 11.4 percent!) on nitro, an apple saison Matrimony Ale, and the Columbus favorite, MacLenny's Scottish Ale. Guest beers included the IPA

from Maumee Bay (Ohio), the popular 90-Minute IPA from Dogfish Head (Delaware), and Bell's Winter White Ale (Michigan).

One beer you will not find at Smokehouse—or anywhere else—was inspired by an Egyptian mummy in the collection of the Ohio Historical Center. Because Lenny Kolada tells this story on his well-written blog (http://www.smokehousebrewing.com/brew-doodblog/), I won't go into detail. But, in brief, Smokehouse Brewing, asked whether it might brew a special-event beer for an evening at the museum dedicated to the mummy, enlisted North High and Actual Brewing as collaborators. Inferring their recipe from the 1800 BC "Hymn to Ninkasi," they attempted several test beers before deciding to serve a saison brewed with ingredients that would have been available to Egyptian brewers: "barley and wheat . . . coriander and lemongrass . . . cracked black peppercorns, bitter orange peel and fresh ginger."

Smokehouse founder and owner Lenny Kolada enjoys performing some "quality control."

Summing up the experiment, Kolada describes it as "part art; part science; part magic." (See also The Actual Brewing Company, below.)

The Food

For the photo with Lenny, the kitchen created a sampler of Smokehouse barbecue. I did not accept the invitation to join an early lunch, but I was sorely tempted by the wonderful aroma and the appealing platter. There are both popular styles of ribs (St. Louis and baby back), hickory-smoked chicken or brisket, pulled-pork and chicken sandwiches, and a "carnivore sampler" that enables you to touch at least three barbecue bases.

Beyond barbecue, burgers appear in a wide range of varieties, and there's a brief but alluring dessert list that includes house-made bread pudding, carrot cake, a Bailey's Cheesecake Martini (you have to see it to understand it), and the Snickerdoodle Ice Cream Sandwich.

The menu changes seasonally, so featured items may change. But I suspect some interesting brewery-based starters such as Spent Grain Pretzel Bites, beer cheese kettle chips, and a beer cheese dip might be "regulars." There are some inviting salads, including one (Southwest Barbeque) that allows you to describe your pulled-chicken and pork meal as "just a salad for lunch." And there are pub favorites such as shepherd's pie and fish and chips.

Newsworthy

A change of name always makes the headlines, even when the change consists of dropping only one word: Barley's. • New releases offer another opportunity to make news—especially when names such as Basin Street Wheat, Saint Joan's Revenge, and Woody Haze 101 capture the imagination. • In the spring, Smokehouse hosts a Mini Real Ale Festival. But "mini" may now be an understatement. The May 2015 list included extraordinarily complex and innovative ales from twelve Ohio breweries.

Other Stuff

There's an extensive take-out menu offering platters and bulk orders. Make entertaining easy! • Or you can schedule a special event at the Smokehouse.

THE SKINNY

LOCATION	It's about ten minutes west of downtown. Exit I-670W to Grandview Avenue and turn right. In a few blocks, turn left on Dublin Road. The brewpub will be on your right in a few blocks. Look for the grain silo.
HOURS	Sun–Thu 11 A.M.–11 P.M. • Fri–Sat 11 A.M.–midnight
PARKING	There's ample parking on the large lot surrounding the brewpub.
KIDS	You bet. The kids' menu includes some barbecue along with more traditional favorites.
TAKEOUT	Beer is not bottled or canned but may be taken out in growlers or in quarter or half barrels.
DISTRIBUTION	Kegs to select local accounts.

WEASEL BOY BREWING COMPANY

126 Muskingum Avenue, Suite E, Zanesville, Ohio 43701
740-455-3767 • http://www.weaselboybrewing.com/#/home/4548152595

Owners Jay and Lori Wince raise ferrets as pets—hence the "pet name" of their brewery. But to my regret, none were in evidence during my visit to the brewery. There probably are laws. But a visit to Weasel Boy Brewing is nevertheless an enjoyable experience. Imagine a leisurely Saturday afternoon hanging out at your college fraternity house. Or joining a good friend for a brew in his den. Or discovering an Old World pub. The comfortable ambience of the Weasel Boy taproom—overstuffed sofas, amiable session beers, light streaming in through the large industrial windows, original art on the walls, congenial patrons, Alison Krauss on the sound system—may make you want to stay a while. I did.

It took a long while for Zanesville to rejoin the brewing scene. Although the city was once home to a major regional brewer, Simon Linser, a long dry spell began when the Eighteenth Amendment went into effect in 1920. When Weasel Boy's brewing operations began in July 2007, the city was able to claim its first brewery in more than eighty years. Jay and Lori have located their brewery near downtown alongside the river, near Zanesville's lovely Putnam Hill Park, the astonishingly Italianate Muskingum County Courthouse, and the famous "Y" bridge, which marks the spot where the Licking and Muskingum rivers merge.

The Winces are among the many successful professionals who earned their first awards as amateurs. They started serious home brewing about twenty years ago, but Jay decided to get *really* serious about ten years ago when he consulted with colleagues in Columbus (Eric Bean at Columbus Brewing and Scott Francis at Barley's) who were willing to teach him the ropes. Spouse Lori Wince, who also draws on home-brewing experience, has since earned the pink boots that identify her as assistant brewer. But in her work on brewery promotions and events Lori draws also on her experience as a journalist. From "ink" to "pink"?

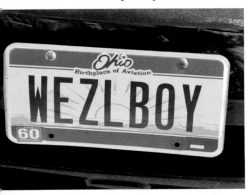

Wherever Weasel Boy owner Jay Wince drives, his message follows him.

The Beers

You have to love the categories: the "year-round litter," the "transient critters," and the "seasonal weasels." Neither filtered nor pasteurized, these beers scurry from amiable session beers to impressive "imperial" styles. I sampled a few.

The **Plaid Ferret Scottish Ale** (ABV 4.2 percent, IBUs 11), a remarkably straightforward expression of this export style, falls into the session category. As the ale is very lightly hopped, there's little aroma, but the rich malt taste, with suggestions of caramel, could entertain you through the afternoon. The **River Mink Mild Brown** (ABV 3.8 percent, IBUs 16) offers a touch of chocolate not always found in this traditional British pub style. Though milds can be nondescript, this beer offers some depth through its light roast and just a touch of hops.

With the **Brown Stoat Stout** (ABV 6.2 percent, IBUs 28) things get even more interesting. A dense dark brown, the beer evokes more than one category: a brief tip of the head to Ireland, a firm nod to American ales. Offering impressions of chocolate, roast malt, and coffee, the beer draws character from unobtrusive but well-placed hops. The Winces justifiably point to a "smooth bittersweet finish." The **Dancing Ferret IPA** (ABV 6.6 percent, IBUs 94) is one of Ohio's great IPAs. The unfiltered color is of hammered copper—not the more familiar yellow/orange but a darker, richer orange/brown. The unfiltered taste is of hops above all. Amarillo, Cascade, Centennial, and Summit hops offer a stroll through the citrus grove: orange, kumquat, grapefruit. The bitterness greets you on the front end and bids you farewell, but there's solid malt taste as well to keep you company.

The "son of Dancing Ferret," **Bitter Sable Imperial Black IPA** (ABV 8.0 percent, IBUs 100), reinterprets the IPA by ramping up the flavor (roasted barley) and the alcohol. But there's nothing intimidating. The full, rich taste has an unexpected softness about it, and there's a note of sweetness in the finish.

The "transient critters" include White Weasel Wheat, Feisty Fisher Amber Ale, Blackfooted Porter, and Wiley Wolverine Rye IPA. Seasonal beers include the prizewinning Anastasia Russian Imperial Stout, Snow

Brewery owners Lori and Jay Wince enjoy Weasel Boy's riverside patio.

A glance at the chalkboard will give you an idea of Weasel Boy's beers—and its ambience.

Ermine Holiday Ale, a mango wheat ale, and Weasel Paw Pawpaw Pale Ale brewed from Ohio pawpaw fruit. I'm not making that up. There's also a commitment at Weasel Boy to revive Zanesville beers brewed before Prohibition by Simon Linser. In addition to a Linser-inspired Vienna lager (summer) and a winter bock, the brewery offers a spring seasonal, American Maid, a "well received" pre-Prohibition pilsner. Check out the full list on the brewery's Web site.

The Food

Pizza is the order of the day at Weasel Boy. Jay's experience as a baker (he is certified by the American Institute of Baking) shows in the crust made daily with whole-wheat flour and beer. Toppings come from local sources as much as possible. There's Rittberger Italian sausage and Gerber naturally raised chicken, for instance. There are also salads made with ingredients from nearby farms (in season, anyway), dressings made on the spot, and breadsticks. The limited menu enables Weasel Boy to focus on quality and creativity.

Newsworthy

In 2010, Weasel Boy earned a bronze medal at the GABF for its Anastasia Russian Imperial Stout. In 2012, they won the gold! • In November 2014, the brewery sponsored a benefit for the Susan G. Komen Foundation featuring a biologist's talk on brewer's yeast as well as a beer tasting, a competition for home brewers, and a silent auction. • In a different approach to collaboration, Weasel Boy traded recipes with an Irish brewery, West Kerry: an imperial IPA from Zanesville in exchange for a red ale from Ballyferriter, so far out on Ireland's Dingle peninsula that Gaelic remains the everyday language there.

Other Stuff

The events room at Weasel Boy regularly hosts exhibitions of local and regional art. (One of the bartenders teaches art, and the pub's traditions include encouraging patrons to try handicrafts as they sip.) The calendar for the bimonthly openings appears on the brewery's Web site. • The room is also available for rental with catering.

THE SKINNY

LOCATION	From downtown Zanesville, cross the Putnam Avenue/South 6th Street bridge and turn right on Muskingum Avenue. Weasel Boy will soon be on your right.
HOURS	Tue–Fri 4:00 P.M.–midnight • Sat 3:00 P.M.–midnight
PARKING	There's a lot across the street—but make sure you're in the Weasel lot, not the one just to the north, which prohibits Weasel Boy parking.
KIDS	They are welcome, and there are soft drinks for them.
TAKEOUT	You can fill a growler.
DISTRIBUTION	Weasel Boy distributes kegs to competitions and to some local bars and restaurants, but there are no plans at present for bottling or canning.

WOLF'S RIDGE BREWING

215 North 4th Street, Columbus, Ohio 43215

614-429-3936 • http://www.wolfsridgebrewing.com/

Between lunch and dinner at Wolf's Ridge there's a lovely space for preparation.

There are two Wolf's Ridge establishments: a serious restaurant operating in tandem with a serious brewery and, right next door, a roomy, inviting taproom offering a limited menu.

The combination is highly engaging, but the restaurant in particular may surprise visitors seeking a quick pint and a burger. Owned and operated by a father-son team, Alan and Bob Szuter, the elegant (a word used sparingly in this book) restaurant expresses the intent of the owners to make a positive contribution to Columbus by offering "a wonderful dining and drinking experience." They are offering also an example of the values celebrated in Chapter 1: the restoration of their strategically positioned location, the enthusiasm for new directions, a commitment to sustainability, and a determination to focus "on craft and locally sourced products and services as much as possible" in order to support the community. The more recent (January 2015) opening of the taproom emphasized these values more fully. Regardless of what you may be expecting, I would lay odds that you will be impressed by Wolf's Ridge—perhaps surprised, but pleasantly so.

The Beers

Begin brewing carefully and deliberately, focusing on just a couple of varieties. Make sure of quality. Eventually expand the variety. Hire a brewmaster: Chris Davison. Meet customer expectations with guest beers. That was the plan for WRB's first months. Since then, with confidence in its quality, the brewery has expanded its list.

I sampled two in the early going. The **3 A.M. IPA** (ABV 7.0 percent, IBUs N/A) offered the expected appeals of a well-made IPA—a pleasing light amber color, an aroma offering cedar and lemon, a malt taste confronting hops bitterness with brown sugar—but came through with a tasting profile that began promisingly with fruit, soon developed a complex balance of malts and hops, and concluded with a sense of bitterness on the back of the tongue that argued for another sip. I write in the past tense because this beer does not appear on more recent listings. If it surfaces again, keep an eye on the ABV because this IPA did not give the impression of a 7.0 percent beer.

My other taste was of **Little Red Riding Ale** (ABV 4.5 percent, IBUs N/A), a companionable red that fits securely within its style, a negotiation of brown and Pale Ales. I found neither great complexity nor a marked profile from start to finish, but the ale is now brewed at ABV 5.4 percent (with IBUs 37) and promises "aromas of clover honey and toasted whole-grain bread." Even in its earlier incarnation, I thought it would accompany well many of the interesting dishes on the menu. The beer list, now far more inclusive, offers Clear Sky (a cream ale), Alpha (a Belgian tripel), Driftwood (a session IPA at ABV 4.6 percent), Ridge Trail (an amber), Howling Moon (an imperial IPA at ABV 8.2 percent), Luck Strikes Twice (an American IPA), Buchenrauch (a smoke lager), and N2 the Night (a milk stout on nitro). It's clearly time to make another visit.

Cofounder and co-owner Bob Szuter draws a Wolf's Ridge brew.

The Food

Wolf's Ridge offered another test of my resolve to refuse offers of food. I successfully resisted—but with great difficulty. While there is much good food to be had at many of Ohio's brewpubs, this restaurant, which embodies chef Seth Lassak's high standard of quality and creativity, promises memorable meals. The photo suggests just how far removed this kitchen

CIA-trained chef Seth Lassak raises "brewpub" dining to a new level.

is from those limited largely to pub favorites. The beautifully garnished pan-seared foie gras resting on a bed of celery root puree, apple compote, and crushed pistachio seems a far cry from fried onion rings! The chef's mentors at the Culinary Institute of America would be proud!

Similarly, you will not find much in common between the WRB fennel salad (shaved fennel, arugula, roasted red peppers, grapefruit, parsnip chips) and your corner tavern's Caesar. There's much at WRB for the hearty appetite, to be sure, but there's not much that is straightforward. Choose the venison, dusted with coriander and cumin. Or a root vegetable risotto. Want a burger? How about a beef and lamb burger with rémoulade?

If you visit for lunch, you will find a different but no less interesting menu. Yes, there is a pulled-pork sandwich, but you will find also mole duck confit tacos. Virtually every item on the menu—from the sweet tea ("Gahanna brewed") to the radishes ("smoked butter, pink Himalayan salt, crushed pistachios") to the ginger ale ("made with agave & real ginger")—reveals a kitchen intent on both intriguing and satisfying its guests. There are separate menus for brunch and for vegetarians.

Newsworthy
Wolf's Ridge received recognition as Best New Restaurant in 2013 from *Columbus Monthly* magazine and was further recognized in 2014 as No. 2 in the magazine's list of ten best restaurants. • WRB has a four-stars rating by the *Columbus Dispatch*. • Special events such as a prix fix New Year's Eve dinner deserve the notice they receive. • So does the opening of the WRB taproom in January 2015. An early review by Columbus's Pat's Pints Web site emphasizes that the new space, offering a limited menu, is above all "a place for drinking beer." Or coffee. A May 2015 collaboration between the brewery and One Line Coffee offered samples of Allegory Brown Ale flavored through infusion with four different coffee varieties. • The WRB pumpkin ale, Pi, weighed in with twice the pumpkin flavor in fall 2015.

Other Stuff

WRB accepts reservations at the number given above, but there are always some tables held for "our neighbors, wanderers, and those of you who prefer to live spontaneously."

THE SKINNY

LOCATION	North 4th Street is of course a downtown Columbus thoroughfare, one-way to the north. To reach 4th, access East Main Street from I-71S or East Broad Street from I-71N. In either case drive west to a right turn onto 4th. Or take the 3rd Street exit from I-670W and drive south to East Long Street. Turn left, then turn left again on 4th.
HOURS	Tue–Thu 10:30 A.M.–11:00 P.M. • Fri 10:30 A.M.–midnight • Sat 10:00 A.M.–midnight • Sun 10:00 A.M.–10:00 P.M. Check the Web site for taproom hours.
PARKING	There is a large self-park lot across 4th Street from Wolf's Ridge.
KIDS	Adults are the primary clientele, but WRB will happily accommodate children, and the chef will prepare child-friendly meals on request.
TAKEOUT	You can purchase growler fills in traditional sixty-four-ounce growlers.
DISTRIBUTION	WRB distributes "to some of central Ohio's best bars, growler shops, and restaurants." There's a list on the Web site.

TAPROOMS

THE ACTUAL BREWING COMPANY

655 North James Road, Columbus, Ohio 43219

614-636-3825 or 614-284-3741 • http://www.actualbrewing.com

Fred Lee, who restored Actual Brewing's brewing system, now supervises the brewing process.

A more unprepossessing location is difficult to imagine. Brewing beer (and roasting coffee, and operating a product-testing lab) in a few bays of a commercial park just beyond the perimeter of the Columbus airport, Actual Brewing offers no pretense of elegance. One reporter memorably suggested that its taproom might remind you of "your first college apartment." What this earnest and enterprising brewery does offer are imaginative, carefully brewed beers distributed throughout Central Ohio and now served fresh Wednesday to Saturday in the most raffish and informal of settings.

The back story is as fascinating as the beer. Phase one: 2010. Dedicated home brewer (and former bank vice president) Fred Lee conceived of an approach to brewing beer without incurring a tax liability. He created a religion, "Actualism." It had (or has) a creed, a version of Polonius's "to thine own self be true." Not surprisingly, that did not turn out so well. Phase two: 2011. Create a business plan. In fact, Fred and his wife, Mira, are clearly shrewd business people. But they needed a stroke of good fortune. In April of that year, in the depths of a barn, behind an old Dodge and some random chairs, they discovered the essential components for a brewing system. Phase three: Initiate the business plan, find a suitable location, and start brewing beer. On the side, they would roast artisan coffee and run a lab for other craft brewers. Ignition! Phase four, which includes a downtown brewpub, lies in the future—one more reason to pay attention.

At Actual Brewing I had an opportunity to taste the beer mentioned in the Smokehouse profile, a collaboration with the Ohio History Center to brew a beer informed by rudimentary knowledge of ancient brewing techniques. (See Lenny Kolada's detailed account of this experiment in his blog: Document7smokehousebrewing.com/brewdoodblog/.) The result? Memorable, to be sure. Don't look for this on the shelves of your favorite beer store. But do raise one of Actual's really good beers in tribute to the brewery's public spirit. Also keep an eye on a tangential outgrowth of this project, the brewery's wild sour tryouts supervised by cellarman Zach Harper.

The Beers

There's much to like about Actual's beers. Brewers Chris Moore and Jonathan Carroll offer a limited range (so far) to allow a consistent focus on quality and consistency. The labels are memorable—among "10 Great Ohio Beer Labels" listed in a sidebar. The beers are memorable as well.

Mira Lee designs distinctive labels for Actual's artisan beers.

The first I tasted was **Elektron** (ABV 6.2 percent, IBUs 27), an American amber ale laced with rye malt. Although I often find amber ales a rather plain cousin to Pale Ales and IPAs, this one has an impressive personality that invites further acquaintance. Just as you anticipate the predictable virtues of this popular style, there is a hint of a tease—perhaps owing to the Ohio-grown hops, perhaps to the soupçon of rye malt. I enjoyed next a taste of **Ingenuity Ale** (ABV 5.3 percent, IBUs 21.5), a lemongrass saison that tastes, the brewery says, "like lemonbears, summer nights and big ideas." Having no clue as to the taste of any of these, I would say instead that this farmhouse-style beer leans more toward the fruit orchard than toward the barnyard. There is a hint of spiciness kept well in check by a level of bitterness that seems just right.

My final sample was **Fat Julian,** an imperial stout (ABV 10 percent, IBUs 45). "Reminiscent of leathery elephants dipped in dark chocolate"? Hmmm, no. At least I don't think so. But this large beer probably would have pleased the czars. The alcohol contributes perceptibly to the taste, both on the front and back ends, but the bittersweet chocolate considerably softens that impression. Very good—but if you choose to enjoy this beer in a twenty-two-ounce bottle by yourself, drink it at home or call a taxi afterwards.

There is also Curiosus, a Berliner Weisse, described by the brewery as "curiously tart . . . with a charming sour bite." Those who know German drinking customs may imagine this style "mit Schuss," with a shot of syrup to take the edge off the sourness. Completing the list in December 2014 was Orthodox, a "winter IPA," brewed with "roasty malts and musky hops" so as to make spices irrelevant. Writing for the January 8, 2014, issue of *Drink Up Columbus,* Paul Gardner observes "the hops are the major flavor, while the malts follow just behind, working with one another in a lovely harmony while allowing each of their strengths to shine through and grace your tongue with wonderful deliciousness."

The Food

Although there is the aspiration to open a downtown brewpub eventually, there are no immediate plans. This is really a tasting room. But Actual encourages you to bring food, and food trucks visit on Thursday and Friday evenings.

Newsworthy

Actual Brewing was recognized as the "best startup business of 2013" by the Columbus Metropreneur. Interviewed by the Web site's Susan Post, Mary McDonald, OCBA executive director, said, "Fred and Mira Lee put a lot of serious consideration into all facets of their business, from the creative science of brewing beer, Fred's forte, to the artistic expression of their branding, Mira's muse." • Actual Brewing released its first canned beer in September 2015: Photon Light Lager.

Other Stuff

As mentioned in the intro, Actual Brewing also roasts coffee and packages it in one-pound bags. There are at least four varieties, each with its own label by Mira Lee. The laboratory specializes in testing beer for specific gravity, ABV, IBUs, and other quantities. Their best deal, unlimited lab services for a monthly fee, was sold out as this book went to press.

THE SKINNY

LOCATION	Take I-670 in the direction of the airport. Exit on East 5th and drive east to North James, which veers off on the left. Turn left onto East 7th for just a few yards and pull in to the parking lot of Airport Plaza. You'll find the brewery in Building 1.
HOURS	Wed–Thu 5:00–10:00 P.M. • Fri 5:00 P.M.– midnight • Sat noon–5:00 P.M.
PARKING	Not a problem.
KIDS	You be the judge.
TAKEOUT	Growlers plus 750-milliliter and 22-ounce bottles. Cans as of 2015.
DISTRIBUTION	To several pubs, restaurants, and taverns in the greater Columbus area. But Actual has plans to invade the Cleveland and Cincinnati markets as well.

COLUMBUS BREWING COMPANY

2555 Harrison Road, Columbus, Ohio 43204
614-224-3626

Well, this used to be confusing. Had you strolled into the Columbus Brewing Company restaurant in, let's say, September 2014, you would have found an exciting range of seasonal offerings, all Ohio, all craft. For instance, there was Jackie O's Barking Pumpkin, Mt. Carmel's Harvest Ale, Hoppin' Frog's Frog's Hollow, and Thirsty Dog's Barktoberfest. What you would not have found on this enticing list is a beer brewed by the Columbus Brewing Company. Despite their shared name and what was formerly a shared location, the Columbus Brewing Company and the Columbus Brewing Company restaurant are not the same company—and never were. The restaurant may be a good one. Its beer listings have been impressive. But this book does not cover restaurants that do not brew beer.

The confusion ended (mostly, anyway) in early 2015, when the brewing company located the space it needed just off of I-70 due west of downtown. The new space makes possible some much-needed elbow room for production brewing. A brewery that had been brewing for statewide distribution in only six thousand square feet now operates a far larger brewing system in nearly ten times the space. But the added space also makes possible some experimentation and product development using a small German-made pilot system. Visitors to the new tasting room

Columbus Brewing's Eric Bean lifts his IPA, an Ohio year-round favorite.

and beer garden will therefore find not only Columbus Brewing's popular staples but also some interesting new departures.

The roots of the brewery in Columbus are deep. It opened in 1988, at the beginning of Ohio's craft beer movement, but its name pays tribute to that of the original Columbus Brewing Company, which began operations in 1830. And its ingredients, many of them anyway, come from local harvests. Now those roots can spread as they should.

The Beers

The ones with which I am most familiar are the **Columbus Pale Ale** (ABV 5.5 percent, IBUs 28) and the **IPA** (ABV 6.50 percent, IBUs 50). The Pale Ale may not challenge an experienced palate, but it is uncommonly satisfying by virtue of its careful balance of German and English malts with American hops. This is neither a traditional English bitter nor a West Coast ale. It is itself. But if you have memories of warm evenings in a British pub or a sunset in San Diego, this beer could put you in touch with them again. The unfiltered IPA adds exclamation points to the appeals of the Pale Ale, especially so far as the malt presence is concerned. Oh, and Simcoe hops are conspicuous in both taste and aroma. If you enjoy either beer, you will enjoy the other. How to decide? Keep both in your refrigerator and plan a showdown comparison in the Columbus taproom.

There are seasonals as well. **Summer Teeth,** which won a medal at the 2010 GABF, honors the Kellerbier tradition of unfiltered lagers with low carbonation and strong hops flavor. Because this style can be a bit opaque, Germans often serve cellar beer in stoneware mugs. That's not necessary with the Columbus interpretation, but it might be a nice touch. Festbier? You guessed it—a beer brewed to honor the Oktoberfest tradition in Germany. And there's Winter Warmer. The Columbus Brewing Web site mentions "England's soggy, gray winters" as the inspiration for heavily malted spiced ales to be "enjoyed in the company of family and friends." Ohioans also know something about gray winters. Columbus Brewing may be performing a public service.

Newsworthy

The opening of the new production brewery and tasting room was a major 2015 headline. • Eric Bean is serving his second term as president of the OCBA. It was under his first-term leadership that the organization secured its first executive director. • In 2014, Columbus Brewing won a gold medal at the World Beer Cup for Uncle Rusty (imperial red), a bronze for Bodhi (IPA), and a gold for Creeper (double IPA). • In January 2015, the brewery announced a thorough "rebranding": new logo, new labels, new bottles.

THE SKINNY

LOCATION	There are several options. To reach 2555 Harrison Road, take 70W, exit on North Hague, and drive south (your only option) to a left on Harrison. Or exit 70E at N Wilson, turn left on N Wilson, turn left on Fisher, and turn right on N Hague to Harrison. Better yet: Follow the up-to-date advice of your GPS device.
HOURS	To be determined. Check the Web site.
PARKING	There appears to be ample parking, but inquire to make certain.
KIDS	Remains to be determined.
TAKEOUT	Probably, but inquire to make certain.
DISTRIBUTION	Columbus Brewing distributes throughout Ohio.

FOUR STRING BREWING COMPANY

985 West 6th Avenue, Columbus, Ohio 43212
614-725-1282 • http://fourstringbrewing.com/

There's not much "street appeal." The taproom is small. The hours are limited. But if you love beer, you'll enjoy the harmony you can taste at Four String, which celebrated its fourth anniversary in October 2015. The name points to owner Dan Cochran's career as bass guitarist for several regional bands, but it signifies also the four essential elements of beer: malt, hops, yeast, water. A home brewer since 1994, Dan had the idea for a brewery while touring with his bands, "sampling every small pub and picking every brew brain from NYC to Seattle." He built the brewery himself. Low moment? During construction, the local hardware store declined

Ram or brass knuckles? Take your pick. Four String's American Pale Ale hits hard.

his debit card. Best moments? In the present, welcoming fans of his beer. He says it best: "It's about taking that chance and delivering the dream one glass at a time. Every sip, every growler that walks out the door had damn well better crush it."

The Beers

In addition to interesting new efforts you may find on tap during your visit, there are four reliable beers, all of which are thoroughly satisfying examples of their styles. I enjoyed sampling the four during my visit—plus one other I purchased later in a six-pack.

Backstage Blonde (ABV 5 percent, IBUs 28), a Belgian Pale Ale, hits the sweet spot between the drinkability of a straightforward ale and the spice of a Belgian. I will avoid the suggestiveness of the brewery's description of this pleasing session ale, but you will enjoy reading it.

Brass Knuckle (ABV 5.75 percent, IBUs 36), an American Pale Ale, lingers on the palette "like a windmill power chord." (Think of The Who's Pete Townshend performing "My Generation.") There's citrus and some evergreen, perhaps a touch of brown sugar from the toasted malts. You may want to have more than one. And that's OK.

Big Star (ABV 7 percent, IBUs 70), Four String's white IPA, is labeled "bright and exciting." True. The Belgian-style ale, brewed with wheat, announces a strong presence of citrus in its aroma and carries through on that promise in the taste. The label emphasizes grapefruit, but I tasted a cross between orange and lemon. While the IBUs number appears formidable, you need not be a hophead to enjoy it. Context is all. Finally, there's **Suncaster** (ABV 5.0 percent, IBUs 28), an American wheat beer. You don't need (and shouldn't request) a slice of orange. All the taste you will need is in the glass of beer.

Having rejoiced in finding the canned seasonal **Vanilla Porter** (ABV 6.0 percent, IBUs 42) in my grocery store at the darkest time of the year, I thoroughly enjoyed its exceptional balance of genuine vanilla flavor (Madagascar beans), a complex malt base, and just the right hops presence.

Four String Brewing's clear Backstage Blonde adds elegance to its informal brewery setting.

The Food
Dan Cochran: "I don't want to run a restaurant." But food trucks visit regularly.

Newsworthy
Four String has joined the fight for grocery store cooler space by working with peripatetic Buckeye Canning to package its beer. The first onto the shelves? Brass Knuckle American Pale. The Vanilla Porter I mention above. Suncaster Summer Wheat reached the shelves in late spring 2015 and Skeleton Red IPA was scheduled to follow in the fall. • Featuring Columbus in its "Worth the Trip" series in February 2015, NBC Chicago mentioned one brewery: this one.

Other Stuff
There's a happy hour with pints for $3 from 4:00 to 7:00 P.M. on days the taproom is open. From time to time, there are new beers in the "solo series" to sample. Recent examples include a farmhouse saison rye ale and an imperial IPA.

LOCATION	The taproom is in the Grandview Heights neighborhood, not far from OSU and the Lennox Town Center. Driving south on Olentangy River Road, turn right onto West 5th, right on Gerrard, and right again on West 6th.
HOURS	Thu–Fri 4:00–11:00 P.M. • Sat noon–11:00 P.M.
PARKING	There's some parking in front of the building and on the street. If you must park in one of the adjacent lots, inquire first.
KIDS	It does not feel like a scene for kids.
TAKEOUT	Fill your growler (sixty-four ounce) or buy a "howler" (thirty-two ounce).
DISTRIBUTION	Four String has expanded its kegging and canning and in July 2015 began distributing as far north as Cleveland.

NORTH HIGH BREWING

1288 North High Street, Columbus, Ohio 43201

614-407-5278 • http://www.northhighbrewing.com/index.php/

As graduate business students at Ohio State, craft brewers Gavin Meyers and Tim Ward knew that making a living from their avocation would require a strong business plan focused on a unique niche. They decided to create "a new kind of brewery . . . one that focuses on the EXPERIENCE of brewing." And that's what North High does. On the north side of its handsome corner location in the Short North Arts District, you can order from the extensive, evolving menu of craft beers brewed there in small batches. On the south side, you can do the brewing yourself, using the North High equipment and benefiting from expert advice.

More recently, the popularity of North High's beers has prompted an expansion in production, from a two-barrel system at the North High location to a twenty-barrel system located nearby on Cleveland Avenue. That will enable the brewery to distribute some of its beers in cans to Central Ohio—to begin with. To help with the move and with the additional brewing it makes possible, Meyers and Ward have added a partner, experienced brewer Jason McKibben. But the experience of North High itself remains a delight. There are almost always the wonderful aromas of beer being

Tim Ward and Gavin Meyers (*left to right*) find pints in their North High mailboxes.

brewed, there's the ambience of authentic "restoration hardware," there is a widely reported "great vibe" (see the brewery's Facebook page), and there is above all a remarkable range of beers to enjoy.

The Beers

Dan Eaton, a reporter for *Columbus Business First,* compared two business models for craft brewing. "Four String Brewing Co . . . started with just two beers and has gradually added from there to build a lineup of four year-round beers with several seasonals. North High has been at the other end of that spectrum, having produced more than 90 beers since opening." With so much from which to choose, I echo North High's encouragement of visitors to "come in and see." But the common thread evident in all of their beers is imagination and quality control.

North High's radiant wheat beer illuminated by North High Street.

The **Chocolate Milk Stout** (ABV 6.0 percent, IBUs 20) is one rich beer. Think of coffee beans covered with bittersweet chocolate. But this is no confection. It's a formidable, well-brewed stout, as appealing in appearance as it is on the palate. One of my Ohio favorites (not a ranking, mind,

Brewer Charles Davis checks on the boil at North High.

just a point of view) is the **Wildcard! English Ale** (ABV 5.2 percent, IBUs 20) served on nitro. From the creamy, long-lasting head to the last sip, this is one delicious beer. Roasted malt and the addition of vanilla beans create a further complexity in what would in any event be memorable. Visiting in the morning, I chose to forgo additional tastings, but I wanted to taste their IPA (ABV 6.8 percent, IBUs 70), their Citra Smash (ABV 4.3 percent, IBUs 85), and their cream ale (ABV 5.7 percent, IBUs 22). I shall return!

The Food
Thanks to a partnership with Café del Mondo, there are some interesting paninis available, from a challenging Diablo (hot Capacolla, pepper jack cheese, banana peppers) to a veggie with artichoke, roasted red pepper, olive, onion, and provolone.

Newsworthy
The major expansion mentioned above certainly qualifies as "newsworthy." • Watch for occasional bottle releases of barrel-aged beers. • North High is a prominent participant in Columbus's Winter Beerfest. • In collaboration with a food truck and the Daily Growler (the taphouse located in Upper Arlington and on Powell Road), North High brewed Carrot Cake Milk Stout in 2015—just in time for Valentine's Day.

Other Stuff
Like Brew Kettle in suburban Cleveland, North High offers aspiring brewmasters an opportunity to brew on their premises with their expert support. "We guide you through the entire process of beer brewing and even clean up all the mess!" You'll need to make a reservation, of course.

THE SKINNY

LOCATION	The brewery, on a corner just a few blocks south of the Ohio State campus, represents an important addition to Columbus's Short North Arts District. Its name is its address. Exit I-71 to 5th Avenue and drive west to North High.
HOURS	Mon–Thu 2:00 P.M.–midnight • Fri–Sat noon–2:00 A.M. • Sun 11:00 A.M.–10:00 P.M.
PARKING	There's an adjacent lot.
KIDS	They're not unwelcome, but I found no particular provision for them.
TAKEOUT	Growler fills are available.
DISTRIBUTION	North High beers are available in many Columbus bars and restaurants. Expanded production facilities should support expanded distribution.

SEVENTH SON BREWING

1101 North 4th Street, Columbus, Ohio 43201
614-421-BEER • http://seventhsonbrewing.com/

The folkloric associations prompted by the name are complicated. The basic assumption is that the seventh son of a seventh son is somehow set apart, either by innate gifts or by a grant of powers by the gods. There's the Irish belief that such a son has gifts as a healer. Many, many works of literature take up this theme, but one in particular, a fantasy novel by Orson Scott Card, has enjoyed particular prominence as an inspiration for a challenging late 1980s album release by the British band Iron Maiden. So what's the connection to the tasting room at 4th and 4th? The brewery's owners and creative brewers understand the seventh son to be "a powerful harbinger of good fortune," much like, one might suppose, a new brewery in an upcoming neighborhood. As an acknowledgment, one of their flagship ales boasts seven different hops.

On ground perhaps a bit less speculative, the front story posted by Seventh Son owners Collin Castore, Jen Burton, and Travis Spencer offers a fascinating account of the complex arrangements, preparations, and support networks a start-up may require. It's worth quoting: "With the help of private investors, a Huntington Small Business Administration loan, coursework at the Siebel Institute of Technology ["America's oldest brewing school"], talented designers, patient architects, extensive tasting (drinking), intensive recipe formulation, inspirational brewers, and countless hours of planning our brewery is complete."

Of course, from the perspective of the customer, what's important is whether these preparations add up to good beers and a good experience. Perhaps with a bit of good fortune emanating from their auspicious name, they do.

Brewer Colin Vent serves a beer—and provides a chemistry lesson.

The Beers

In the relatively short time that Seventh Son has been brewing, brewer Colin Vent has created a list that offers a rotating selection of enterprising creations in addition to three mainstays. Those are the ones I sampled.

Seventh Son American Strong Ale (ABV 7.7 percent, IBUs 40) is a worthy addition to an influential lineup known best for Stone Brewing's Arrogant Bastard. The category allows considerable variation but is reserved for beers with ABV levels above 7.0 percent. But the strength of Seventh Son's version is not its defining characteristic, however. The aroma is extraordinary, memorable by any standard, perhaps inimitable. Recall the seven hops mentioned above. And the taste, while not as remarkable, graciously balances the fruitiness and bitterness of the hops with a weighty malt presence.

Stone Fort Oat Brown Ale (ABV 5.25 percent, IBUs 25) honors a small, isolated Coshocton county building reputed to be Ohio's oldest. The beer is larger than the "fort," in that its rich toasted grain conquers the palete at once. Its English pedigree is patent. The brewers want you to taste "roast coffee, cocoa, leather and biscuit flavors." With that list in mind, perhaps you will. This is a good solid ale.

If you can't remember "**Humulus Nimbus Super Pale Ale** (ABV 6.0 percent, IBUs 53)," you can simply order Hops Cloud. (Humulus evokes the scientific name of the hops plant, while nimbus of course refers to clouds likely to bring rain.) The hops in this instance, Mosaic and Simcoe, greet you at once in the aroma of this fresh, fruity beer that maintains its seriousness with a less-than-subtle but fully delightful bitterness.

I want to return in the hope of encountering one or two of the "great new beers" Vent and his associate, Max Lachowyn, create from time to time. For example, there's Stone Rabbit (displaying the pleasures of dry hopping), Glad Tidings (an orangey winter beer), an Ale of Two Cities (Dickens might enjoy this double IPA brewed in collaboration with Jackie O's), a Belgian-style double IPA, and various farmhouse ales and stouts.

The Food

Seventh Son publishes an inviting list of scheduled food trucks that visit from Tuesday to Sunday and takes the additional step of providing the Facebook listings for each. On Fridays, Saturdays, and Sundays there's a sequence. In effect, a "lunch" truck gives way to a "dinner" truck.

A Colin Vent creation awaits the first sip.

Newsworthy

Interviewed by the Columbus NPR station about the decision to can two Seventh Son brews, Colin Castore defended the taste of canned beer ("you'd never be able to tell the difference") but urged buyers to pour his beer "into a proper glass." • Columbus Underground picked Seventh Son as the city's best local brewery in 2013 and 2014.

Other Stuff

There are some inexpensive logo mementoes available such as beer koozies, stickers, and a pint glass, as well as an elegant wooden tap handle and apparel. On Saturdays, Seventh Son welcomes Columbus Beer Adventures.

THE SKINNY

LOCATION	Seventh Son is easy to find. Take the 5th Avenue exit off I-71 and drive west (on East 5th) to North 4th Street. Take a left for two blocks and you're there. If you are on North High, drive east on East 5th to North 4th and turn right.
HOURS	Tue–Wed 4:00 P.M.–midnight • Thu 4:00 P.M.–2:00 A.M. • Fri–Sat 11:00 A.M.–2:00 A.M. • Sun 11:00 A.M.–midnight
PARKING	Appears ample, though I was not there during peak evening hours.
KIDS	Not really, at least according to my intuition. But you may want to inquire.
TAKEOUT	Growler fills are available.
DISTRIBUTION	In addition to more than fifty keg accounts with restaurants and taverns in the Columbus area, the brewery is now canning two of its beers.

ZAUBER BREWING COMPANY

909 West Fifth Avenue, Columbus, Ohio 43212
Telephone 614-456-7074 • http://www.zbeers

Mozart's entertaining opera, *Die Zauberflöte,* tells the story of a romantic couple that endures a series of ordeals in order to be wed and presumably live happily ever after—all through the aid of a "magic flute." Similarly, brewer/owner Geoff Towne says that all brewing requires a "leap of faith—a moment of trust in the magic of fermentation." Of all Columbus breweries, Zauber focuses most closely on creating zauber (i.e., magical) beers in the Germanic and Belgian brewing traditions. Indeed, a beer fan planning or recalling a trip to Zauber might enjoy reviewing the styles of German beer, described in detail on the Web site of the German Beer Institute (http://www.germanbeerinstitute.com/styles.html).

The brewery started operations at a different address in 2012 as a growler-filling nano-brewery with aspirations for growth. Building on his experience in Austria, on a UC-Davis certificate in brewing science, and on his experience at Great Lakes (Cleveland) and Boston Beer (Cincinnati), Towne opened the current taproom, roomy and hospitable, early in 2014.

Brewer Cameron Lloyd and Zauber founder Geoff Towne (*left to right*) share a hearty Zum Wohl!

The Beers

Since the opening of the new brewing system (see Newsworthy) brewers Pat Tyznik and Cameron Lloyd have been demonstrating its capability. I sampled five of Zauber's wide range of beers.

Vertigo (ABV 5.4 percent, IBUs 12) makes a good case for an unfiltered wheat beer, that is, a hazy Hefeweizen, as a year-round pleasure. Rather than experiencing a sensation of vertigo, you should instead experience balance inspired by a careful straddling of German and Belgian brewing traditions. It has an intriguing sweetness that is far from simplistic thanks to the hints of spice, citrus, and banana. **Myopic Red** (ABV 5.0 percent, IBUs 16) will take you to the beer halls of Düsseldorf for an ale lovely in color and amiable in taste. Roast malt with a hint of plum and cherry and an overarching nuttiness will be what you remember—and your memory will be acute, thanks to this true session beer.

The **Buxom Blonde** (ABV 6.3 percent, IBUs 30) and her first cousin, **Berzerker** (ABV 6.3 percent, IBUs 60), together introduce the distinctive aromas and tastes of Belgian beers. There the comparison becomes more complicated. To borrow from Zauber's mischievous copy, the Blonde is "well proportioned, soft, and beautiful." All true. By contrast, Berzerker concedes the family resemblance but offers a taste of international diplomacy: the distinctive fruity edge created by Belgian-style yeast married to the satisfying bitterness of a British IPA.

Poltergeist (ABV 5.0 percent, IBUs 31), another fusion, adds to the straightforward accessibility of a British dockworker's porter the depth and complexity of a German Schwartzbier to create a dark Altbier, the ancient (alt = old) style most closely assorted with the Rhineland. Neither Berzerker nor Poltergeist is a blend of separately brewed beers.

Zauber's efficient brewing system continues to expand.

They're much more interesting than that. They are beers brewed with reference to different traditions so as to develop fresh interpretations. There are many ways in which such an approach might have created discords, but, fortunately, with these beers Zauber has managed to capture both Mozart's inventiveness and his command of harmony.

I concluded by tasting a small sample drawn from a tank holding the brewery's remarkable holiday seasonal, **X-Mas** (ABV 6.1 percent, IBUs 35). Like the brewery's stronger Holiday Ale (ABV 8.7 percent, IBUs 35), this one forgoes the customary flavorings many Christmas ales feature. There are no spices, and there is no honey. But there are lots of spice and fruit in the taste of the ale, thanks to a remarkable blend of aromatic and bittering hops.

A beer I wish had been available during my visit, Zauber's Roggen Rye, recreates an ancient German style by emphasizing the malts of the brew—barley, wheat, and rye—rather than its mild hops. This promises to be a highly creative interpretation. To quote from the brewery's Web site: "the unique banana, clove, vanilla flavors of Weizen still apply with the addition of an herbal backbone, reminiscent of Rye bread." Other beers you may find at Zauber include Stodgy Brown (an ABV 5.2 percent German altbier), Magnum (an ABV 5.4 percent Belgian copper ale), and Kitschy Kolsch (ABV 5.3 percent). I list these ABV levels to make the point that the brewery focuses on Zauber (a magical charm) rather than Rausch (intoxication). That's with the possible exception of Ominous, an ABV 9.0 percent Belgian-style stout checking in at 55 IBUs, which sounds like another Anglo-Germanic fusion. Note to self: must schedule an Ominous experience.

Zauber's Cameron Lloyd stands ready behind a rank of Zauber taps.

The Food

Zauber doesn't serve food, but the brewery coordinates an interesting rotation of food trucks with a wide variety of offerings. Here, too, the Zauber Web site will tell you what you need to know.

Newsworthy

Since the opening of its attractive taproom on West Fifth, Zauber has begun production with its expanded brewing system, which is well worth a look. The heart of the twenty-barrel system is a temperature-controlled lineup of three tanks that align initial brewing stages into a single linear process, thereby permitting more consistent production—as much as two hundred kegs a month. • A fall 2015 Oktoberfest offered seasonal beers, special food truck selections, and live music. In fact, Zauber can be counted on to create events around most holidays.

Other Stuff

Brewers Night on Mondays will give you the chance to talk beer with Geoff Towne and the other Zauber brewers. There's usually live acoustic music on Tuesday nights. Every so often, it's "game night." The brewery stocks familiar board games to create camaraderie—and perhaps to emphasize the advantages of its session beers. You can also watch sports on the large-screen TVs. Soccer appears to be a particular taproom theme. There's a gift shop with apparel, glassware, etc.

THE SKINNY

LOCATION	To reach the Grandview Heights neighborhood from OH-315S, exit to Kinnear Road, turn left, and follow Olentangy River Road to West Fifth. Take a left and look for Zauber on your left after three long blocks. If you are headed north on 315, take the exit for West Goodale Street, turn right, then turn right on Olentangy and left on West Fifth.
HOURS	Mon–Tue 4:00–11:00 P.M. • Wed–Thu 11:00 A.M.–11:00 P.M. • Fri–Sat 11:00 A.M.–1:00 A.M. • Sun 11:00 A.M.–10:00 P.M. If you are visiting during the holiday season, check for special hours.
PARKING	There's some head-in parking in the back along the side of the brewery.
KIDS	I can't quite picture kids in this mix. But you may want to inquire.
TAKEOUT	Most beers may be purchased in growlers.

CONSIDER ALSO

BUCKEYE LAKE BREWERY (5176 Walnut Road, Suite A, Buckeye Lake, Ohio 43008) opened in early 2012. About midway between Columbus and Zanesville, it is highly accessible to Central Ohio. It is located on OH-79 in a former service station—not squarely on the lake, but close. There's an interesting lineup of beers, a restaurant, visiting food trucks on occasion, and equipment that enables them to sell thirty-two-ounce "fresh fill" cans of their beer. Telephone: 740-535-6225 Web: buckeyelakebrewery.com/ Current information is also posted on the brewery's Facebook page, https://www.facebook.com/buckeyelakebrewery

BUCK'S BREWING COMPANY (1046 Stewart Street, Suite E, Newark, Ohio 43058) brews for local taverns and restaurants. Examples of their brews include a black imperial IPA, an IPA, a Pale Ale, a porter, and a stout. Telephone: N/A Web: https://www.facebook.com/pages/Bucks-Brewing-Co/528852127200449

THE GRANVILLE BREWING COMPANY (5371 Columbus Road, Granville, Ohio 43023) focuses closely on Belgian-style ales, e.g., The Betrayer (a tripel brewed with honey), The Reaper (a saison), and The Oppressor (an imperial Belgian amber). Their twenty-two-ounce bottles are available in the college town and on the eastern rim of the Columbus area. Telephone: N/A Web: http://www.granvillebrewing.com/

Deep in the hills southeast of Columbus, the microbrewery at the HIDE-A-WAY HILLS LODGE (29042, Box 1, Hide-A-Way Hills Road, Ohio 43107) uses water from the lodge's well to brew Rushcreek lager ("a light beer that produces an almost true Czech pilsner") and a British-style Pale Ale. The brewpub is open evenings Tuesday through Saturday as is the lodge restaurant. Note that visitors who are not members must arrive with a reservation and must secure a pass at the security gate. Telephone: 740-569-7944 Web: http://www.hideawayhillslodge.com

Part of a growing franchise that "brings Bavaria to you," HOFBRÄUHAUS (800 Goodale Boulevard, Columbus, Ohio 43212) is "modeled after" the ancient beer hall in Munich. Open seven days a week, it offers German beer brewed in-house and German food that offers "an authentic German experience." (There's also a location in Cleveland.) Telephone: 614-294-2437 Web: http://hofbrauhauscolumbus.com/

Determined to defy the "spiraling arms race of more alcohol, more hops, more bitter beer," HOMESTEAD BEER COMPANY (811 Irving Wick Drive West, Heath, Ohio 43056) seeks to "restore the roots of American beer." To be clear, that does not mean reverting to insipid lagers. There's a full range of styles from three different IPAs to an American stout and a Pale Ale. You can sample the beers in the tasting room or the adjoining patio and beer garden, or you can fill your growler. Thanks to a distribution deal, the beers are more widely available throughout Ohio. Heath is just south of Granville and Newark. Telephone: 740-358-0360 Web: http://homesteadbeerco.com

Ignore the sophomoric pun and the, ahem, "distinctive" graphics. The beers brewed by HOOF HEARTED BREWING (300 Country Road, Marengo, Ohio 43334), once available only on draft in selected Central Ohio locations, are now well worth seeking elsewhere. An expansion in early 2015 enabled more production (thanks to a larger brewing system), more accessibility (thanks to a tasting room opened in July 2015), and wider availability (thanks to canning). In July 2015 HH began distribution of two notable IPAs, South of Eleven Double IPA and the award-winning Musk of the Minotaur. Keep an eye out also for a brewpub in Columbus's Italian Village, just north of downtown. In February 2015 Dan Eaton reported in Columbus Business First on the planning then under way. Telephone: 419-253-0000 Web: hoofheartedbrewing.com/ and facebook.com/hoofheartedbrewing/timeline?ref=page_internal

LAND-GRANT BREWING COMPANY (424 West Town Street, Columbus, Ohio 43215), in the Franklinton neighborhood, has a big footprint: 12,000 square feet in a former elevator factory. Every day, principals Adam Benner and Walt Keys open the taproom to offer four year-round beers: a Kölsch, a session IPA, a brown ale, and an IPA. New fermenters as of fall 2015 will expand capacity to 500+ barrels a year. Food trucks and guest beers offer a further invitation. In spring 2015 Land-Grant began distributing canned beer. Franklinton is just across the Scioto from the heart of downtown. Telephone: 614-427-3946 Web: https://landgrantbrewing.com

LINEAGE BREWING (2971 North High Street, Columbus, Ohio 43202) opened its "inevitable craft brewery" in the Clintonville neighborhood in the spring of 2015. "Inevitable"? Yes, given the home-brewing experience and success of the founders. Its Bricky Briffon English Pale is reputed to be about as close as we're going to come to a classic British bitter. Hours are Tuesday through Sunday. Telephone: 614-461-3622 Web: http://www.lineagebrew.com

MARIETTA BREWING COMPANY (167 Front Street, Marietta, Ohio 45750) opens seven days a week to offer an ambitious restaurant menu based on local ingredients, an inviting lineup of house brews featuring at least two IPAs, live music on weekends, and a charming downtown ambience near the confluence of the Muskingum and the Ohio. There's space for private parties as well. The city's slogan—"Bold Beginnings, New Adventures"—describes the brewery as well. Telephone: 740-373-2739 Web: http://mbcpub.com

MILLERSBURG BREWING COMPANY (60 East Jackson Street, Millersburg, Ohio 44654) brings craft brewing to Amish country. In fact, it stands squarely adjacent to the Holmes County Courthouse, equidistant between Columbus and Cleveland. One of my "Fifteen Great Architectural Experiences" among Ohio breweries, this one serves ten or so beers named mostly for local points of reference. For instance, there's Major Andrew

Hunter Holmes (a double IPA), French Ridge (an IPA), State Route 39 (a stout—and the street on which the brewery lives), and Killbuck Creek (a Kölsch). Distribution of canned beer—the IPA, for starters—began in March 2015. Open every day but Monday. Telephone: 330-674-4728 Web: http://millersburgbrewing.com

While planning for their grand opening in 2015, PIGSKIN BREWING COMPANY (81 Mill Street #150, Gahanna, Ohio 43230) kept Columbus beer (and sports) fans interested with regular Facebook postings of equipment deliveries, holiday greetings, construction updates, and beer-related commentaries. Founder Tarry Summers told Columbus CEO reporter T. C. Brown "we want to make sure people are wowed." The sports-centric taproom anchors Creekside Plaza, an upscale development close to Big Walnut Creek. Hungry fans can order from an inventive and expanding menu. Telephone: 614-944-9311 Web: http://pigskinbrewingcompany.com/

ROCKMILL BREWERY (5705 Lithopolis Road NW, Lancaster, Ohio 43130) opens its charmingly rustic tasting room Friday through Sunday to serve the Belgian-style beers much sought in distinctive craft bottles as well as some varieties available only on draft. An accomplished wine connoisseur, Matthew Barbee converted to brewing on discovering that the water on his family's farm, southeast of Columbus, corresponded to water used by certain Belgian brewers. The beers are distributed throughout Ohio. Telephone: 740-205-8076 Web: http://rockmillbrewery.com

SIDESWIPE BREWING (2419 Scioto Harper Drive, Columbus, Ohio 43204) is at present adjacent to the Scioto Trail, near Valley View. Owner Craig O'Herron is brewing with a 2.5 barrel system, but he says he's eager to move to a larger system in a larger facility. Its taproom opens on Thursdays from 5:00 to 9:00 P.M., and the brewery's beers in twenty-two-ounce bottles with eye-catching, boldly sketched labels are available at many taverns and beer stores in the Columbus area. Telephone: 614-719-9654/ Web: http://www.sideswipebrewing.com/

STAAS BREWING COMPANY (31 West Winter Street, Delaware, Ohio 43015) maintains a focus on "classic Belgian and English" styles that proprietors Liz and Donald Staas describe as "Delaware inspired." Because they emphasize the classic roots of their beers, they have imported British "beer engines" to enable authentic service from the cask. So the "Delaware inspiration" must be sought in the names of the beers. Their ESB is named The Runner Up to recall that Delaware almost became the capital of Ohio. Their "Presidential" IPA recognizes Delaware native Rutherford B. Hayes. And so on. They're open Thursday to Saturday, when food trucks visit on a fairly regular basis. Sign up for the shuffleboard league. Telephone: N/A Web: http://www.staasbrewing.com

I first met Scott Francis, the influential Columbus brewer, during my visit to Barley's in fall 2013. He left Barley's. Now he has left retirement to guide a new brewery, TEMPERANCE ROW BREWING COMPANY (41 North State Street, Westerville, Ohio 43081), which is located at the rear of Uptown Deli and Brew. The name reflects Westerville's role as national headquarters of the Anti-Saloon League in the early twentieth century, and the beers echo episodes of this history. For instance, Hatchetation Ale recalls Carrie Nation's vigorous attacks on saloons, while Corbin's Revenge is a posthumous attempt to honor the publican whose Westerville saloon was bombed—twice. But this new brewery also contributes to Columbus's brewing history, in that Scott Francis, a true Columbus brewing pioneer, is the brewmaster—assisted by his son! The Deli and Brew is open seven days a week. Telephone: 614-891-2337 Web: http://www.uptowndeliandbrew.com/ and https://www.facebook.com/temperancerowbrewingco

TWENTY-NINE BREWPUB (1692 Marion Mt. Gilead Road, Marion, Ohio 43302) opened in late 2014 serving wood-fired pizza and a range of guest craft beers. House-brewed beers arrived in 2015. Why "twenty-nine"? According to John Jarvis, writing for the *Marion Star,* the number honors the twenty-ninth president of the United States, Warren G. Harding. OK. Open seven days. Telephone: 740-751-4586 Web: https://www.facebook.com/pages/TwentyNine-BrewPub/544010975707246

ZAFTIG BREWING COMPANY (545 Schrock Road, Worthington, Ohio 43085) brews and bottles "full bodied ales" and opens its doors at least three times a week, Wednesday and Thursday evenings and Saturday afternoons. Though just kitty-cornered from Columbus's huge Anheuser-Busch plant, Zaftig's big beers will not be overshadowed. One hopes. After all, it's hard to imagine a mass-produced beer that could compete, say, with the result of Zaftig's collaboration with Crimson Cup Coffee & Tea, namely, BamBaLam Breakfast Stout. Telephone: 614-636-2537 Web: http://www.drinkzaftig.com/

AND DON'T OVERLOOK

COLUMBUS'S DAILY GROWLER. Even though it is neither a brewery nor a brewpub, it earns a mention for three reasons. First, it offers pint drinkers and growler fans a remarkable array of sixty craft beers "with a focus on local and regional microbreweries." Second, its two locations (2812 Fishinger Road, Upper Arlington, Ohio, 43221, and 258 West Olentangy Street, Powell, Ohio, 43065) are open every day. There's even a daily Happy Hour, 3:00–7:00 P.M. Most important, the Daily Growler respects growlers. They make them available at a reasonable price and fill only their own. I quote: "Each time you bring back your Growler we swap it out for a sanitized chilled one and then put your old Growler through our dedicated Growler dishwasher." That's a good precedent that should become an industry standard. Telephone: 614-656-2337 (Upper Arlington), 614-987-8277 (Powell) Web: thedailygrowler.com/about/

4

SOUTHERN EXPOSURE
CINCINNATI AND THE SOUTHEAST

Cincinnati can claim one of Ohio's newest production breweries, Rhine-geist, or "Ghost of the Rhine." Just about one hundred miles to the east, along the Ohio River, the Portsmouth Brewing Company makes its claim: "the oldest brewery in Ohio." From a resurgence of once-proud brewing traditions in historic buildings to the emergence of new, innovative traditions, the Ohio River is once again inspiring beers that will justify a beer fan's "southern strategy."

As was the case in the nineteenth century, most of the action can be found in and around Cincinnati. Prior to Prohibition, Cincinnati was one of the nation's brewing centers. German beer barons such as Christian Moerlein and Ludwig Hudepohl built breweries (and mansions) in Cincinnati. They also introduced the popular new style of beer, lager, which soon captured the public taste. A brewery tour of Over-the-Rhine (a neighborhood just north of downtown Cincinnati) offered throughout the summer will show you many of the remnants of this proud past. But the brewery district, now recognized by the city's Community Urban Redevelopment Corporation, is not just a showcase for past glories. It is an active site for brewery development. No fewer than three craft breweries, all with taprooms, are now operating in OTR, and that does not count the craft beers brewed in Cincinnati by Boston Brewing.

Cincinnati craft brewing today is by no means limited to this one historic area. There are craft breweries in warehouses and industrial parks. Mt. Carmel operates out of the brewing family's former homestead. Fifty West, having discovered that a legendary suburban restaurant had closed, has given the historic building new life as a brewpub.

The variety of locations suggests the variety of the beers. Cincinnati and its environs can support more than ten craft breweries in part because they largely avoid duplicating one another. While nearly all brew IPAs, wheat beers, and stouts, most have also identified a distinctive niche. Some have achieved regional distribution by bottling or canning their beers. Others focus on keg sales to area restaurants and other outlets. All make a virtue of focus and consistency. Some attract beer fans seeking the experimental.

Writing for the NewMediaBureau Web site in 2012, a University of Cincinnati journalism student, Kristin Vinci, reported on the camaraderie that characterizes the city's brewing culture. "There appears to be little or no competition among the group. At times they can be seen enjoying each other's company at one of the city's many pubs. Each is willing to lend a hand to the next." Even as the competition becomes more intense, that continues to be the case. Along with a widely shared interest in architectural restoration and innovation, a strong sense of ecological responsibility, customer service (and education), and product experimentation, Cincinnati's craft brewers are a collegial group, celebrating each other's success on the premise that a rising yeast lifts all worts.

While any industry experiencing rapid growth may face a shakeout at some point, the business models of Cincinnati's breweries appear to be thoughtful, pragmatic, and strategic. The brews they are producing are memorable, and the experiences available at their sites no less so.

BREWPUBS

FIFTY WEST BREWING COMPANY

7668 Wooster Pike, Cincinnati, Ohio 45227
513-834-8789 • http://fiftywestbrew.com/

If your interest in well-crafted beer prompts you to consider a road trip, you should set your GPS for the brewery that takes its name from its highway, Fifty West. From downtown Cincinnati, you reach Fifty West via a scenic drive eastward along the Columbia Parkway leading you through the picturesque suburb of Mariemont to a charming property that was once one of Cincinnati's dining destinations. Having restored (a challenging undertaking) and repurposed a lovely old building formerly occupied by The Heritage, Fifty West makes good use of the ample space it reopened in 2013.

Your first impression of the neocolonial home set against large stands of native trees suggests unhurried attention to quality, balance, and good taste. The beer brewed inside will confirm that impression. From the compact, efficient brewing system, where the words TRADITION—INNOVATION—CRAFTSMANSHIP—PATIENCE are conspicuously emblazoned on the walls, beers emerge that are both consistent in quality and widely diverse in style. Memorable in themselves, the beer and food served at Fifty West partake of a charming synergy arising from the balance of historic architecture, a sylvan environment, and a determination to maintain high standards of craftsmanship in both the beer and the food.

Fifty West's psychedelic chalkboard describes what's on tap.

The Beers

Brewmaster Blake Horsburgh attempts to satisfy a wide range of tastes with a wide range of beers—twenty on the current list for my snapshot, most with intriguing names such as Mooving Violation and Loneliest Road Stout. Although the Fifty West Web site does not always offer detailed information on the beer, there are Web sites such as http://www.beeradvocate.com that will provide much of the information you may want prior to a visit. A photo of the beer board, itself a memorable exercise in psychedelic chalk, indicates what I found on tap during my visit: a double IPA, a Kölsch, a wheat beer, a porter, a barley wine, etc.

From this wealth of possibilities, I sampled first the **Coast to Coast IPA** (ABV 7.0 percent, IBUs 70) and found its otherwise firm balance between malt and hops tilted just a bit toward the citrus and cedar aromas of West Coast hops. As the IBUs number suggests, this is indeed a bitter beer, but not so much so that you are distracted from the finish of caramel malt and toast. **Sour Wagon Cherry** (ABV 7.0 percent, IBUs 15) was a morning's tasting mouthful—one of the first samples tasted from a beer that had been "under construction" prior to my visit. Fifty West begins with a Flander's Brown Ale, a Belgian sour, then ages it in oak wine barrels with "an organic cherry purée" for nearly a year. Your first taste of this extraordinarily complex beer announces its Belgian roots. It is sour! But that is for only a moment until the fruit makes its presence known—decisively. Then, just when you think you have had the full experience, there blooms on the back of the tongue an impression of malt that adds weight and balance. It is then time for another sip.

Eastern Standard Bitter (ABV 4.2 percent, IBUs 45), served on nitro, is in its way "extra special" but not in the sense that the British use the term to refer to a Pale Ale brewed to a somewhat higher ABV. This is in fact a pleasant session beer. While not extraordinary, it should be perfectly suited to an afternoon of Bengals football or Reds baseball.

The Food

Chef John Tomain describes the Fifty West menu as "tapas style." If you choose to define an eight-ounce bone-in pork chop, a chicken pot pie, or a Maple Dijon Flank Steak as a "tapas," OK. By any name, the menu is invitingly diverse. For lunch, there are soups, interesting salads, and hearty sandwiches such as one featuring a locally sourced rib eye, served thinly sliced on salted rye. Sandwiches, salads, and, yes, "tapas" lead to "large plates" such as those I have mentioned. What Fifty West describes as "a disclaimer" I call an affirmation of quality: "The chef chooses to use seasonal ingredients for all food menu items. What is reflected on the website is not always up to date. Please call the brewery for the most up-to-date information." A bravo to the chef but a word to whoever maintains the Web site: please do.

Fifty West's brewmaster Blake Horsburgh and distribution coordinator Bobby Slattery (left to right).

Newsworthy

Fifty West is a lively place, if its Facebook time line is any indication. There are lots of events throughout the year, special releases, and special menus. The Fifty Fest, held in the early fall, brings together lots of live music on outdoor stages with releases of special beers—some of which have been brewed for the occasion by Fifty West and cooperating breweries. • The brewery won gold for its Punch You in the EyePA, silver for its imperial stout, Death, and bronze for its barley wine at the 2015 New York International Beer Competition.

A nineteenth-century Cincinnati landmark, now an upscale brewpub, Fifty West.

Other Stuff

There's a shuffleboard table. Brewers' Brunches on Sunday mornings feature collaboration with another restaurant and brewery. A loyalty program called Penny's Pints rewards those who drink at least fifty pints in the course of the year with an invitation to a party at year's end.

THE SKINNY

LOCATION	See the introduction above for one route. Another? Exit I-275 on the east side of Cincinnati at OH-28 and follow it southeast toward the city. At the intersection with U.S. 50, continue straight. As the name of the brewery suggests, the highway will lead you directly to the brewery on your right after you pass the Kroger Hills State Reserve and Avoca Park.
HOURS	Tue–Thu 11:00 A.M.–midnight • Fri 11:00 A.M.–2:00 A.M. • Sat noon–2:00 A.M. • Sun 11:00 A.M.–9:00 P.M.
PARKING	There's ample parking in the adjoining lot.
KIDS	Yes, especially for lunch and brunch. For the late evening, perhaps not.
TAKEOUT	Growler fills are available.
DISTRIBUTION	Self-distribution so far.

MOERLEIN LAGER HOUSE
115 Joe Nuxhall Way, Cincinnati, Ohio 45202
513-421-2337 • http://www.moerleinlagerhouse.com

MALT HOUSE TAPROOM AT THE CHRISTIAN MOERLEIN BREWERY
1621 Moore Street, Cincinnati, Ohio 45202
513-825-6027 • http://christianmoerlein.com

This is a tale of two breweries—but of one impressive multifaceted mission and its visionary advocate.

We begin with the Moerlein Lager House, built from the ground up on Cincinnati's riverfront adjacent to the Great American Ball Park (the Reds) and not far from Paul Brown Stadium (the Bengals). The building itself commands attention. A large, modern, angular structure, the 28,000-square-foot Lager House offers commanding views of the Ohio

A seal in the entry hall of Moerlein's Lager House marks the spot where first base was located in Riverfront Stadium.

River and of Northern Kentucky, provides several distinctive dining (and drinking) areas and offers private dining rooms. When the weather is inviting, diners enjoy tables on its balconies. Tables in a first-floor beer garden are always open.

In addition to furthering Cincinnati's brewing tradition by sustaining or reviving many of the area's former brands, including that of Christian Moerlein, the Lager House honors and celebrates that tradition with displays of brewing memorabilia, with signage that honors historic Cincinnati breweries of the past, and with its Beer Barons Hall of Fame. In short, the Lager House can gratify the beer aficionado, impress the tourist, accommodate large baseball or football crowds, and give locals a reason to return often. It is an impressive complex and one of the largest brewpubs in the world.

The other location, the Malt House Taproom and a small kitchen at the Christian Moerlein Brewery, lies in the heart of Over-the-Rhine. Like the Lager House, this property is owned by Gregory Hardman. Unlike the new Lager House, however, the Moerlein Brewery restores a nineteenth-century brewery, most recently the location of a potato chip factory, to its original purpose. This historic site offers an invitation to local archeology, an opportunity for further expansion, and an attractive

TEN GREAT TAPROOMS

Brewpubs are terrific, especially when you want a meal accompanied by a good beer. But there are times when you just want to enjoy the beer. A great taproom offers not just great tastes, but a comfortable environment and an inviting conviviality. Some may encourage you to bring food or order it delivered, but the focus is on the beer.

- At **JAFB** in Wooster, the regulars make a newcomer feel welcome, and the handcrafted picnic tables encourage conversation. You can sit at the handsome bar and stare into your pint if you wish, but this taproom invites a sense of community. And it's family-friendly. Bring the kids.
- **Thirsty Dog** in Akron welcomes you to an informal and friendly space more or less in the midst of an expanding brewery. Even though this brewery focuses on distribution, you will have the satisfaction of knowing that some of the beers on tap are meant for you and your taproom friends alone. Another taproom is in the cards.
- **Warped Wing** in Dayton (which also appears on the list of Ten Great Up-Close Breweries) makes this list as well because of its friendly ambience. Because there's no restaurant, visitors aren't bound to particular tables. They can wander about, visit the bar, join new conversations. There is a distinct culture here—an engaging one.
- **Zauber Brewing Company** (Columbus) combines the verve of a tasting room that has clean lines and reminders of the English Premier League with a clear focus on ales and lagers principally in the German and Belgian traditions.
- **Star City** (Miamisburg) may eventually install a full kitchen and offer meal service. Its building was once a much-loved restaurant, after all. But in the meantime there's a real pleasure in knocking about from one engaging room to another, sampling the games, examining the artifacts, sipping a beer.
- The so-called **13th Floor Taproom** at Elevator Brewing (the production brewery on North Fourth St., Columbus) may appear as though it has been cobbled together just for your visit. There's not much that's elegant here other than the beers—but that's the point, isn't it?
- Could you find a more pleasant place to spend a dark winter afternoon or a summer evening than the taproom (and art gallery) at **Yellow Springs Brewery**?
- **Toxic Brew Company** has multiple personalities—but there's no disorder involved. On nights when the Dayton Dragons (longest sellout streak in the United States) are playing at nearby Fifth Third Field there are likely to be fans at the bar before and after the game. On a sleepy summer afternoon the bar offers a mellow and undemanding space. If there's a new release the beer aficionados come schooling around the bar.
- **North High** in Columbus offers a convenient central location, a comfortable space enhanced by restored architectural details, and the buzz of the in-house and home brewing happening in the next room.
- **Catawba Island Brewing Company** in Port Clinton may look unprepossessing from the road, but its gleaming wood tables, its sturdy bar, and the brewing system clearly visible through its large windows create an ideal environment for a leisurely visit.

Perhaps the largest brewpub in the world anchors the Cincinnati riverfront.

haven for beer aficionados seeking to drink beer brewed on the premises. The cavernous taproom with its magnificent arched ceiling was in fact a malt house in the nineteenth century. It is well worth a visit.

If you should have sufficient time and stamina and are fortunate enough to come by an invitation, a tour beyond the most accessible rooms would be well worth your time. The cellars descend for three levels, each more rough-hewn than the one above. Even in the summer, they hold a chill, offering a reminder as to why they proved ideal for conditioning beer. There's obviously much work to be done beneath the streets of Over-the-Rhine before these vast spaces again serve a useful purpose. Given the considerable space that remains available at street level, there's no real urgency. But the Moerlein brews seem to taste even better when you're standing on hallowed brewing ground.

The one story behind both locations describes a present-day "beer baron." By the time he was thirty-four, Hardman had found early success as a beer distributor in the Athens area, which enabled him to become CEO of Warsteiner USA, the domestic importer for one of Germany's oldest and most popular beers. That appointment put him in touch with Warsteiner's Cincinnati distributor, Hudepohl-Schoenling, and acquainted him with the regional brewer's "better beer," Christian Moerlein, brewed according to the 1516 German purity law. He became familiar as well with other brands long associated with Cincinnati.

There remains much to explore beneath Moerlein's nineteenth-century production facility in Over-the-Rhine, Cincinnati.

Gregory Hardman envisions a beer garden on the roof of Moerlein's Over-the-Rhine Malt House.

In the course of our conversations, Hardman explained that he had begun to realize elements of his present mission around 2004, when he made a commitment to invest his experience, resources, and business acumen to revive the brewing heritage of Cincinnati. He proceeded to buy the rights to Little Kings, Hudepohl, Hudy Delight, Burger, and others and to create the capacity to brew them again—first under contract at other breweries, but more recently on home turf. He then found the opportunity to make the significant investments now evident in both the riverfront and OTR locations.

His timing could hardly have been better. The brewpub stands as a flagship for Cincinnati's rediscovery of the Ohio River and revitalization of its riverfront, while the production brewery and its Malt House taproom represents a significant advance for a historic neighborhood showing impressive vitality. One measure of Hardman's contribution to craft brewing and to Cincinnati may be found in the readiness with which colleagues, competitors, and civic leaders give him credit. Cincinnati is once again on the map as a city known for fine brewing, and Hardman's two locations are an appropriate starting point for the modern beer explorer.

The Beers

The Moerlein beers—both those brewed on the premises in a small but efficient state-of-the-art facility at the riverfront location and those originating at the Moore Street production facility—are well worth tasting. While Hardman's commitment to collegiality and collaboration appears in his making many other Cincinnati craft beers available, the range of the house brews suggests there's hardly any reason on a first visit to stray from the Moerlein list.

With two breweries operating simultaneously, the variety of beers is unusually extensive. That means my sampling could touch only a fraction of the available beers. But my report of a few carefully chosen tastings can reveal three principles that Moerlein brews express. First, there is a deep respect for brewing tradition, for the history of Cincinnati beer, to be sure, but for the German, Czech, and Belgian traditions as well. Second, there is an evident commitment to quality in the choice of ingredients and in the brewing process. Finally, with the principle of respect for tradition as a given, there is a willingness to innovate.

House beers on draft include both year-round and seasonal Christian Moerlein offerings. I sampled three of the year-round beers. **Over-the-Rhine Ale** (ABV 6.0 percent, IBUs 35) recalls a staple brew from the early days of the neighborhood, when German settlers having to make do with limited refrigeration pitched hops as a preservative but leveraged a strong malt presence to make the result palatable. With three malts in today's menu as well as a combination of citrus and earthiness from domestic hops, you should find this (as the brewery says) a "crisp, quaffable ale." The **CM Helles Lager** (ABV 5.2 percent, IBUs 19) interprets the style most typical of German (especially Bavarian) beer by creating a version of "the light one" that you might enjoy at a Munich bierhaus. ("Light" refers to the blond clarity of the beer, not to its ABV or calorie count.) Having enjoyed this style of beer in Munich, I enjoyed CM's version more. It tastes fresher, hops are somewhat more prominent, and the finish avoids the distracting off-tastes of some German beers.

CM Zepplin (ABV 5.0 percent, IBUs 40), a Bavarian-style Pale Ale (in contrast with Bavaria's traditional lagers), relies on German noble hops (see the Word List) as well as Czech and German malts to create an appealing but far from ordinary impression. Enabling an anticipation of the taste, the aroma offers both malt and citrus. But the taste adds both malt richness and a suggestion of stone fruits. Given the choice among the three I sampled, this would be my beer ("constantly smooth and balanced in flight") for an afternoon on the Lager House balcony, gazing across the Ohio to bustling Northern Kentucky.

Other CM beers on tap during my visit included Barbarossa (a double dark lager named for Frederick I, German emperor from 1155 to 1190), a double IPA, a "robust" American brown ale brewed with a substantial quotient of malted rye, and an IPA named Northern Liberties to honor a Cincinnati neighborhood once known for its free spirit.

The Food

The menu at the Lager House recreates some dishes that would have accompanied beer brewed more than a century ago. For instance, there's a hunter's stew, a bone-in pork rack, a hops-smoked pork belly, and a wide variety of sausages. The Beer Baron Brat, for instance, showcases

Silhouetted against the windows of Moerlein's Lager House, luncheon diners enjoy a view of the Roebling Bridge connecting Cincinnati and Northern Kentucky.

the brewery's "signature sausage," a bold, oversized, fine-ground pork sausage laced with ground chili peppers. Cincinnati was once known as "Porkopolis," after all. But there are also familiar offerings—burgers, steaks, salads, and seafood—and a good selection of imaginative vegetarian fare. The Malt House taproom in OTR serves a limited but appropriate pub menu: sandwiches, sausages, and a few side dishes. They provide a satisfactory accompaniment for the brewery's beers, but if you are seeking a more ambitious menu, choose the Lager House.

Newsworthy

In December 2014, Moerlein announced that a Cincinnati native and well-regarded beer authority, Eric Baumann, had been hired to take charge of brewing at both the brewpub and production breweries. • The brewery also made the headlines with its decision to distribute canned craft beer—a double IPA for starters—throughout southern Ohio and Kentucky. • There are occasional exhibits at the Malt House taproom. • In 2015, the New York International Beer Competition named Moerlein "Cincinnati Brewery of the Year." • To celebrate the 2015 All-Star Game in Cincinnati, the Lager House made available a beer for every Major League team—most of which had a close association with at least the team's location. • The brewery's and Moerlein's Lager House's Facebook page offers the most immediate resources for tracking what's making the news.

Other Stuff

There's much good stuff at the Lager House. • To begin, there are loyalty programs, the Hogshead Union and the Old Jug Society. • Except in December and January, there are tours of the production brewery available through Cincinnati Beer Heritage and Brewery tours. • Events include specials on growler fills and bottled beers. • Mondays feature "blues, brews, and BBQ." • Private dining is available in different rooms of varying size; the private dining menu can be modified to accommodate preferences. • Mementoes at the Lager House store include tap handles, authentic bartender shirts, various kinds of apparel (including winter clothing), logo items celebrating renewed Cincinnati beer brands, and glassware.

At the Malt House taproom, the prime attraction is the building itself. But you will find indoor shuffleboard, a pool table, and a few other diversions.

THE SKINNY FOR THE MOERLEIN LAGER HOUSE

LOCATION	Because of its location on Cincinnati's newly developed riverfront, directions are complicated. Trust your GPS, follow the signs to the Great American Ball Park, or see details at http://www.moerleinlagerhouse.com/hours-and-directions/
HOURS	Mon–Thu 11 A.M.–midnight • Fri–Sat 11 A.M.–1 A.M. • Sun 11 A.M.–11 P.M.
PARKING	The Central Riverfront Garage is right below the Lager House door. The only time you will have trouble finding a place is when there's a Reds or Bengals game—and the spot you do find will then be more expensive. There is also off-street metered parking within walking distance.
KIDS	Welcome. They'll enjoy it. And there's a kids' menu.
TAKEOUT	Available in growlers, bottles, and cans.
DISTRIBUTION	Available in bottles throughout much of Ohio south of Columbus and on tap in selected restaurants and bars.

THE SKINNY FOR THE MALT HOUSE TAPROOM

LOCATION	In the heart of Over-the-Rhine. From I71 N take Liberty Street west and turn right on Moore Street. From I75 S take the Findlay St./Liberty Street exit and turn left on E Liberty. Turn left on Moore Street.
HOURS	Variable according to demand and special functions. Call.
PARKING	There is ample parking in three adjacent lots.
KIDS	Kids would prefer the riverfront location.
TAKEOUT	Available in growlers, bottles, and cans.
DISTRIBUTION	Available in bottles throughout much of Ohio south of Columbus and on tap in selected restaurants and bars.

PORTSMOUTH BREWING COMPANY AND MAULT'S BREWPUB
224 Second Street, Portsmouth, Ohio 45662
740-354-6106 • http://www.portsmouthohbrewing.com

You can't get much further south in Ohio than Portsmouth. The city's slogan is "Where Southern hospitality begins." Roughly two hours east of Cincinnati, Portsmouth grew in the 1800s into a prominent industrial center. The city's location on the Ohio River next to the mouth of the Scioto River and the Ohio and Erie Canal encouraged its growth as a nexus for railroads and supported shoe manufacturing, firebrick and paving brick production, and a growing steel industry. The original Portsmouth Brewery was a part of that early story. Opened in 1843, it prospered with the arrival of German immigrants. Unlike many of its competitors, it managed to survive the Civil War.

The story of Portsmouth brewing thereafter prior to 1919 is one of entrepreneurship, improvisation, and adversity—floods, repressive legislation, and high taxes. But Prohibition ended the story once and for all. Until now, that is. In 1995, a local home brewer, the aptly named Steve Mault, bought the Portsmouth Brewing building and began its restoration. And in October 2011, the rechristened Portsmouth Brewing Company began distributing its beer.

Portsmouth's river heritage inspires the brewery's beers.

The Beers

Portsmouth bottles Portsmouth Pilsner, Red Bird Ale, and Peerless Pale Ale. The pilsner hearkens back to the brewery's Germanic legacy, and the brewery traces the recipe for its Red Bird Ale to its early years. In these days of intense IPAs, the **Peerless Pale Ale** (ABV 6.0 percent, IBUs N/A) offers a satisfying alternative as it honors an era when Portsmouth's nickname was Peerless City, USA. Without compromising the distinct bitterness a Pale Ale should present, Peerless rounds off its satisfying edge with a pleasant fruity aroma, the result of adding aromatic Cascade hops to the keg following fermentation, and with a subtle but solid malt presence. (Facing a long drive, I did not sample any of the beers on-site, but I picked up a six-pack of Peerless Pale Ale to enjoy at home.) A nearby lookout, Raven Rock, provides the name for the brewer's spring Doppelbock, a dark German beer brewed with double malt. It seems a pity that Dortmunder Spartan Export is no longer brewed.

Portsmouth's "peerless" flagship beer recalls the city's and the brewery's long history.

A welcoming, flower-decked window at Portsmouth Brewing.

How else will we remember the Portsmouth Spartans, the NFL team that Portsmouth "exported" to Detroit as the Lions? The brewery bottles also Crystal Gold Light Lager.

While five of Portsmouth's beers are available regionally in six-packs and kegs as far north as Columbus, there must be a particular pleasure in enjoying them on draft at the comfortable brewpub located within the brewery building. There are always six beers on tap. "Beer should be drunk, not sipped," Portsmouth advises. "It should roll down easy." Beer brewed according to the German Beer Purity Law—such as Portsmouth's—usually does.

The Food

There are several different rooms in the brewpub, one dominated by the brewpub's handsome bar, another offering long tables and booths, and a large room adjacent to the brewery, capable of accommodating large parties. The brewpub menu is fairly predictable, but the kitchen makes many of the items from scratch, and the prime rib available only on Friday and Saturday is described as "good enough to be presented to royalty." Other notable exceptions to the expected fare of burgers, chef salad, chicken wings, and pizza are the Stromboli (a rib-eye steak served on toasted sourdough with pizza sauce and mozzarella) and the baked spaghetti. In the summer, the brewery grows its tomatoes just outside.

Other Stuff

In the summer, there's a beer garden. • Portsmouth offers tours of its brewery regularly and on request. It also publishes for its visitors a succinct summary of the brewing process and a list of guidelines for tasting and evaluating beer.

THE SKINNY

LOCATION	Second Street (OH-73 and OH-104) is a major Portsmouth thoroughfare. The brewery lies within two blocks of the confluence of the Scioto and Ohio rivers, a stone's throw from the city's high flood wall.
HOURS	Mon–Thu 11 A.M.–10 P.M. • Fri–Sat 11 A.M.–11 P.M. • Sun 12 noon–10 P.M.
PARKING	Easy, along the street and in a lot across the street.
KIDS	At lunch and dinner kids would fit in—perhaps not as well in the late evening on weekends.
TAKEOUT	Growlers are available but so are six-packs and cases.
DISTRIBUTION	Five bottled varieties are available in six-packs.

ROCK BOTTOM RESTAURANT AND BREWERY

10 Fountain Square, Cincinnati, Ohio 45202

513-621-1588 • http://www.rockbottom.com

On a warm summer's day, a light mist from the Tyler Davidson Fountain can drift toward the shaded outside tables at Cincinnati's Rock Bottom Restaurant and Brewery, a charming reminder that this versatile restaurant and serious brewery stands at the heart of Cincinnati. The address, 10

In the heart of downtown Cincinnati, Rock Bottom draws in both locals and tourists.

Fountain Square, could hardly be more central. An easy stroll from the Reds' Great American Ballpark, the National Underground Railroad Freedom Center, the Contemporary Arts Center, and classy shops, the brewpub is well situated to serve locals and tourists alike.

Having grown from a single location in Denver to nearly forty locations, the Rock Bottom chain now belongs to CraftWorks, a Chattanooga, Tennessee, corporation that also owns the Gordon Biersch and Old Chicago Pizza chains. The two brewery networks appear in a sense complementary, with Rock Bottom specializing in ales, Gordon Biersch in German lagers. Will Rock Bottom continue to maintain its commitment to local creativity as a member of an even larger corporate family? Time—and taste—will tell.

During my fall 2013 visit, one of the first in my project, Gerry O'Connell, an Irishman who describes his dedication to brewing with more than a trace of a brogue, was brewing Rock Bottom's staples according to company recipes. There is consistency in such quality that a traveler may find reassuring. But O'Connell described also his ample opportunity to express himself through a rotating range of "specialty dark" and "brewmaster's choice" beers and through his selection of beers for cask conditioning. "What keeps us relevant is the variety," he explained.

I asked whether he had seen a change in customer preferences. "These days, everyone's going after IPAs," he says. What might be the next trend? "It's difficult to predict." What style would he like to spend more time brewing? "Good lagers," he says. "But they take more time. That's the problem. They tie up the brewery." His favorite beer other than those served by Rock Bottom? "Well, I would never say no to a pint o' Guinness."

Rock Bottom presents a selection of its beers with information to match.

The hospitality is what develops loyal customers, O'Connell says. The advantage of working for Rock Bottom over working in a larger brewery is that "you see your guests." Rock Bottom brews for the customers who come through its doors. They may take a growler of their favorite home after a meal or happy hour, but that's it—no cans, no bottles, and no kegs to be served in other bars and restaurants. That makes it easier for a brewmaster to monitor what is selling well and what emerging demands may suggest the next "brewmaster's choice."

The Beers

Like all Rock Bottom locations, Cincinnati's offers both a comfortable corporate consistency in its standard beers and an occasional opportunity to try the unexpected. Four of its beers—the **IPA** (ABV 6.5 percent, IBUs 60), **Kölsch** (ABV 5 percent, IBUs 20), **Red Ale** (ABV 5.7 percent, IBUs 38), and **White Ale** (ABV 5.3 percent, IBUs 11) are competently brewed year-round according to standard recipes. I tasted all of them. Indeed, I have tasted all of them in multiple locations over many years. Every one is a faithful, well-brewed, thoroughly satisfying example of its style. And that deserves respect. You will not be amazed by these beers. You may not find them particularly memorable. But you will enjoy them. And a few months later, at another Rock Bottom, you can enjoy them again.

Seasonal specialties such as Fire Chief (early spring), Summer Honey, Oktoberfest, and Winter Tartan, a Scottish ale, are also brewed according to franchise recipes but add variety to the regular offerings and provide the occasion for tapping celebrations aligned with chosen charities. No question: Like the regular offerings, the seasonal beers are solid, well-balanced, flavorful beers. Only the Kölsch is filtered. From Seattle to

Nashville to a concourse at MSP (Minneapolis-St. Paul, Minnesota), many a traveler seeking a good meal and a locally crafted beer has found a haven at Rock Bottom.

The colorful nachos are a popular starter at Rock Bottom.

The Food

The menu at Rock Bottom will not startle, but the broad variety should have something for everyone. There may be a hint of Cincinnati's history in the "baby brats" appetizer and the German Sausage Platter, though these recent menu additions also appear on the menus at other locations. There are a few choices for vegetarians (a veggie quesadilla and the predictable veggie burger) and a colorful children's menu that offers expected choices (buttered noodles, grilled cheese sandwich), interesting information (e.g., about renewable energy), and outline drawings for coloring.

Newsworthy

In 2013, the Rock Bottom family of breweries to which the Cincinnati restaurant belongs won "brewpub group" recognition at the GABF. Despite its focus on serving its beers in-house, the corporate home of Rock Bottom, CraftWorks Restaurants & Breweries Inc., places in the top forty of craft brewers for total production.

Other Stuff

Rock Bottom participates in many of the Cincinnati beer festivals such as Oktoberfest, the Starkbierfest (that celebrates stronger brews), and the Volksfest (that revels in session beers).

LOCATION	In the heart of downtown Cincinnati on Fountain Square.
HOURS	Sun–Thu 11 A.M.–11 P.M.; Fri–Sat 11 A.M.–midnight
PARKING	City garage at 416 Vine and other garages and lots within easy walking distance provide ample parking—usually.
KIDS	They are indeed welcome. There is even a special kids' menu.
TAKEOUT	Beer is not bottled or canned but may be taken out in growlers.
DISTRIBUTION	No.

TAPROOMS

LISTERMANN BREWING COMPANY

1621 Dana Avenue, Cincinnati, Ohio 45207

531-731-1130 • http://listermannbrewing.com/

Located near Xavier University in a neighborhood showing signs of progress, Listermann Brewing Company will not attract you by an impressive facade, though its understated brick building is not without charm. Nor will its recently enlarged tasting room give you pause to dwell on its architecture or interior design. Clearly, for this small, innovative brewery, beer is the priority. With a first sip, beer enthusiasts will appreciate a single-minded devotion to craft.

Listermann operated initially as a supply house for home brewers. Having brewed beer for more than forty years, Dan Listermann realized that considerable improvements might be made in supplies and equipment available to hobbyists. So in the early 1990s he began manufacturing equipment optimally suited to home brewing and began contracting for improved ingredients. That led him to develop kits for home brewers that would enable them to brew a variety of beer styles. Listermann's salesroom remains a magnet for craft brewers, professional and amateur alike. Indeed, some of his craft-brewing colleagues and competitors began their brewing careers with ingredients purchased at 1621 Dana.

But about five years ago Listermann decided to expand his business to include craft brewing on his own terms. He converted part of the building into a brewery and taproom. The result has been a steady stream of remarkable, small-batch beers that have earned the brewery a distinct identity within Cincinnati's burgeoning craft-brewing environment.

The Beers

At Listermann, head brewer Patrick Gilroy used to brew on an efficient ten-barrel system. Because there were only three year-round beers, "there was always something new and interesting on tap." There still is. The twenty-barrel fermenters added in fall 2014 not only create expanded capacity but, given Gilroy's ingenuity, should encourage the development of new styles. As brewery spokesperson Jason Brewer told the *Cincinnati Business Courier,* when popular beers can be produced in greater quantity through the larger tanks, smaller tanks can be redirected to experimentation and product development.

Examples of more-or-less dependable regulars would include an oatmeal sweet stout named 562 Lateral (for Cincinnati's connector between I-75 and I-71), an American Pale Ale called Jungle Honey, and a Belgian blonde ale that takes its name after the Belgian King Leopold.

I sampled the GABF medalist, **Nutcase Peanut Butter Porter** (ABV 6.7 percent, IBUs 28). It is a robust, splendid porter spiked with peanut adjuncts that significantly impact flavor and aroma. To be sure, you will experience peanuts in this beer, especially in the aroma, but you will experience also the coffee and chocolate you expect in a well-made porter. The roast of the malt creates an exceptionally smooth beer with considerable depth and nuance. Compared to Willoughby's entry in the peanut competition, Listermann's is the more restrained. If you want a memorable first-time experience, try Willoughby. If you want to drink more than one pint, you may prefer Listermann.

Seasonals may include a smoked bock (Friar Bacon), a bourbon barrel-aged stout (Cincinnatus), an IPA (Intergalactic), and a holiday ale with the charming name of White Death. Specialty beers include a Belgian-style sour ale named Julia and an oatmeal stout named SlideJob fermented in oak barrels.

An affiliated enterprise at the same address, Triple Digit Brewing Company, focuses on "high gravity" (high in alcohol) beers. Dan Listermann describes these beers as "Listermann's premium brand." Aftermath, a Scottish wee heavy (ale), clocks in at 10.5 percent with 25 IBUs. Chickow! (ABV 10 percent, IBUs 28), Triple Digit's most popular

Beer aging in barrels once used for bourbon.
One result is Listermann's bourbon barrel-aged specialty, Colonel Plug, that comes with a narrative.

offering, is a hazelnet double brown ale bittered with Magnum hops. Cranium (ABV 10.5 percent, IBUs 50) is an ale laced with coffee and vanilla before developing further in bourbon barrels. Decimation (ABV 10 percent, IBUs 70) is an imperial white IPA, but one that pours a lovely golden hue.

Gravitator (ABV 10.5 percent, IBUs 23), brewed with lager yeast, is a German double bock and is as black as its style demands. Finally there is Reanimator, an imperial pumpkin ale. This ale, beautiful to behold, checks in 10.5 percent ABV with 25 IBUs. So far as these styles are concerned, the brewer states an interest in taking you "past the limits of what you think is possible" in craft brewing. These beers stand at the other end of the spectrum from a "session IPA." They are to be drunk very slowly, savored carefully, and noted appreciatively.

One more beer deserves mention, especially if you find yourself afflicted with a headache each year around April 15. Audit Ale hearkens back to medieval England, when large landholding universities brewed strong ales to compensate (or distract) their tax-paying leaseholders. Fermented in bourbon barrels, the beer develops and gains complexity over time. A different barrel will be tapped each year. Once you file your return, perhaps 1621 Dana should be your next stop.

The Food
Listermann occasionally cooperates with restaurants in the area in order to offer beer dinners.

Newsworthy
In 2014, Listermann took home a bronze medal from the GABF for its Nutcase Peanut Butter Porter. Between GABFs, Listermann participates in beer festivals throughout Ohio and often provides a home for Cincinnati beer events. Perhaps the most notable is the Volksfest that Listermann hosts for Cincinnati's craft brewers. • Listermann has added mead, cider, and wine to its production agenda. creative work of local craftpeople such as glass artist David Armacost.

Other Stuff
Still committed to the home-brewing community, Listermann offers classes for home brewers—teaching brewing with extracts to beginners and all-grain brewing to advanced students. When the classes were offered at no cost, they swelled to more than seventy, hardly an optimum pedagogical situation. Now there is a $20 charge (which comes with a $20 gift certificate) and you must reserve your place in advance. If you show up without a reservation? There are worse fates: "You will be forced to drink beer in our tasting room."

The Skinny

LOCATION	Exit I-71S at Dana and turn right. Exit I-71N at Dana/Montgomery, turn right on Duck Creek, turn right on Montgomery, and turn left on Dana. The taproom is just down the street from Xavier University and just three blocks from the Cintas Center.
HOURS	Mon–Thu noon–8:00 P.M. • Fri–Sat 10:00 A.M.–11:00 P.M. • Sun noon–8:00 P.M.
PARKING	There's an informal parking lot across the side street (Idlewild) and limited on-street parking. Changing regulations and enforcement suggest a call might be in order before visiting.
KIDS	Kids often visit. "We are fully kid-friendly."
TAKEOUT	You can have your growler filled.
DISTRIBUTION	Not at the moment.

MADTREE BREWING COMPANY

5164 Kennedy Avenue, Cincinnati, Ohio 45213

513-836-8733 • http://www.madtreebrewing.com/home.html

Owner and brewer Brady Duncan makes the point clearly: "one word, capital M, capital T." The brewery's handsome stone sign just off the road in a light industrial area north of downtown Cincinnati suggests MadTree's characteristic inclination to rethink conventions, test innovations, and celebrate imagination. Craft brewers bottle their beer. So why not can? There's such a thing as a porter and such a thing as an IPA. Why not attempt to combine the styles? With a successful tasting room, no one needs food. So bring in a vendor to provide food! Or invite local restaurants to collaborate on an

MadTree founders (*left to right*) Jeff Hunt, Brady Duncan, and Kenny McNutt enjoy a cool one.

evening to remember. Or reconsider the whole thing and install an in-house pizza kitchen. You've made your reputation on canned beer. Maybe it's time to consider bottling. See what I mean?

If you enjoy drinking a beer that has been brewed within a few paces of your glass, you will enjoy MadTree. The challenge for MadTree will be to manage its growth while retaining its verve. In the spirit of the T-shirts that plead "Keep Austin Weird" (a lost cause, by the way), MadTree fans must share the hope that as new tanks arrive and the brewing plant capacity moves past twenty thousand barrels a year, the spirit of entrepreneurship, experimentation, and exuberance will continue to inform the space and the taste and the people.

The Beers

There are four beers more or less readily available in cans. **Happy Amber** (ABV 6.0 percent, IBUs 30) announces at once that MadTree's cans deserve respect. Don't even think of drinking from the can! And don't throw them in the refrigerator and forget them. This aromatic amber comes across as unusually sophisticated for a relatively new brewery. The malt taste is rich and complex, the nose an inviting suggestion of

It's time to shovel out the grist at MadTree following lautering.

citrus and cedar, the finish a balance of malt and hops. **Psychopathy IPA** (ABV 6.9 percent, IBUs 70) adds Centennial to Happy Amber's mix of Cascade and Chinook hops, with the result that there's a fresh, verdant anticipation of tasty bitterness the moment you pop the top.

Gnarly Brown (ABV 7.0 percent, IBUs 32) turns the wheel decisively toward the malts, which bring tastes of chocolate and roasted barley. MadTree describes the beer as striking a balance between brown ale and porter, and that seems right. With overtones of coffee, vanilla, and caramel, it is far more complex than traditional porter and deeper and richer than traditional brown ale. **Lift** (ABV 4.7 percent, IBUs 11), the fourth in the lineup, might conceivably be the one MadTree beer you could drink from the can without disgracing yourself—in a pinch. The most accessible of the four, it has its own virtues. As Cascade and Pacifica hops provide a stimulating aura of citrus, the addition of hops from Germany's prime hops-growing region (Hallertauer Mittelfruh is one of the noble hops associated with lager) moves Lift into a somewhat different but no less thought-provoking category.

Year-round beers available in limited quantities include Identity Crisis (well-named for its references both to the maltiness of a porter and the hoppy pleasures of an IPA), Galaxy High (a powerful imperial IPA), and Axis Mundi (an only slightly less powerful imperial stout). You will find full information on these beers, on MadTree's four seasonals, and on a wide range of interesting experiments on the brewery's uncommonly

An Ohio pioneer in canning craft beer, MadTree fights for shelf space with strong visuals.

informative Web site. A Kölsch "brewed with lime, ginger, and a hint of Ancho" would be worth a trip! In fact, it would be a trip!

The Food

First there were occasional "Hop Up" dinners and visiting food trucks. Now there's the Catch-a-Fire Café at the brewery serving wood-fired meat and veggie pizzas, breads, and bites. You can choose from a wide choice of toppings in order to create a custom-made pizza, but standards such as Satisfy My Soul (bacon, crème fraîche, kale, red onion, cheeses) and Jammin' Jerk Chicken (spiced chicken, jerk sauce, bell pepper, red onion, four cheeses) may satisfy your creative impulse.

Newsworthy

MadTree was a marquee attraction at Indianapolis's 2014 "CANvitational," a festival limited to canned beers. • The brewery played host for Cincinnati's 2014 FreshFest. • MadTree has addressed an obvious need for additional space by expanding into a former office supply store next door. • Celebrating its second birthday and its expansion, the brewery's annual Winter Bonanza in January 2015 offered a wide selection of Ohio beers, live music, and food trucks. • Citra High, an imperial IPA, is now available in cans.

Other Stuff

There's a patio, now enlarged and nicely fenced, where you can drink beer and throw a cornhole bag—though not at the same moment, presumably. • Dogs were welcome prior to the in-house pizzeria. Are they still? Worth a check. • Saturday brewery tours begin at 3:00 and

4:00 P.M. • You can reserve the party room for a special event. • Few breweries post their beer recipes online. This one does. • The store stocks the usual items (T-shirts, glassware) but some unusual ones as well: an etched metal MadTree sign, some attractive beer posters, and a calendar.

THE SKINNY

LOCATION	From I-71N take exit 8A. Turn left on Ridge, right on Duck Creek, left on Kennedy for about a block. Brewery will be on your right. From I-71S take exit 8 (Ridge/Kennedy) and turn right on Highland, left on Kennedy. Brewery will be on your left after several blocks.
HOURS	Tue–Wed 4:00–10:00 P.M. • Thu noon–midnight • Fri–Sat noon–1:00 A.M. • Sun noon–8:00 P.M.
PARKING	There's a lot adjacent to the tasting room and in front of the "new" building next door.
KIDS	With foosball, TVs, and cornhole, MadTree welcomes kids.
TAKEOUT	Have a growler filled or pick up a couple of six-packs as you leave.
DISTRIBUTION	MadTree's six-pack cans are available throughout most of Ohio as far north as Columbus. Their aim is to distribute throughout Ohio and much of the Cincinnati tri-state area by 2016. The map of availability on the MadTree Web site shows they're making progress.

MT. CARMEL BREWING COMPANY

4362 Mt. Carmel-Tobasco Road, Cincinnati, Ohio 45244
513-240-2739 • http://mtcarmelbrewingcompany.com/

As you drive down Mt. Carmel-Tobasco Road, a thoroughfare too far out to be urban but not far out enough to be rural, look carefully for the small water tank and front porch that announce the brewery, taproom, and front porch of Mt. Carmel Brewing Company. While there are many Ohio locations where you can enjoy a leisurely beer in congenial surroundings, there are few that offer anything like the combination of the front porch and back patio at Mt. Carmel. The importance of these

There's a good reason Mt. Carmel celebrates the "front porch" quality of its beers.

spaces lies neither in their architectural distinction nor in stunning views. Rather, they represent the spirit of well-ordered priorities that inform a creative and consistent brewing operation.

These spaces offer an invitation that the brewery's taproom fulfills in more than one way. When you step inside the "public house," with just a bar and a few tables, you find amiable surroundings in which to sample what's available. But there are additional rooms in this former family home that offer more spacious if no less comfortable surroundings. And if you visit when it's warm enough to sit outside, you should. There's even a small pond where you can relax under an awning, sip a beer, and meditate on the marriage of hops, water, grain, and yeast.

Wherever you choose to alight, you will not be able to ignore the brewing operation, which is visible through large taproom windows and which stands adjacent to the pond. Astonishingly compact for a brewery that bottles for a statewide market, Mt. Carmel's plant celebrates resourcefulness, efficiency, and economy of scale. If they're in production during your visit, you will come away impressed by what can be accomplished in a little space. The bottling line is especially memorable. Two staff members, manning a complex, gleaming assembly line with hoses hissing and bottles clanking, move the beer from the tanks to six-packs ready for labeling, stacking, and pickup.

The story is that cofounder and director of brewing Mike Dewey was

What's on tap (not the clueless photographer) is the real appeal at Mt. Carmel.

becoming a more and more serious craft brewer, managing to turn out some memorable brews from a jerry-rigged system in the storm cellar of his home, which is now the home of Mt. Carmel. One day, his wife, Kathleen (now cofounder and president), came to the top of the stairs and said, in effect, "Either make a business out of this—or clear out the lot." The result of that prompted decision appears in the three domains of Mt. Carmel: the farmhouse with its taproom, the attached brewery and bottling line, and the spaces to sit and sip a spell. Having recently obtained additional property nearby, Mt. Carmel continues to develop even more comfortable, hospitable, and accommodating environs.

The Beers

Mt. Carmel divides its beer into year-rounds, seasonals, and a "snapshot series" that includes creative forays in styles such as imperial coffee stout, an imperial brown ale, and a Belgian quad. There are five year-rounds. They may be familiar because of their statewide distribution but should never be taken for granted. Poured into a glass, the popular **Amber Ale** (ABV 6.0 percent, IBUs N/A) offers a reminder that humankind has always prized golden brown amber. But the taste of this ale has nothing to do with fossilized tree resin. A graceful, straightforward balance of tasty malts and aromatic hops, Amber Ale is the stuff of which leisurely fall afternoons are made.

The **Blonde Ale** (ABV 5.5 percent, IBUs N/A) is a most pleasant beer that might benefit from just a slightly heavier hand with the hops. Perhaps a bit of dry hopping would do the trick. The issue is not one of making a major change but of accentuating the positive already present—hints of citrus, hints of malt. I was not able to taste the IPA (ABV 7.0 percent, IBUs N/A) or the stout (ABV 6.0 percent, IBUs N/A), but the **Nut Brown Ale** (ABV 6.0 percent, IBUs N/A) at once confirms its eye appeal. It is dark brown and as clear as the Amber Ale but offers tastes of roasted grain, molasses and maple, and bread. The bitterness indeed recalls nuts, not pecans, to my taste, but walnuts—there is just that touch of astringency that a raw walnut offers. Some beers you put down until you're thirsty enough for the next swallow. This one you sip repeatedly as you try to get to the bottom of the complex impression it makes. Well done.

The Food
Mt. Carmel does not operate a kitchen.

Newsworthy
The "snapshot series" beers usually stay behind the bar, but both the Coffee Brown Ale and the Imp IPA are now available in bottles—perhaps the signal for a fresh marketing initiative. The spring 2014 release on tap of an imperial IPA drew attention for its commitment to an extraordinary quantity and variety of hops. Earlier releases of a Belgian quad and a rye IPA also made the news. • The Clermont Chamber of Commerce awarded Mt. Carmel its 2015 Emerging Excellence Award.

Brewed, bottled, packaged, boxed, and ready for shipment.

Other Stuff
That back patio mentioned in the introduction becomes a heated beer garden in the winter. Inside there's art to enjoy at all times, but especially when the brewery hosts art shows. Watch the Web site (updated irregularly, alas) for details.

THE SKINNY

LOCATION	From I-275N or I-275S on the east side of Cincinnati, exit to OH-32, the James A. Rhodes Appalachian Highway. Drive east and turn left on Bells Lane, which, after a block, becomes Mt. Carmel-Tobasco Road. Keep your eye out for Mt. Carmel on the left.
HOURS	Wed–Thu 4:00–8:00 P.M. • Fri 4:00–11:00 P.M. • Sat noon–11:00 P.M.
PARKING	Can be a problem, but one Mt. Carmel is likely to solve before long. For special events, the brewery runs a shuttle to a nearby church parking lot.
KIDS	There isn't much to keep them occupied, in my view, but you may want to check.
TAKEOUT	Growlers and six-packs are available.
DISTRIBUTION	Throughout Ohio and Northern Kentucky.

RHINEGEIST BREWERY

1910 Elm Street, Cincinnati, Ohio 45202

513-381-1367 • http://www.rhinegeist.com/home

On the day of my visit, because Rhinegeist was remodeling its front door, I had to climb in using the fire escape. There are worse ways to sneak up on a geist (ghost). In a way, it was fortuitous, because having to watch my step on the climb up meant that my first glimpse of this brewery's remarkable cathedral space was without preconception or preparation. I was simply astonished—by the expanse, by the size of the brewing system, by the impression of lots happening at once in a building that once served as the bottling plant for Moerlein beers. I felt thus properly introduced to a brewery committed to supporting its Over-the-Rhine neighborhood, to expanding the distribution of its beers, and to providing a memorable experience at its taproom. It doesn't hurt, by the way, that Cincinnati's new streetcar, which will connect the riverfront with OTR, will stop right in front.

The Rhinegeist "story" appears on its Web site. I will not replicate it here but would offer two summary bullets:

- The building harkens back to the late nineteenth century, when it was constructed to house bottling operations for what was then Cincinnati's largest brewery, Christian Moerlein. (See the Christian Moerlein entry above for the story of Greg Hardman's restoration of the CM brewhouse.)
- When two of the current partners, Bob Bondor (a former coffee entrepreneur) and Bryant Goulding (then a salesman for prominent West Coast breweries), visited the "empty and defunct warehouse" on Elm Street, they could somehow envision what they have since achieved and continue to develop. Brewers Jim Matt and Luke Cole soon signed on to undertake the task of installing a brewing system and brewing beer with it, and Dennis Kramer-Wine arrived with ideas for distribution.

The Beers

Rhinegeist cans seven of its beers. Three—an IPA (Truth), a blonde ale (Cougar), and a session IPA (Zen at ABV 4.8 percent)—are available year-round. The other three are seasonals: an "American robust porter" (Panther), an Oktoberfest (Franz), a "Hoppy Holiday Ale" (Dad), and a "Hoppy Pale Ale" (Pure Fury).

But this is a book primarily about drinking beers where they are made, and Rhinegeist makes that experience special with an impressive list of creative beers available on tap at the bar, many of which appear for a limited time only. Because I would have to negotiate the fire escape again on my way out, I sampled only three of the beers on draft, but enjoyed them all. Their **Cougar** (ABV 4.8 percent, IBUs 25) hits the right notes for a blonde ale: crisp, clear, flavorful. But there is a welcoming aura of citrus and evergreen that distinguishes this beer from some of its less interesting cousins. I am no great fan of British milds, but Rhinegeist's **Uncle** (ABV 3.8 percent, 17 IBUs) could make me rethink. Unlike many of its British forebears, the Rhinegeist version presents a malt profile that has some vigor. The taste therefore is several stages beyond simplicity. Finally, I found in **Truth** (ABV 7.2 percent, IBUs 75) an uncompromising IPA, enticing on the front end with lovely intimations of fruit and impressive on the back end with a three-malt blend anchoring a firm hops bitterness.

Rhinegeist's Bryant Goulding evaluates a new hops shipment.

Primed to offer a brewed awakening to those who visit Rhinegeist's cavernous hall.

Among other beers that you may find during your visit are Conquistador (a Pale Ale), Gramps (an American barley wine), Homie (a double IPA based on collaboration with another craft brewer), Fiction (a Belgian IPA), Ink (an imperial stout), Puma Pils (a Bohemian pilsner), Saber Tooth Tiger (an imperial IPA), Panda (an oatmeal stout), and Squirt (a "tangy ale"). Rhinegeist's good Web site provides information about the recipe as well as calendar availability. Squirt is available only during the summer, for instance.

The Food

"Visitors are more than welcome to bring in food or have orders delivered," but Rhinegeist does not serve food. If you visit when the nearby Findlay Market is open, you might combine two distinctive Cincinnati experiences.

Newsworthy

Rhinegeist is often in the news for its releases and its gatherings. Their double IPA festival in the autumn of 2014 drew examples from fifteen Ohio brewers and from more than twenty others, while their Franztoberfest featured live music and gourmet bratwursts. • Bryant Goulding, one of the cofounders, took a prominent turn for *GQ* magazine in October 2014 by contributing to an article on the fifty best craft beers. • Rankings released by RateBeer in early 2015 ranked the cavernous taproom as Ohio's best. • In early 2015, WCPO Cincinnati reported on a Rhinegeist beer brewed collaboratively with Six String Brew Works to honor a Cincinnati policeman who had died from a brain aneurysm. Sales of S23 (the officer's badge number) raised funds for the support of his family. • In the spring of 2015, the brewery announced that it would plant a small brewing system in Columbus. There will be no taproom, at least at first, but the expansion will enable Rhinegeist to offer specialty beers to Central Ohio. • In April 2015, *Beer Advocate* ran an article, "9 Steps to Beerdom," featuring head brewer Jim Matt. "We have this goofy, edgy attitude, and we put a modern spin on tradition," Matt told the magazine. • Baseball fans vote for All-Star players. Rhinegeist invited beer fans to vote for a beer it would introduce at the 2015 All-Star Game in Cincinnati. Goulding told Shauna Steigerwald of the *Enquirer:* "There's so much excitement for the All-Star Game in Cincinnati. We thought this would be a fun way to capture that." • The brewery won its first GABF medal in 2015 for Sherry Ink, an imperial stout that is barrel aged.

Other Stuff

There's foosball (remember that?) and there are large-screen TVs tuned to sports. Free tours of the brewing plant begin Monday, Wednesday, and Friday at 4:30 P.M. and on Saturdays at 1:00 P.M. • Rhinegeist can accommodate sizable parties and will welcome your inquiries about hosting one. • Clothing with the brewery's sobering logo is available at the gift shop—as is apparel that will not frighten the grandchildren.

THE SKINNY

LOCATION	It's in Cincinnati's bustling Over-the-Rhine neighborhood. Exit I-71N on E Liberty Street, which becomes W Liberty as you cross Vine. Turn right on Elm, pass the Findlay Market, and you're there. Or from I-75S exit on Findlay, turn left, then turn left again on Elm.
HOURS	Mon–Thu 4:00–11:00 P.M. • Fri 4:00 P.M.–midnight • Sat noon–midnight • Sun noon–7:00 P.M.
PARKING	Just a couple of doors down from the entrance, there's a Rhinegeist lot across the street.
KIDS	They are welcome, but not after 8:00 P.M. on Fridays and Saturdays.
TAKEOUT	Growlers and "crowlers" (thirty-two-ounce cans of fresh beer) are available as are six-packs of twelve-ounce cans.
DISTRIBUTION	Their self-distribution model for their kegs has achieved broad coverage of greater Cincinnati. Their canned beers are available at bars, restaurants, and grocery stores in Cincinnati, Dayton, and Northern Kentucky.

RIVERTOWN BREWING COMPANY

607 Shepherd Drive, Lockland (Cincinnati), Ohio 45215

513-827-9280 • http://rivertownbrewery.com

Brewer Jason Roeper pulls a pint at Rivertown Brewing.

Former brewery supervisor Nugget directing operations from a keg-top perch.

In the introduction, I comment on the both the vitality and the volatility of craft brewing. While the industry is moving in a positive direction, things are changing all the time. Having written a draft profile on Rivertown following a fall 2013 visit, I checked with president and owner Jason Roeper as this book was going to press. He responded that major revisions would be necessary. There have been changes in staff, a considerable expansion in the brewing system, and—but I'll let Jason tell the story. "We have changed our logo, look, marketing approach, and of course our beers." And their feline brewing supervisor, Nugget, had accepted a job offer elsewhere. So there was a lot to be changed.

Not everything has changed, however. If you enjoy the Belgian-style ales of Rivertown, you might picture fermenting tanks open to the wild yeasts of sylvan meadows and picturesque glades. But your search for its taproom will lead you to a long, nondescript metal building in a far-from-scenic inner suburb of Cincinnati. Neighbors include a ready-mix concrete plant, a truck leasing lot, and a compressed-air facility protected by chain link and barbed wire. Beer fans who persevere will find Rivertown's taproom well worth the trip, however. And they will find Roeper well worth getting to know. Pursuing a deep interest in home brewing, he began to dream of opening a craft brewery. It's a familiar story, but it rarely turns out this well.

A spool of labels that will wrap bottles of Rivertown's Pumpkin Ale.

The Beers

Rivertown once made the most of a limited brewing system. Since then the brewery has added four sixty-barrel tanks, a fully automated seventy-two-head bottling line, and a six-thousand-pound grain silo, so as to brew fifteen thousand barrels annually. Year-round, they make five beers available on draft and in six-packs.

I have tried **Lil Sipa** (ABV 4.5 percent, IBUs 55) in a six-pack. In several six-packs from my local grocery store. An early entry in the expanding session IPA category, this beer does not make you regret the reduction in alcohol. Nicely hopped, with lots of citrus (and just a hint of clove?) on the nose, Lil Sipa invites and then retains your interest without clouding your judgment. The **Roebling Porter** (ABV 7.8 percent, IBUs 35) I enjoyed on draft at the Rivertown taproom. This imperial porter, named for the architect of the iconic Cincinnati bridge, which served as a model for the Brooklyn Bridge, offers subtle suggestions of both Manhattan and Brooklyn. No, actually, of vanilla and espresso. Perfectly balanced with no aberrant notes, it is an exceptional example of a demanding style. The coffee? It's from a small roasting company "within a day's drive from the brewery." Also in the year-round lineup are Divergent (a Berliner sour ale), Jeaneke (a Belgian blonde ale), and Soulless (a Flanders red ale brewed with Belgian malt and a wild lacto strain from Belgium).

Seasonal beers include a Belgian-style wit ale brewed with spices (spring), a blueberry lager (summer), a Märzen lager released in July as the brewery's Oktoberfest offering, and a winter ale. I sampled Rivertown's **Pumpkin Ale** (ABV 5.0 percent, IBUs N/A), which might convert many a beer fan otherwise opposed to flavored brews. Concocted with molasses, cinnamon, and spices, in addition to pumpkin, it offers less a taste of pumpkin than an impression, a presence. It is, first of all, an ale.

Three very special limited-release beers, two of which are occasionally available in 750 milliliter bottles and one of which was in the planning stage when I hit my deadline, deserve mention as well. Available March to September, Insurrection is a double IPA (ABV 9.0 percent, IBUs 90) brewed with lots of Galaxy, Citra, and Mosaic hops. Available October to February, Death is seasoned with hot peppers and checks in at ABV 11.7 percent (IBUs 38). The one I found being planned was to be brewed in collaboration with Nashville's Yazoo Brewing Company. This will be, and I quote, "a rye beer base fermented with Yazoo's wild yeasts and aged in tequila barrels with lime and lemon peels."

There is one project that remains fascinating even though the beer, named Triumvirate, is no longer in production. It required a collaboration between the brewery, the Rookwood Restaurant (a popular Mt. Adams spot located in the old pottery plant), and a distillery in West Virginia. The brewing process began conventionally enough, with pilsner malt, wheat, oats, and Perle and Cascade hops. The resulting wort was then exposed to "Rivertown's house wild strains" of yeast. Then the process became even more interesting. To what was a fairly straightforward sour ale, the brewers added tonic water concocted by the restaurant, raw sugar, Persian lime peels, cinchona bark, lime zest, juniper berries, and simple syrup. And for aging? Aged gin barrels from West Virginia. Sorry I missed it!

The Food
Although Rivertown does not prepare food, the brewery does not discourage patrons from bringing their own.

Newsworthy
The recent expansion of the brewing system mentioned in the lead is worth a headline, as are the brewery's collaborations, which in 2014 included working with New Holland Brewing Co. (Michigan) on a geuze. A caution: If you seek information on the Web, do not confuse Cincinnati's Rivertown with Pittsburgh's Rivertowne. Mind the e.

Other Stuff
For $6, a visitor can receive a Rivertown Brewing glass, a pint of beer, and a tour of the premises—Fridays at 6:00 P.M., Saturdays at 3:00 P.M. Some deal! (But wear closed-toe shoes for the tour.) • Other products

available for sale include baseball caps, glassware, T-shirts, skull caps, and hoodies. • There are arcade games to test your skill between pints— or to give your kids something to do while you're at the bar. • You can rent a private room at Rivertown for your event.

THE SKINNY

LOCATION	Located north of the Reagan Cross County Highway and just west of I-75, this taproom justifies the purchase of a GPS. It will direct you reliably to the address in Lockland.
HOURS	Wed 4:00–9:00 P.M. • Thu–Fri 5:00–10:00 P.M. • Sat noon–10:00 P.M.
PARKING	There's no problem with parking. Just drive around to the right of the building and keep driving until you see the sign for the taproom.
KIDS	Children are welcome in the taproom but are not allowed to sit at the bar.
TAKEOUT	Six-packs, growlers, and kegs are available, though the brewery requests a five-day notice for sixth- and half-barrel kegs. Some limited-edition beers are not available for growler fills, and there is a two-bottle sales restriction on limited-release twenty-two-ounce bottles.
DISTRIBUTION	By using the services of a local distributor, Rivertown has been able to reach four states in addition to Ohio: Indiana, Kentucky, Tennessee, and—a surprise—Florida. Future plans call for possible expansion into Pennsylvania if the commonwealth amends its restrictive laws regulating the sale of beer.

CONSIDER ALSO

Hanged in 1895 as a murderer, "Bad Tom" Smith blamed his fall on bad drink. His great-great nephew, Sean Smith, offers the beers of BAD TOM SMITH BREWING (4720 Eastern Avenue, Cincinnati, Ohio 45226) purportedly to make amends. Just off the Columbia Parkway not far from Lunken Airport, the taproom is open Wednesday through Sunday with six or so craft ales such as Addlehead IPA, Kloppenburg (a Helles), and

Black Kettle Stout. Will Sean's good beers restore the honor of the family name? You can decide, sip by sip. Telephone: 513-871-4677 Web: http://www.badtomsmithbrewing.com

BLANK SLATE BREWING COMPANY (4233 Airport Road, Unit C, Cincinnati, Ohio 45226), which opens its "pourhouse" Thursday through Sunday, sets itself apart by foregoing a "flagship" beer in favor of seasonals—unusual ones such as Indian Amber Ale, Cherrywood Smoked Porter, a brown ale brewed with Shitake mushrooms, an Opera Cream Stout brewed in concert with a Hyde Park bakery, the Bonbonerie, and a collaboration beer brewed with Colorado's Oskar Blues but inspired by Cincinnati's famous chili. Note that Airport Road is adjacent to Lunken Airport on the Cincinnati side of the Ohio River. Telephone: 513-979-4540 Web: http://www.blankslatebeer.com/ and https://www.facebook.com/blankslatebeer

CELLAR DWELLER (2276 East U.S. 22 and 3, Morrow, Ohio 45152) is another of Ohio's vineyard/brewery pairings, to wit: "We at Valley Vineyards have created . . . craft beers for our family and friends." By starting a brewery underneath the roof of a winery, you can open every day and serve a wider span of tastes and interests: a dry-wine sampler for one, a beer-tasting tray for another, and a cheese tray and pretzels for both. Distinctive brews include Dead Dweller (an English ale) and Jeremiah's, an IPA brewed from a recipe found in a bible owned by Jeremiah Morrow, Ohio's ninth governor. Telephone: 513-899-2485 Web: https://www.valleyvineyards.com

DOGBERRY BREWING LLC (7865 Cincinnati Dayton Road, West Chester Township, Ohio 45069) introduces itself memorably: "We brew the beers we love and share them with you! If you want them, come see us, we will keep on being Dogberry!" Among the possible offerings? Prodigal is an American Pale Ale aggressively dry-hopped—but with different hops each time! Maiden Flight RYEPA updates the classic rye ale with a strong presence of aroma hops. It appears that you can explore what "being Dogberry" means on Friday and Saturday afternoons—but check before going. Telephone: 513-847-8208 Web: http://twitter.com/DogBerryBrewing or https://www.facebook.com/pages/DogBerry-Brewing-LLC/759533604089454?sk=timeline

MUNICIPAL BREW WORKS (20 High Street, Hamilton, Ohio 45011) is good news for downtown. Named for the former municipal building that is its site, the brewery has plans to brew for local distribution as well as for its taproom. There's no food service planned, but trucks and local restaurants are expected to pick up the slack. In fall 2015, the brewery's Facebook page proclamed, "Opening 2016." Telephone: N/A Web: https://www.facebook.com/municipalbrewworks

OLD FIREHOUSE BREWERY (237 West Main Street, Williamsburg, Ohio 45176) opened in September 2014 with the motto "Great Beer, Great Friends, Great Fun." The building, "a tribute to firefighters and emergency personnel," displays firefighting and emergency equipment. Four of the "signature brews" are predictable. One, the Hoser Gose, "flavored with coriander and sea salt," interprets a German tradition once almost lost. All are available Wednesday through Sunday at this dog-friendly taproom just to the east of Cincinnati. In fall 2015, the brewery announced statewide distribution. Telephone: 513-536-9071 Web: http://www.old-firehousebrewery.com/

QUARTER BARREL BREWERY AND PUB (107 East Church Street, Oxford, Ohio 45056) is serious about the nano part of nano-brewery. With their current system, they can produce roughly just one-and-a-half kegs per brew—not much for a pub open seven days a week to serve a thirsty university town. So they focus on quality and fill in the gaps with a judicious selection of guest beers. The menu offers food a cut above standard pub fare. Telephone: 513-523-2525 Web: http://www.facebook.com/Quarter-Barrel-Brewery

SIX STRING BREW WORKS (5618 Arnsby Place, Cincinnati, Ohio 45227) received much favorable attention in early 2015 for its collaboration with Rhinegeist on a beer honoring a deceased Cincinnati policemen. (See the Rhinegeist profile for details.) In its promising Facebook page (https://www.facebook.com/sixstringbrew/timeline) the brewery describes itself as "a new and local start-up microbrewery" specializing in collaboration beers. Production of beer on-site was scheduled for late 2015. Telephone: N/A Web: http://sixstringbrewworks.com

Appropriately, TAFT'S ALE HOUSE (1429 Race St., Cincinnati, Ohio 45202) opened its doors for the first time on Opening Day, April 2015. And there was a priest to bless the newborn beers. Located in what was once St. Paul's German Evangelical Protestant Church in Over-the-Rhine, the three-level brewery, bar, and restaurant shows "attention to detail." Writing in the *Cincinnati Enquirer* on April 6, 2015, Shauna Steigerwald described a 220-seat space that "features 46-foot ceilings and a large chandelier that draws the eye up to them." Antiques placed strategically throughout re-call the brewery's namesake, William Howard Taft. A $9 million project according to Steigerwald, Taft's Ale House is, in the words of partner Dave Kassling, "something that Cincinnatians have never seen before, and a place for them to call home." Telephone: 513-334-1393. Web: http://taftsalehouse.com

TAP AND SCREW BREWERY (5060 Crookshank Road, Cincinnati, Ohio 45238) honors Cincinnati beer (tap), Ohio's wine industry (screw), and the city's manufacturing history. The first brewpub on the city's west side offers the ambience of a sports bar and the beers of a craft brewery. Having opened informally in fall 2014, T&S began serving its own beer in De-cember 2014 following its grand opening. Dr. Kool IPA is worth seeking out for its bracing hops flavor that somehow does not translate into for-midable bitterness. There's also Irony, a Belgian ale that balances a mild sweetness from Belgian brewing sugar with the sour edge of a dubbel. Telephone: 513-451-1763 Web: https://www.tapandscrew.com

A NOTE ABOUT SAMUEL ADAMS

SAMUEL ADAMS BREWERY
1625 Central Parkway, Cincinnati, Ohio 45214
• http://www.samueladams.com and http://www.bostonbeer.com

In 1997 The Boston Beer Company, brewers of Samuel Adams, was seek-ing a significant expansion in production. So the company purchased the Hudepohl-Schoenling brewery on the Central Parkway in Cincinnati. Why Cincinnati? In addition to finding the brewing capacity he needed as well as an opportunity for expansion in an area of the city with relatively inviting real estate prices, Jim Koch, brewer and founder and owner of Boston Beer, was returning to his hometown. In the 1940s, Koch's father worked as an apprentice at the brewery.

Unlike Boston Beer's Germania Street brewery in Boston, a compact brick Federal-style building with flower boxes at its windows and hop vines screening its patio, the Cincinnati brewery welcomes beer fans for tours just once a year, during Oktoberfest Zinzinnati. Although the immense, rambling assortment of industrial buildings just a few blocks north of Washington Park and the Music Hall may give an impression of architectural anonymity, Koch points out some interesting original features, such as "art deco ornaments on Central Parkway and flour-ishes above several of the inside doorways." There are recent features as well. The brewery has installed several stained-glass windows in its new barrel room. According to Koch, "one celebrates Cincinnati's brewing history and Boston Beer's history and the other celebrates traditional brewing motifs." (You can see photos of the most recent Oktoberfest tour at http://www.hoperatives.com/?p=15303.)

Boston Beer has earned its prominence both by its undisputed leadership as a craft-brewing pioneer and by brewing accessible, noteworthy lagers and ales in a remarkable diversity of styles. In addition to its flagship beers, Boston Lager and Sam Adams Light, the company's three breweries (Boston, Cincinnati, and Breinigsville, Pennsylvania) produce a changing array of seasonals, "brewmaster's special releases," small-batch beers, limited-release beers, and a "barrel room" collection. Although there's no tasting room at 1625 Central Parkway, Samuel Adams beers are of course widely available. And thank goodness for that!

....

5

NORTH BY NORTHWEST
THE ISLANDS AND GREATER TOLEDO

Comparative latecomers to the craft-brewing scene, the brewpubs and breweries of northern and northwest Ohio—those of Toledo, the Lake Erie islands, and a few others here and there—are making up for lost time. Through their creative brews, personable welcomes, and, for some, inventive cooking, they are emerging as a distinctive asset of their region and an attraction to aficionados from throughout Ohio and beyond. One caveat: A couple are seasonal, so it would be wise to check opening times with the breweries themselves.

BREWPUBS

KELLEYS ISLAND BREWERY

504 W. Lakeshore Drive, Kelleys Island, Ohio 43438
419-746-2314 or 419-656-4335 • http://kelleysislandbrewpub.com

On a warm summer afternoon, sitting under a green umbrella with a pint of Island Devil in your hand, looking out over Lake Erie and luxuriating in "island time," you may be tempted to check the island's real estate listings. The brewery, the restaurant, and the grounds are compact, but the location is matchless—and well worth the short ferry ride from the mainland. There are three comfortable spaces: on the lawn, under the canopy of the outside rock bar, and inside the brewpub/restaurant.

The brewery's story, as told in its colorful menu, began in 1999 with the remodeling of a former custard stand. (The brewery still serves milkshakes.) Longtime Kelleys Island resident Patti Johnson, who proudly wears the pink boots of an experienced brewer, affirms that "the restaurant makes the most of what we know about making island visitors welcome and comfortable [and] the microbrewery enables us to bottle a bit of Kelleys Island magic and offer it to beer lovers both on and off the island."

As is the case with many businesses on the islands, the brewery closes for the winter, roughly from October through April.

Dachshund Petey Turkelton and brewer Doug Muranyi extend a welcome to the brewery.

The Beers

In this small brewery with a big view—the full expanse of the lake—Doug Muranyi crafts his beers in two-hundred-gallon releases. The range is not expansive, but each beer that Doug brews tends to bear a stamp of individuality. The **Anglers Ale** (ABV 5.5 percent, IBUs N/A), which the brewery describes as a "standard English bitter," offers one interpretation of the British pub staple. It is more effervescent, offers a more prominent hops presence, and is served colder than its English cousins. It may not make an English visitor homesick, but it might encourage her to order another. The brewery's most popular offering, **Dawg Bizkit Brown** (ABV 5.5 percent, IBUs N/A), is by contrast lightly hopped. Its rich taste arises from roasted barley complemented with chocolate and crystal malts. Although the brewery's Web site warns that "it ain't for poodles," the resident dachshund, Petey, has been known to scarf a few drops here and there. **Gale Force Ale** (ABV 6.5–7 percent, IBUs N/A) will please IPA devotees. Centennial hops dominate the taste up-front, but a smooth return of malt completes the sip. The real surprise on the Kelleys Island list may be the **Island Devil**, a double Belgian-style ale that manages to achieve a remarkable balance. Fairly strong by Ohio standards at ABV 8.5 percent (IBUs N/A), the beer appeals more by its smooth taste and rich plummy aroma than by its alcohol content. Sipped with discretion, the ale offers the rewards of German hops, Trappist yeast, and crystal malts. Superb. There is also a good single Belgian-style ale, **Anniversary Ale** (ABV 3.5 percent, IBUs N/A), which has enough character to sustain interest while allowing enjoyment over a long

and lazy session. Finally, for those who prefer light beers when summer fun beckons, there's **Summer Haze** (ABV 4.5 percent, IBUs N/A), a true craft beer that any beer lover can enjoy. You're likely to find several of these on tap when you visit, but "availability varies." And Doug may surprise you with something unexpected.

The Food
The Kelleys Island Brewery is one of only a very few Ohio brewpubs serving food all day: breakfast, lunch, and (on Thursdays, Fridays, and Saturdays) dinner. There's nothing fancy—but the fare is local (or at least regional) and the servings are generous. Breakfast favorites range from the Hash Brown Heaven (good fuel for hikers and cy-clists) to a healthy Breakfast Parfait of yogurt and granola. The menu for the rest of the day features Cream Cran-

A perfect day on Lake Erie calls for a sample of what Kelleys Island Brewery can do.

berry Almond Salad, with chicken and mixed greens, Sauerkraut Balls, a Brew Cheese Soup incorporating the brewery's ale, a hearty soup-of-the-week, such as Shrimp and Corn Chowder, and the signature Perch Sand-wich. There are also lots of appetizers, burgers, and sides. If you share your travel plans and food restrictions with Patti (at the number above) she will try to accommodate you.

Newsworthy
The most important news each year are the dates of opening (announced on the Web site, but typically late April) and closing for the season (around Halloween). • The brewery introduced a stout, The Devil's Shadow, in summer 2015. "Goes great with eggs," according to the brewmaster.

Other Stuff
The brewery caters for special occasions and can host private parties. "Weddings, birthdays, and reunions are becoming a trend on this natu-rally laid-back island," says the brewery. • Also available: wine (by the bottle or the glass), some mass-market beers, and a full bar offering

some exotic drinks as well as traditional spirits. The Brandy Alexander and Love in a Glass have a reputation. • There is a cottage just across the street (on the lake side) that the brewery rents during the summer. The views are lovely, and you would never be more than a few steps from a good beer.

When she's brewing, Patti Johnson wears the pink boots at Kelleys Island Brewery.

The ferry services to Kelleys Island from the mainland arrive at a dock about a mile from the brewpub. If you take the passengers-only ferry in the summer (Jet Express by Put-in-Bay Boat Line from Sandusky) or choose to park your car in Marblehead before taking the auto/passenger ferry (Kelleys Island Ferry Board Line), you can opt for a pleasant walk along the coastline to the brewpub, rent a golf cart, or call a taxi. Or you can take your car on the ferry from Marblehead.

THE SKINNY

LOCATION	When you disembark from the ferry, take a left on East Lakeshore Drive, which soon becomes West Lakeshore Drive. The brewpub is on the western side of Kelleys Island, just about a mile from the ferry docks. It is a pleasant walk if you have not brought your car. Or you can rent a golf cart at or near the dock.
HOURS	Sun–Thu 8:00 A.M.–11:00 P.M. • Fri 8:00 A.M.–11:30 P.M. • Sat 8:00 A.M.–midnight. Call to confirm hours. CLOSED IN WINTER.
PARKING	It's easy. There's an ample lot for your car or golf cart.
KIDS	Why not—especially during the day? There's an appealing kids' menu with a perch basket in addition to the usual chicken bites and mac and cheese.
TAKEOUT	There is as yet no canning or bottling, but most beers may be purchased in growlers.
DISTRIBUTION	The brewery makes its keg beer available through distributors.

Oliver House, home to Maumee Bay Brewing, offers an impressive beacon for downtown Toledo.

MAUMEE BAY BREWING CO.

27 Broadway Street, Toledo, Ohio 43604

419-243-1302 • http://www.mbaybrew.com/maumee-bay-brewing-co/

Breweries typically occupy one of three kinds of properties: new construction, rented space, or restorations. Maumee Bay falls decisively into the third category. The brewery boasts that its home, Oliver House, is "the oldest working commercial building in Toledo." It is a striking building that dominates its corner, Broadway and Ottawa. Given its restoration, it seems ideally suited to house a brewery and four restaurants. The capacity and complexity of the site might suggest less of an emphasis on distribution, but that is not the case. Maumee Bay's bottled and draft beers, now with bold new labels, continue to spread throughout Ohio—reaching Columbus and Cleveland in late 2014 and heading for Cincinnati. According to brewery manager Craig Kerr, the challenge these days is not finding customers but the logistics of distribution—securing sufficient warehouse space and brewing beer for a longer shelf life.

TEN GREAT OHIO BEER LABELS

L abels do far more than shout for attention on cooler shelves. They offer an impression of both the brewery and of what's inside the can or bottle. They express personality. They provide information. This list should be far longer, but here are ten great labels.

- The intriguing silhouettes on colorful but artfully monochromatic labels of **Actual Beer's** twenty-two-ounce bottles suggest stories you would enjoy hearing. But as you enjoy a large bottle of, say, Fat Julian (an imperial stout), you should be able to complete the story in your imagination.
- **Maumee Bay's** new label, which features a striking silhouette of the suspension bridge that looms above its neighborhood, may have to persuade fans of the lonesome heron on the former label, but it conveys the increasing authority of an expanding brewery.
- **Rivertown's** redesigned labels, which emphasize simplicity, clarity, and color, reflect the brewery's emerging focus on distinctive beers with distinctive names such as Divergent (a sour ale in the Berliner style) and Soulless (a scarlet sour ale in the Flanders style).
- The elegant majesty of **Rockmill Brewery's** lone horse silhouetted against a sky of unbroken cloud establishes a strong identity for Belgian-style beers brewed by creative brewers committed to consistent quality. **Thirsty Dog's** canines may not be as elegant, but they are amiable and amusing.
- **Sideswipe** takes an aggressive approach with its beer names (such as Elegant Hoodlum Smoke Stout and Coop Looter Saison) and with its brilliant scratch-art labels.
- The labels of **Great Lakes** beers have been works of art—literally. The 2015 label redesign has not changed that.
- The sylvan imagery of **Mt. Carmel's** year-round beer labels offers a reassurance of consistency and makes the beers instantly recognizable in the cooler. Only the colors and names change. The seasonals continue this theme, but the scene more vividly reflects the season. That graphic continuity gives the brewery license to experiment in labeling its "snapshot series" with bold, mostly monochromatic images. Check out the squirrel taking a nibble from the label on Squirrel Bite, an imperial brown ale.
- **Rhinegeist** brews large, no-nonsense beers in a large, no-nonsense industrial space, so it makes sense that its distinctive, colorful cans are well designed, direct, and informative.
- The sixteen-ounce cans that constitute the "three-can trilogy" of **Warped Wing** are "busy," with bold colors and extravagant graphics, and so detailed that the brewery provides on its Web site an explanation of "the inspiration behind the can." Here's a sample: "The whale is shown smoking a rye silo as he brings rye grain back to the brewery for production. Eclectic clouds are forming from the silo smoke symbolizing innovative ideas and thoughts that can come from anyone, anywhere at any time." Recall when you chose cereals for the reading content on the boxes? These cans will repay your study as you enjoy the contents. The cans won an ADDY award in 2015. That is the largest competition for advertising.

The beautiful brewing system in Oliver House appears to be the same generation as the building.

The Beers

Maumee Bay is really three breweries: a beautiful classic fifteen-barrel system on two floors of the Oliver House, a modern thirty-barrel production facility with a bottling line across the street, and a three-barrel nano-brewery for producing small brewpub releases. Brewery manager Craig Kerr's beer menu is formidable, offering styles as far apart as Blood Orange Wit and Brewedwitch Barley Wine, some of which are now barrel aged. The nano-brewery encourages varieties that can be really quite creative. I'm ready to return for the Mojito Wit. Or perhaps the Lemon Peppercorn Saison.

The few beers that I sampled were memorable. The one exception was the iconic **Buckeye Beer** (ABV 5.2 percent, IBUs 14). While any preservationist should commend Maumee's continuing to make Toledo's "hometown beer" available—it has been brewed since 1838—the beer itself offers to my taste a reminder of just how much better modern craft beers are than their predecessors. However, I would never question anyone's affection for a local brew, and I admire brewmaster Jon Koester for avoiding the adjuncts that I expected to taste. The **Glass Hopper India Pale Ale** (ABV 7 percent, IBUs 80) is all about the hop blend, a mix of varieties that offers both strong bitterness and overtones of citrus. Maumee Bay's dry hopping adds some floral overtones on the nose. There really is extraordinary balance in this moderately strong beer.

Maumee Bay's **Pumpkin Ale** (ABV 5.2 percent, IBUs 22) begins with locally grown pumpkins and squash roasted on-site with brown sugar. Built on an English base malt to which specialty malts and flavorings (nutmeg, cinnamon, etc.) are added, this is a highly drinkable autumn and winter ale, more dry than sweet, rich on the tongue but not cloying. I concluded with what turned out to be one of the most memorable beers of my statewide sampling, the **Total Eclipse Breakfast Stout** (ABV 9.1 percent, IBUs 31). Although this remarkable beverage is said to be Maumee's "version of breakfast in a glass," you would have to be a hardy soul to face this powerful brew in the morning! But if you are a hardy soul, it would offer you the espresso con cioccolato (strong espresso flavor that is laced with dark chocolate) you might need to get moving. The beer is as opaque as a cup of espresso and as rich. Could it be improved? I would love to taste this beer from the cask or on nitro so as to drink it less cold and with less carbonation. But in any form this beer justifies a trip to Toledo.

The Food

The ample four-page pub menu offers reliable pub favorites such as pizza, burgers, mac and cheese, and a rib eye, but there's a distinctive creativity evident in two respects. There are dishes that convey a sense of place: the Oliver House Salad (romaine with provolone, bacon, red onion), the Oliver House Pizza (artichoke hearts, two cheeses, sausage, mushrooms), and the Mud Hen Pie (named for Toledo's famed AAA baseball team). But of even greater interest are the dishes that reflect a partnership of brewer and chef: the beer wort cheesecake, IPA pancake syrup, the cheddar beer soup made with Buckeye Beer, the hIPstA sandwich combining IPA cured pork and IPA sourdough, and the beer-marinated baby back ribs.

According to general manager Neal Kovacik, "beer and food pairings are all well enough, and we suggest them, but what really works for us is a collaborative approach to beer and food." Beer is, after all, "a food," Craig Kerr reminds. Although I consistently honored my pledge "not to eat free food," there were times when I was tempted, and this was one of them. Weekly specials are listed on the brewpub's Web site. Note that there are other venues on the premises with different menus. For instance, Rockwell's Steakhouse broils USDA prime beef at 1800 degrees! And The Café, entered from the Ottawa Street side of the building, opens for breakfast and lunch with homemade pastries, salads, and sandwiches. It is billed as "an international bistro . . . in a hip urban atmosphere." The Web site for all Maumee Brewing establishments,

Ashley McAninch tenders a Total Eclipse Breakfast Stout.

If you're looking for the Maumee Bay brewpub, this is your entrance.

http://www.mbaybrew.com, will enable you to make an appropriate choice from among the Oliver House restaurants.

Newsworthy

One highly visible change has been a dramatic rebranding based on a striking artistic interpretation of the nearby Anthony Wayne Bridge (OH-2, OH-51, OH-65), now the only suspension bridge in the Ohio state highway system. (I will miss the heron, but the new look is eye-catching.) • New beer offerings and new menu items are often noted on the Web site.

Other Stuff

Monday nights offer a trivia game in the brewpub and $6.50 pitchers before 9 P.M. • During October, there are "haunted brew tours" of the brewery's historic site. • There's a rewards program that credits you with 5 percent of every purchase you make.

THE SKINNY

LOCATION	The brewery is near the western foot of the Anthony Wayne Bridge, but the easiest way to reach it is by exiting I-75N at Exit 201A to Logan Street. Take the next right onto Erie, then another right onto Newton, then a left onto Broadway. The brewpub is about four blocks north on your right. If you do happen to cross the Anthony Wayne Bridge driving into Toledo from the east, simply take a right on Broadway.
HOURS	The hours for Maumee Bay's different venues are not the same, but one or more of the dining and bar areas are open Mon–Tue 8:00 A.M.–midnight and Wed–Sat 8:00 A.M.–2:30 A.M.
PARKING	There is considerable parking in the lot that wraps around the Oliver House, but there is free parking also in a lot just across Broadway.
KIDS	Kids will enjoy the nooks and crannies of Oliver House, and there's a section of the menu just for them.
TAKEOUT	Many of the beers bottled by Maumee Bay are available for purchase in a large cooler just behind the checkout. Or you can fill a growler or half growler. All beers are available in kegs.
DISTRIBUTION	See the introductory note. Maumee Bay's beers should soon be available throughout Ohio.

PUT-IN-BAY BREWING COMPANY

411 Catawba Avenue, Put-in-Bay, Ohio 43456

419-285-4677 • http://putinbaybrewery.com/index.html

The beer is enjoyable, the expected brewpub fare (burgers, wings, nachos) comes with a few twists, and the house-distilled spirits are well worth sampling, but this "summer place" stands out above all for its

Put-in-Bay Brewing Company offers easy parking for the island's preferred transportation.

ambience. Just a few blocks up the avenue from Lake Erie, across the street from the Grand Islander Hotel, the brewpub captures the seasonal spirit of its resort. When it opens its wide fire station doors on a warm spring day after the long, dark winter months, the town and the island can begin to stir. It's time to tap a keg.

The Beers

For a small craft brewer operating principally during the summer and early fall, PIB offers a considerable range of craft brews. I did not sample the beers, and the brewery does not post ABV and IBU levels, but I can pass along the brewery's information that their most popular, Summer Brew, is an unfiltered wheat beer that is "the perfect beer to cool off and refresh on a hot summer day." Summer Brew also provides a starting point for the brewery's fruity variation, Watermelon Wheat. The list becomes more interesting with Ole Cotton Top Irish Red, which honors one Cotton Duggan, a Lake Erie commercial fisherman and "a grand historian" of the island. Malt dominates the ale. Hops are said to offer a distant echo. The West Shore IPA also offers a story, that of the captain who met defeat at the hands of Oliver Hazard Perry in the naval battle just offshore, the largest of the War of 1812. PIB brews one stout in two varieties: South Bass Oatmeal Stout, described as offering a "fantastically full finish," and Pass Out Bourbon Stout, the oatmeal stout aged, as the name suggests, "with Kentucky bourbon." A final offering, counterintuitive given the brewery's seasonal operation, is its Christmas Ale, available in July. Shown in the photo, the ale is a striking red in color. It is said to offer the familiar seasonal notes of honey, ginger, and cinnamon. PIB Brewery also serves "guest beers" from craft brewers such as Great Lakes, Thirsty Dog, and Left Hand, as well as commercial staples such as Budweiser, Miller Light, and Labatt.

The Food

The brewpub standards are all here and appear to be well prepared and served in ample portions: cheese sticks, smothered nachos, Caesar salad, and a range of burgers. But there are some more interesting offerings

Put-in-Bay's Brian DeFrank and Tom Dailey (*left to right*) introduce Christmas Ale in July.

as well, such as Guinness onion soup, described as rich and smoky, Walleye Bites, a Caprese salad with local tomatoes, mozzarella, and pesto, and a perch sandwich. (There is also a perch dinner.) The "famous" PIB pizza comes in several interesting variations (Greek, barbecue chicken, Alfredo), but the most interesting may be the Island Stoner Pizza baked for a group. Essentially two pizzas in one, the pie layers coleslaw, chicken, ham, onion rings, macaroni and cheese, french fries, and mozzarella cheese sticks. Perhaps not the recommended choice for diners anticipating a rough ferry return to the mainland!

Newsworthy

As with other island businesses, the most important headline each year is the announcement of the opening date. The hours listed below are for the summer, but the brewery opens for limited hours from spring until fall.

Other Stuff

There's often an Oktoberfest beer brewed for the annual island festival on the second weekend in October. • The restaurant closes at 10 P.M. • Ferry services to Put-in-Bay serve two different docks. The JetExpress dock (passenger ferry from Sandusky and Port Clinton) is just blocks away from the brewery, a short stroll through Perry Park. The Miller Boat Line (vehicles and passengers) from Catawba Island docks a little over two miles down Langram Road from downtown PIB and the brewery, perhaps ten minutes by golf cart or taxi.

LOCATION	In downtown Put-in-Bay, on the north coast of South Bass Island.
HOURS	Daily 11:30 A.M.–2:30 A.M., Memorial Day through Labor Day. Call the brewery for opening hours in the off-season. CLOSED IN WINTER.
PARKING	On the street or in nearby lots. Golf cart parking at the door.
KIDS	There are kid-friendly entrees on the menu, including a mini cheese pizza.
TAKEOUT	Most beers may be purchased in growlers.
DISTRIBUTION	There are no plans at the moment for distribution.

TAPROOMS

CATAWBA ISLAND BREWING COMPANY

2330 East Harbor Road, Port Clinton, Ohio 43452

419-960-7764 • http://catawbaislandbrewing.com/home.php

Look for it! Your GPS should get you into the general vicinity, but if you fail to see the sign, you may drive a few more blocks down nondescript East Harbor Road before turning around. You will be rewarded for your perseverance. These are dedicated year-round brewers crafting highly creative beers, lovely to the eye and the palate, in a large custom-designed facility. The contrast between the industrial park modern exterior and the gleaming, comfortable interior could hardly be more dramatic.

Shad Gunderson had been home brewing for about twenty years when his cousin, Chad, also a home brewer, issued a challenge: There was a building in a good location that would accommodate a brewery. The RV repair shop and pet store were no more. Why not now? As fourth-generation Catawba Islanders, they knew the territory. And so Shad and his wife, Cindy, recruited coinvestor Mike Roder to join them in a leap of faith. They have landed on East Harbor Road, Port Clinton. And beer fans should be grateful.

The Beers

There may be as many as fifteen beers on tap when you visit, thanks to a state-of-the-art fifteen-barrel brewing system. You can check out the full listing at the Web site above. During my visit, I found several I thought particularly memorable.

Insularium Black IPA (ABV 7.5 percent, IBUs 96) may be Ohio's most challenging beer name. The reference is to the Lake Erie water snake that recently emerged from the protection of the federal list of endangered species. Its scientific name is Nerodia sipedon insularum. Hence the brewery describes the beer as "not for the faint of heart." Indeed, lurking beneath the placid surface there lies a menacing presence of dark malt and intense hops awaiting the opportunity to seize your palate. But you needn't feel endangered. You will find the notes of coffee and chocolate promised by the color, but you will find as well a straightforward toast more suggestive of a porter than an IPA. I will let this snake bite me anytime.

I next considered (a counterintuitive move) an even bigger snake, the **Double Couple Three Hops Imperial IPA** (ABV 8.5 percent, IBUs 100+). The three hops in question—Apollo, Cascade, and Summit—are all American in origin, and two of the three are especially effective in bittering. That the strongest of the three, Apollo, is one of the most expensive gives some insight into the commitment of head

Whether or not it rains, Cindy Gunderson pours at Catawba Island Brewing.

Head brewer Mike Reynolds enjoys one of the world's great aromas.

brewer Mike Reynolds to memorable IPAs. But the beer's balance represents even more persuasive evidence. The hefty IBUs find their match in a gratifying caramel presence, with the result that you emerge smiling. If you enjoy a sip every now and then rather than quaffing with abandon, you will be able to use the colloquialism with authority: "I told him a couple three times to order me another pint!"

The Insularium Black IPA makes a shining impression at Catawba Island Brewing.

After these two formidable (but approachable) IPAs, I imagined that the **Back'er Forward Brown Ale** (ABV 4.6 percent, IBUs 42) might prove underwhelming. Not so. Evocative of a bowl of good nuts covered with dark chocolate, this dark ale finds its discipline in a hops presence that emerges over time. The mouthfeel is especially generous. I was in fact relieved to discover a beer one could enjoy over the course of an afternoon and still be able to execute the local directive, "back'er forward." Finally, could I resist a few sips of **Intentionally Shitty Lager** (ABV 4.6 percent, IBUs 19)? Of course not. The warning could hardly be more explicit: Following the example of macrobreweries, Catawba Island has "utilized cheap/improper ingredients (like corn and rice) and spent all of our money advertising our exceptionally shitty beer." I regret to report that the beer is not that bad. Perhaps my taste buds had been anesthetized by the hops and the alcohol of previous tastes, but I found the ISL a clean, pleasant, unexceptional but far from off-putting beer. Anyway, wouldn't it be worth a lot to step up to the bar, pull out a crisp bill, and say, "Bartender, give me . . ."?

The Food
Catawba Island is a tasting room, not a brewpub, but, in addition to pizza by the slice or by the pie, the brewery sometimes announces special dinners.

Other Stuff
Locals know that Catawba Island is an island in name only. As the directions below suggest, there is no ferry needed. Live music occasionally takes the stage in the tasting room, of both professional and "open mic" quality. There's pinball for those who bring quarters. Sometimes there is trivia or euchre for those who don't.

LOCATION	Exit I-80 (Ohio Turnpike) to OH-53 and drive north toward Port Clinton. Before you reach the town, take OH-2 east to the next exit, 1-21A, which will deliver you to East Harbor Road. A short drive east and Catawba Island Brewing will be on your right. Keep your eyes peeled.
HOURS	Wed–Sat 5–10 P.M. • Sun 3–8 P.M.
PARKING	Ample, just outside the front door.
KIDS	Not really a scene for kids, to my eye, but there shouldn't be a problem. Perhaps inquire?
TAKEOUT	Most beers may be purchased in growlers.
DISTRIBUTION	Beer is available on tap in some bars and restaurants in the area. There is some canning as well for distribution in the immediate area.

CONSIDER ALSO

BLACK CLOISTER BREWING COMPANY (619 Monroe Street, Toledo, Ohio 43604) has invited those who "believe in local craft beer" to join the Order of the Black Cloister at this heart-of-downtown brewery. It's located near Fifth Third Field, home to the legendary Mud Hens. Details are available at http://www.blackcloister.com/index.html and from brewery founder (and Lutheran pastor) Tom Schaeffer. Martin Luther, who was later to commend the spiritual values of good beer, served in a "black cloister" during his pre-Reformation days as a monk. Telephone: 419-214-1500.

Army veteran, Toledo native, and craft brewer Chris Harris has opened a garage-based nano-brewery, BLACK FROG BREWERY, in the Toledo suburb of Holland (address N/A). For additional information, e-mail the brewery at http://blackfrogbrewery.com or Chris himself at charris@blackfrogbrewer.com Telephone: 419-389-7136.

What John Wesley would have to say about a microbrewery in a former Methodist Church is anyone's guess, but FATHER JOHN'S BREWING COMPANY (301 West Butler Street, Bryan, Ohio 43506) offers "honest, handcrafted fare" that can prove surprisingly sophisticated. There are also more than a dozen house-brewed beers here in Ohio's far northwest corner. The brewery's commitment "to the highest standards of quality and sustainability in everything we put on the plate as well as what we put in our brew kettles" suggests that they are keeping the faith. Church doors are open Tuesday through Saturday from lunchtime to late evening. Telephone: 419-633-1313 Web: http://www.fatherjohnsbrewery.net/

FINDLAY BREWING COMPANY (227 ½ North Main Street, Findlay, Ohio 45840) is an interesting nano-brewery with aspirations of becoming a microbrewery. Even now, there's an interesting range of available styles, including a molasses porter, a black IPA, and a stout named Floodwater—"not brewed with floodwater," the brewery promises. Because hours open may be limited to Fridays 5:00–10:00 P.M., check the Web site (http://www.findlaybrewingcompany.com) before you visit. Telephone: 419-722-7395.

FLATROCK BREWING COMPANY (215 Railway Avenue, Holgate, Ohio 43527) opened its Napoleon Taproom at 621 North Perry Street, Napoleon, in late 2014. (It's due west of Bowling Green on U.S. 6.) You can order pints of its year-round beers as well as taproom-only specialty brews such as a Wild Yeast IPA Thursday through Saturday. And you can fill your growler. Appetizers from nearby restaurants are available at the bar. Telephone: 419-966-1440 Web: https://flatrockbrewery.squarespace.com

GRANITE CITY FOOD & BREWERY (2300 Village Drive W, Suite 130, Maumee, Ohio 43537) offers reliable food and craft beers at this outpost of its thirteen-state franchise. Unlike Rock Bottom, which brews its beers in-house using company recipes, GCFB begins its fermentation process using wort provided by a central commissary. Telephone: 419-8789054 Web: http://www.gcfb.net/ (Note: In February 2015 the business press reported that GCFB's parent corporation had retained an investment bank to guide its interest in possible sale or merger.)

GREAT BLACK SWAMP BREWING COMPANY (3323 Monroe Street, Toledo, Ohio 43606) does not operate a taproom but distributes its beers—a red ale, stout, Pale Ale, IPA, and golden ale—in kegs to many restaurants and taverns in the Toledo area and in bottles to many specialty markets and liquor stores. Telephone: 419-973-1256 Web: http://www.greatblackswampbrewing.com

SUGAR RIDGE BREWERY (109 S. Main St., Bowling Green, Ohio 43402) brews "heavier beers with full rounded flavors leaving behind a portion of the residual malt sugars to balance slightly to the sweet side." They make a few varieties available Thursday to Saturday at their site. A recent offering included a blueberry ale, a light lager (Joe Beer), and a foreign extra stout. Sometimes there's music. Telephone: 419-373-6553 Web: http://www.sugarridgebrewery.net

6

THE SURPRISING SOUTHWEST
DAYTON AND ENVIRONS

In the early nineteenth century, Dayton settlers founded breweries to assuage the thirst of travelers discovering the region. By mid-century, with the Miami and Erie Canal operating at capacity, there was a substantial demand for beer—and a sizable brewing industry. The ales produced by that industry needed little refrigeration, which was a good thing. But then came the J & M Schiml brewery on Wayne Street, which in 1852 adopted new technology to brew Dayton's first lager. Other lager breweries followed. By the late nineteenth century, Dayton's brewing industry was the equal of that of many a metropolis. There were at least twelve breweries in operation.

Where are we now? When this book was planned there was to be a single chapter covering Cincinnati and Dayton—or Columbus and Dayton. That had to change. In January 2012, the number of breweries in Dayton was equal to the number of tigers in your kitchen: zero, I trust. (I remember elementary math!) But as I wrapped up the work on this book, there were twelve. Shades of the nineteenth century! While Cincinnati, Cleveland, and Columbus still offer Ohio's greatest concentrations of craft brewing, Dayton and its near neighbors now represent an increasingly attractive and competitive beer destination. From Miamisburg, where you can stroll easily from one craft brewery to its nearby neighbor, to Dayton's downtown Oregon District, and to always interesting Yellow Springs, there's good reason to recall those early travelers and "stay thirsty."

BREWPUBS

LOCK 27 BREWING
1035 South Main Street, Centerville, Ohio 45458
937-433-2739 • http://www.lock27brewing.com/home.html

Distinct among craft breweries in the Dayton area, Lock 27 Brewing offers a creative menu in addition to its house beers and its impressive selection of guest beers on draft and in bottles. The suburban strip mall

Stephanie Doe offers an IPA at Lock 27.

location may be far from distinctive from the outside but once you step inside or take a seat on the artfully screened patio, you'll forget about the environs and enjoy the environment. The guiding spirit behind a welcoming balance of food and beer is owner Steve Barnhart, a former corporate executive who discovered that brewing beer at home was more satisfying than flying around the world with a long to-do list. With the help of his wife, Michelle, he created a methodical business plan providing first for the development of a strong local presence. He envisions a production brewery eventually: bottling, canning, and distribution. But "great breweries take twenty years to develop," he says. "And there's risk in trying to achieve too much too soon." When you visit Lock 27, named for a landmark on the Miami-Erie Canal, you'll find that a lot has been achieved already.

The Beers

Like many brewpubs, Lock 27 offers a wide selection of well-selected guest beers, both on tap and in bottles, so that it can focus on brewing a limited range of interesting house styles. I sampled three Lock 27 brews. The **Sunfish Pale Ale** (ABV 5.7 percent, IBUs 40), their approachable house American pale, offers a worthy introduction to the brewery's straightforward focus on balance and quality. There's a good balance of malt and hops resulting in citrus and herbal hints. The brewery's signature IPA, **Mouth Breather** (ABV 7.2 percent, IBUs 65), is a well-balanced, straightforward, not particularly complex version of the style. There is again a hint of citrus in the aroma, and more than a hint in the taste, together with a bit of cedar. Such transparent beers are not easy to brew well. Any misstep will be conspicuous. No missteps are evident here. **Bear Trap** (ABV 5.8 percent, IBUs 21) should not be served quite so cold as

Brandon Frank checks on the boiling wort at Lock 27.

Lock 27 pours it. The real virtues of this brown ale—the softness on the tongue of its malts and the overtones of honey and brown sugar—will be far more apparent if you drink your pint after allowing it to warm up a bit. On the list of Lock 27 beers you may find also a dark Russian imperial stout, a Belgian ale, a classic British extra-special bitter (ESB), an oatmeal stout, and the occasional barrel-aged sour ale.

The Food

At Lock 27, food is a costar, not just a supporting cast member. The "eclectic kitchen" turns out a limited but wide-ranging menu of interesting dishes that change with the seasons. Appetizers on one visit included a stout-flavored version of the Canadian favorite, poutine (fries with beef gravy, cheese, and a fried egg), but there were cheddar-and-bacon pierogies as well. And there's beer-cheese soup, which combines the brewery's amber ale with three cheeses (smoked gouda, cheddar, and parmesan). Entrees include standard fare such as mac and cheese and fish tacos, but even these offer some points of interest. And there is a not-so-standard Thai Curry (see the photo), which can be served with chicken or shrimp. For many British pubs, a good curry provides the perfect companion for a pint, and it is good to see that Lock 27 offers that combination. Noteworthy among the sandwiches is the Chicken Fresca Panini, which combines house-roasted chicken with feta cheese, apples, bacon, and honey mustard. You can finish with a good stout or with a stout brownie, a remarkable wedge made with the brewery's stout and accompanied by your choice of artisan ice creams.

Newsworthy

Lock 27's expression of interest in expansion has attracted media attention. Reporting for the *Dayton Business Journal,* Olivia Barrow describes Barnhart's search for industrial space to enable a ramping up of production and distribution. He told Barrow, "I think our brand and our reputation are where we wanted to be, and the time is right for us. We certainly have more demand than we could possibly fill."

Other Stuff

Events have included beer dinners just about every month. There are Bacon Nights as well: bacon served in Mason jars to accompany the pints of beer. • In addition to offering menu specials, the kitchen sometimes contributes to the brewing process, as when it once prepared the sweet potatoes for a Belgian strong ale. • The tables and walls of the restaurant offer a rustic ambience thanks to the repurposing of salvaged barn wood.

At Lock 27 the kitchen and the brewery combine efforts to create memorable dining.

THE SKINNY

LOCATION	Take I-675 to the exit for OH-48 and OH-725: Centerville's North Main Street, which is also known as the Dayton Lebanon Pike. Drive south beyond the intersection with Spring Valley Road to a large strip mall on your right. Look for the brewery's blue roof.
HOURS	Mon–Tue 11:30 A.M.–10:00 P.M. • Wed–Thu 11:30 A.M.–11:00 P.M. • Fri 11:30 A.M.–midnight • Sat noon–midnight • Sun noon–9:00 P.M.
PARKING	There's a large lot in front of the brewpub.
KIDS	Yes, there is a good selection of nonalcoholic beverages and a children's menu.
TAKEOUT	Growler fills are available.
DISTRIBUTION	Yes, there's an intent, but expansion depends on establishing a remote production facility.

TAPROOMS

STAR CITY BREWING COMPANY

319 South Second Street, Miamisburg, Ohio 45342

937-701-7827 • http://www.starcitybrewing.com/

Star City's bubbling growler welcomes beer fans to its nineteenth-century tasting room.

In the nineteenth century, Star City's downtown Miamisburg building was a sawmill, strategically located just two blocks from the Miami River. In 1929, the building found a new life as a popular restaurant, the Peerless Mill Inn. Now the historic structure, with its exposed hand-hewn beams and rustic paneling, has a new life again as the home of Star City Brewing—thanks in part to the "phenomenal" support of a city newly focused on (in the words of owner Justin Kohnen) "unique experiences for tourists." The potential for growth, given the brewery's many large rooms and fireplaces, is considerable, but the owners—Justin and his brother Brian Kohnen—plan to expand slowly and methodically. Part of the plan calls for focusing first on "entry-level" beers that enable locals new to the craft scene to approach slowly. But it already seems apparent that there's a new star in Miamisburg, Ohio's "Star City."

The Beers

Brewing at least for the present with a three-and-a-half-barrel system, Star City focuses on a few well-crafted beers. I tried four served by amiable bartender Dylan Sage. The **Blonde Ale** (ABV 3.8 percent, IBUs 21), meant to evoke a Kölsch, lacks the transparency of taste that style should present but offers instead a deeper, richer maltiness balanced more by bitterness than fruitiness. Star City's blonde is in a way more interesting than Kölsch. The

Dylan Sage pulls an Irish red at Star City.

Weizen Star (ABV 4.8 percent, IBUs 10) is more interesting still. A lovely Hefeweizen, this unfiltered wheat beer presents an appealing yeasty haze with banana and clove both on the nose and the palate. There are just enough hops to provide a sense of balance.

The brewery's notes for its first release of **Dry Lock IPA** (ABV 6.3 percent, IBUs 57) refer to its British ancestry, but its appearance and aroma are more suggestive of an American IPA. Intriguingly cloudy (my sample, at least) and fragrant with cedar and citrus, this beer offers a solid malt base that complements but does not really compete with the dominance of the Centennial and Cascade hops. Despite a relatively modest IBU level, this IPA is packed with a strong hop aroma and flavor. Finally, there's the **Old Mill Stout** (ABV 5.8 percent, IBU 28). Say "old mill" quickly and you'll hear an important ingredient in this very smooth, slightly sweet, and entirely opaque variation on the classic Irish version. Here the IBUs level may be a bit higher than customary in beers of this style, but bitterness is but one element, and not a pronounced one, in a beer that creates a memorably silky mouthfeel. (Note the reservations expressed in the Word List and elsewhere concerning IBUs measurement as an indicator of taste. This brewery's offerings illustrate those reservations.)

The Food

The building could easily accommodate a restaurant. There's already a kitchen. But there's also a long-range plan, Justin Kohnen explains. First, move production elsewhere, presumably in order to move to a more capacious system. Then, rehab the kitchen and restore food service. In the meantime, local food trucks visit and visitors may order from nearby restaurants poised to deliver.

Newsworthy

A friendly rivalry between Star City and its new neighbor, Lucky Star, has led to increased attention for both.

Other Stuff

Events regularly listed on the brewery's Web site include live music, food truck visits, and happy hours. There's a rewards program that promises gifts for frequent flyers—er, drinkers. • Works by local artists hang on the walls. • There are board games to enjoy.

The Skinny

LOCATION	From I-75, follow OH-725 west toward Miamisburg, where it becomes East Central Avenue. Turn left on South 2nd Street. After a couple of long blocks, you have arrived.
HOURS	Mon–Thu 4:00–10:00 P.M. • Fri 4:00–11:00 P.M. • Sat 1:00–11:00 P.M.
PARKING	There is a large lot immediately adjacent.
KIDS	There is a lot of room and a few board games.
TAKEOUT	Growler fills are available.
DISTRIBUTION	The beer is available at several locations in Dayton.

TOXIC BREW COMPANY

431 East 5th Street, Dayton, Ohio 45402
937-985-3618 • info@toxicbrewcompany.com

Opened in 2013, Toxic Brew, downtown Dayton's first brewery in half a century, brings a charmingly idiosyncratic presence to the city's historic and increasingly popular Oregon District. Before the development of the neighborhood, patrons sitting upstairs at a bar on one side of the street would speculate about the destination of pedestrians on the other. Headed for the pawnshop on 5th Street—where the brewery is now located? Or for the XXX-rated emporium next door? Toxic Brew recalls those days with its Porn or Pawn Pale Ale and its Porn or Pawn Pepper. Presumably, if you can say that name three times without stumbling, it would be OK to order another.

There's a strong sense of neighborhood in other ways as well. In addition to Porn or Pawn, their Hefeweizen is named for their address, 5th

Street. One of their IPAs, Practice Yoga, gives a nod to neighbors kitty-cornered across East 5th and Jackson. And Gem City Ruby echoes one of Dayton's historic nicknames. The neighborhood is well represented also in the small booklet you will find on the bar. Instead of operating its own kitchen, Toxic features local restaurants willing to deliver. Order a pint, call in your order, and await your meal! Because Toxic has become a popular neighborhood fixture in just a short time, walking in for the first time can feel a bit intimidating for a moment or two—but only for a moment. Toxic really is a very friendly place, and you will soon feel part of the neighborhood, which includes many other small restaurants and bistros and the Fifth Third Field, home to Dayton's highly successful minor league baseball team, the Dragons.

The Beers

Like many start-ups, Toxic began its brewing with beers it describes as "very approachable." But now it draws many of its customers to more creative high-gravity releases, some brewed for limited release. Brewers Patrick Sullivan and Shane Juhl cite the inspiration of Belgian and Bavarian brewing tradi-

Brewmaster Shane Juhl poses with Toxic's well-deserved award for architectural restoration.

Toxic Brew's healthful Gem City Amber reflects the brewery's restored surroundings.

tions, and you will find both well represented in the list. On the day of my visit, the range was considerable. There were more than ten available beers. Now there are nearly twenty taps—sixteen Toxic beers and three locally made craft sodas.

Abby Blonde (ABV 5.6 percent, IBUs 28) offered a pleasing introduction to the list. With its yellow-to-orange haze and yeasty aroma, this Belgian style recalls a Hefeweizen but is both fruitier (banana, perhaps kiwi) and sharper than wheat beers brewed to please all palates. While amiable, the beer may not disarm the anxieties of all craft-beer novices.

Christina Gamble serves pints of ISO-Heaven IPA to Patrick and Stephanie.

As its name promises, **Gem City Ruby** (ABV 6.9 percent, IBUs 24) offers first a treat for the eye: It is a brilliant *red*. But again, there's a twist. Instead of the malty nose you may anticipate, there's more than a hint of yeast—in this instance, *American* yeast. The taste confirms the flowery aroma but the beer surprises with a nice bite of hops more pronounced than the posted IBUs would indicate. As suggested above, the beer recalls a Dayton nickname conceived by a nineteenth-century mayor. In his "Toast to Dayton," African American poet Paul Laurence Dunbar, a Dayton native, refers to "the brightest gem" in "Ohio's diadem."

Feeling the need for a brief workout, I tried the **Practice Yoga** (ABV 5.1 percent, IBUs 69), an IPA well suited for an afternoon at the bar. I like very much the *idea* behind this and other session IPAs, but true IPA fans may find that this pleasantly hopped interpretation lacks the authority of its stronger cousins. Toxic refers accurately to its "clean, dry finish," but an IPA often leaves a more pronounced impression. Finally, I sampled the alliterative **Porn or Pawn Pepper** (ABV 6.2 percent, ABVs 37) mentioned above. It offers a pleasant deception. At first, you taste only a good Pale Ale, albeit one that has a somewhat darker yellowish hue than some. But after a couple of sips, the roasted poblano and habanaro peppers begin to introduce themselves to your palate. And after half a pint, you may want to have a glass of water alongside. Interestingly, the heat does not mask but rather reinforces the backbone of the well-hopped ale. As the board indicated at the time of my visit, other beers that may be available include a more traditional IPA (ISO-Heaven) and a double IPA (Cap City Hustler), a Belgian tripel (Abby's Cure), and a black IPA (Derailed on 5th).

The Food

Toxic prides itself on giving business to neighborhood restaurants. There's a collection of take-out menus in the booklet on the bar. Toxic's long-term planning includes possibly a niche kitchen offering a small seasonal menu.

Newsworthy

As another confirmation of the craft-brewing culture, Toxic chose to celebrate its first birthday by brewing a collaboration beer with Lock 27.

On a leisurely afternoon Toxic Brewing visitors neglect the shuffleboard for the beers.

Other Stuff

There's an old-fashioned machine that pops "toxic" popcorn, art from the neighborhood on display, and a shuffleboard table. • In the summer, a few tables outside enable you to enjoy watching the traffic on East 5th. • Origins of the brewery's name? According to Shane Juhl, there are several. The required health warnings on bottled beer as well as the "classic toxic warning label" on laboratory ethanol suggested a tongue-in-cheek echo. And there was an earlier experiment by the Toxic brewers creating a "tinctured" limoncello, the astringent liqueur of southern Italy. Adding coffee beans produced a "very, very, very bitter" concoction that justified the comment, "This stuff is just toxic." That experiment has not been repeated. But the name has stuck.

THE SKINNY

LOCATION	Downtown Dayton, in the Historic Oregon District. From I-75, take West 3rd Street to South St. Clair and turn left on East 5th for a couple of blocks.
HOURS	Mon–Thu 3:00 P.M.–midnight • Fri–Sat 1:00 P.M.–1:00 A.M. • Sun 1:00 –11:00 P.M.
PARKING	Some of the streets in the neighborhood have parking, but a better bet might be the Oregon District guest lot a couple of blocks east, adjacent to the railroad overpass.
KIDS	There's not much here for kids, to my eye. Call to inqure?
TAKEOUT	You can have a growler filled.
DISTRIBUTION	Toxic is serving a growing number of accounts in the area.

TEN GREAT LOCATIONS FOR *UNA BIRRA ALL'APERTO*

When the weather is pleasant for a change in Ohio, there's reason to celebrate, and there's no better way than with a cool pint in the outdoors. Some of the spaces on the list are taprooms. Others are brewpubs. They all offer a memorable sense of place. (By the way, al fresco means "in the refrigerator.")

- At Kelleys Island Brewery on a good day, you can sit on the lawn under a garden umbrella and gaze out at beautiful Lake Erie. Or you can sit at the outside bar and gaze at those sitting on the lawn. There are not many more congenial beer-drinking experiences than this!
- The hop garden at Willoughby Brewing in suburban Cleveland is not large, but its vine-covered trellises create an ideal ambience for enjoying the brewery's creative brews.
- If you can snare one of the few tables in front of Toxic Brew, you'll be in a great spot to view the eclectic promenade along East 5th in Dayton's Oregon District.
- Step through the side door at Weasel Boy Brewing to a charming rustic patio overlooking the Muskingum River and downtown Zanesville. Take a sip. Enjoy the view. Repeat.
- At Market Garden in Ohio City, a Cleveland neighborhood, you need not wait for good weather. Even in the cold and snow, there are hardy souls who like to gather around the outside fireplace to enjoy a hearty porter or stout.
- Take your pint "out the back" at Mt. Carmel in suburban Cincinnati, find a chair, and let the placid pond work on your spirit. If you would prefer to watch the passing scene, enjoy your pint on the front porch. Either way, you'll be the better for it. The beer helps.
- Tables in front of Gordon Biersch offer a pleasant three-season perspective on the pedestrian parade through Columbus's Arena District.
- The deck at Moerlein Lager House offers a splendid view of the Ohio River, Northern Kentucky, and, just in front, a lovely riverfront park.
- Try the patio behind Yellow Springs Brewery, which overlooks the Little Miami Scenic Trail. Or take the scenic approach and pedal your bicycle there.
- Star City Brewing in Miamisburg has made the most of its nineteenth-century location. You'll enjoy sipping a beer outside in a quiet neighborhood with a lovely "growler fountain" creating music for the ear.

The beers at Warped Wing will give you a lift.

WARPED WING BREWING COMPANY

26 Wyandot Street, Dayton, Ohio 45402
937-222-7003 • http://www.warpedwing.com

Warped Wing Brewing pays homage through its name to Dayton's rich history of invention. So as to enable their "flyer" to move right and left, the Wright brothers engineered the controlled "warping," or curving, of the wing surfaces—the innovation that made controlled powered flight possible in the early stages. While the fixed wing with elevator flaps would eventually serve the same purpose more reliably, the warped wing remains a paradigm of elegant and effective design.

That balance between a respect for origins and a commitment to improving on them is evident as well in the beer that Warped Wing brews and pours at its tasting room in downtown Dayton. There's a lovely balance also between the conviviality you'll find at the bar and tasting tables in a beautifully restored industrial space (formerly Buckeye Iron & Brass Works), on the one hand, and the seriousness you'll appreciate in the brewing, in the other. Look up. The huge crane that once served the foundry is still there.

If you drive into Warped Wing's large parking lot on a weekday afternoon in the summer, you will be greeted by a happy sight: professionals dressed for the office, college kids in shorts and T-shirts, truck drivers in company uniforms, all sitting at communal-style tables in the center of the tasting room enjoying their pints. These repurposed library tables from a closed high school encourage mixing. Of course, people don't flock to Warped Wing just to be sociable. They come for the beer. New acquaintances are a bonus, one suggested by the brewery's catchphrase, "Share a Pint, Make a Friend."

Warped Wing's sampler will get you off to a flying start.

The Beers

As Warped Wing has brewed more than fifteen (and counting) beers in its brief history, there's even less reason to rely on any one report of a tasting. You will want to check out brewmaster John Haggerty's current lineup on UNTAPPD (https://untappd.com/WarpedWingBrewery). But even a single visit will reveal three characteristics of what Warped Wing can create through its impressive thirty-barrel brewhouse.

First, there's a strong creative streak evident in naming the beers to capture local references. The **Self Starter Session IPA** (ABV 5.2 percent, IBU 67) honors Charles Kettering (1876–1958), Dayton's renowned inventor, a self-starter extraordinaire. The use of Amarillo hops during the boil and in later dry hopping results in a characteristic balance of fruitiness and assertive bitterness while giving the welcome impression of a traditional (that is, higher in alcohol) IPA. Another beer with a strong local reference? The Mr Mean Imperial/Double IPA recalls the name of a 1970s album by a band known as The Ohio Players. (Yes, some of the references are obscure.) I enjoyed the **10 Ton Oatmeal Stout** (ABV 7.0 percent, IBUs 30), which honors the foundry (and its ten-ton crane) that is the brewery's home. It is a solid, unsurprising, thoroughly agreeable stout offering more chocolate than coffee. It provided an ideal capstone for my tasting. Why not enjoy a good dinner in downtown Dayton, then visit Warped Wing for your nightcap?

Second, there is a clear commitment to experimentation across a broad variety of styles: the list includes most of the familiar ones, from a Belgian tripel to an oatmeal stout, but you will find also a dark rye beer (Jolly Tar), a Thai saison, a smoked porter (CreepShow), and a chili beer (Gypsy Queen). I enjoyed **Ermal's Belgian Style Cream Ale** (ABV 5.4 percent, IBUs 20) for its, yes, creaminess (a rich mouthfeel), its pleasing bouquet of citrus (grapefruit, to be sure, but also an interesting hint of lime), and the piquant hops notes. Daytonian Ermal Fraze invented the pop-top can.

Finally, Warped Wing likes to "warp" a familiar style to create interesting variations. For instance, the Ermal's Cream Ale may be available also as Ermal's Spice Blend. The Flyin' Rye IPA is sometimes dry hopped with Amarillo hops and sometimes with Centennial hops. And the 10 Ton Stout is laced on occasion with Grand Marnier and with cherry, peach, and orange bitters. Other beers may be aged with vodka staves, cocoa nibs, mango, lemon peel, etc. As you might expect, such varieties are worth queuing for. They're all limited in quantity: five-gallon casks or pins (see the Word List) only.

In spring 2014, the brewery collaborated with Wood Burl Coffee Roasters on a Belgian black tripel named Pirogue, the small boat used by pioneers navigating the Great Miami upriver to Dayton. And in fall 2014 a collaboration with Esther Price Candies provided caramels to brew Esther's Lil Secret, a holiday Scotch ale. Through repeated visits, you could become an expert on the many hops (Cascade, Centennial, Boadicea, Amarillo, Bravo, Belma, etc.) used to create carefully focused variations. There are many less worthy research projects!

The Food

Warped Wing is above all a place to enjoy beer, but you can bring in any commercially prepared food, order for delivery from several local establishments, or patronize a visiting food truck.

Newsworthy

Joe Waizmann, Warped Wing's president, initiated Dayton Beer Week in 2010, and the brewery is now a regular participant. • In October 2014, Warped

Suzanne Switzer, Katie Schwartz, Tara Michel, and Erika Ross (*left to right*) offer their welcome to the Warped Wing bar.

As soon as the weather opens up, so do Warped Wing's industrial doors.

Wing premiered its first barrel-aged beer, Whiskey Rebellion, the result of a collaboration with The Century Bar. • In late 2014 the brewery announced the lease of a second location at 1226 Schaeffer Street. • In early 2015 Rate-Beer named Warped Wing Ohio's best new brewery for 2014. • In May 2015 two Mexican brewmasters arrived to take part in an international collaboration, an IPA for Cinco de Mayo, Tres Carnales (Three Bro's?). *Dayton Daily News* writer Mark Fisher reported also that Warped Wing brewmaster John Haggerty would travel to Mexico in fall 2015 to reciprocate.

Other Stuff

Warped Wing offers some beers in the Dayton area in colorfully illustrated sixteen-ounce cans. The first three canned for distribution were the Flyin' Rye IPA, Ermal's Belgian Style Cream Ale, and 10 Ton Oatmeal Stout. Warped Wing is only the second brewery in Dayton's history to can beer, the first being Miami Valley Brewing Company, which canned beer only from 1949 to 1950. Note the news about the ADDY award in the sidebar about labels.

LOCATION	From I-75, exit on to West 3rd eastbound. After you cross North Patterson Boulevard, look carefully for Wyandot on your right. You're there!
HOURS	Wed–Thu 5:00–10:00 P.M. • Fri 4:00 P.M.–midnight • Sat 1:00 P.M.–midnight • Sun 1:00–6:00 P.M.
PARKING	Could hardly be easier. There's a dedicated lot in front.
KIDS	Warped Wing has been family- and kid-friendly since its opening.
TAKEOUT	Yes, growlers, canned beer, and kegs.
DISTRIBUTION	Once the needs of the Dayton area are satisfied, there's a strategy for continued expansion throughout Ohio.

YELLOW SPRINGS BREWERY

305 North Walnut Street, Suite B, Yellow Springs, Ohio 45387
937-767-0222 • http://www.yellowspringsbrewery.com

"Crafting Truth to Power." According to co-owners Nate Cornett and Lisa Wolters, that motto is meant to capture a "simple concept, one that holds within it the purpose of self-expression and the promise of a stronger community." When you step into the warm, informal tasting room, already forgetting the building's nondescript exterior, the Age of Aquarius will not seem that far off. The convivial conversation, the adjacent Little Miami Bike Trail, the art on the walls, and the good beer will conspire to persuade you that it's time to relax, to savor the moment, and to smell the—well—hops.

The Beers

Like many of their colleagues in the craft-brewing industry, the brewers are late converts to the profession. Nate Cornett was an IT expert. Jeffrey McElfresh managed a large bookstore. By sampling their beers, you will discover that they have now found their true calling, to make life, in their words, "better and richer and fuller for everyone." (Nate's mechanical background

was evident in the seven-barrel brewing system. I saw one that features some repurposed dairy equipment. That background is no doubt being put to further use as the brewery increases its capacity.)

Their extended list of beers shows a broad range of styles, including five different IPAs (one "intensely hopped" in the American style, one with freshly harvested Ohio hops, one "black" owing to toasted malt, one approaching "imperial" status, and a Belgian style), a saison ale, an American cream ale, an American smoked brown ale, and many others.

I enjoyed two versions of their saison, **Captain Stardust.** Their "regular" brew (ABV 6.5 percent, IBUs 18) is good. There's a pleasant citrus aroma from the Comet hops to balance a not at all unpleasant impression of freshly turned earth arising from the malt. Because saisons are paradoxical—complex in taste but humble in their farmhouse lineage—it's possible to take a wrong turn, but Yellow Springs Brewery is on the right course. Then (drumroll) I tasted Captain Stardust that had been aged for two months in gin barrels (ABV 8.0 percent, IBUs 18). Remarkable! The

Owners Lisa Wolters and Nate Cornett "craft truth to power" at Yellow Springs.

Resourcefulness is adapting discarded dairy equipment to the brewing of imaginative beer.

closest comparison might be Rogue's Juniper Pale Ale, but this was better, both more subtle and more interesting. Doing the research for this book, I ordinarily restricted myself to 1–2-ounce tastes, but I asked for a second small taste of this one. The gin did not dominate. The saison offers the spicy, fruity edge traditional for the style, but its typical rusticity has been domesticated. The farmhouse maid has become a sophisticated and alluring mademoiselle.

For an English major, **Wyatt's Eviction** (ABV 5.0 percent, IBUs 30) might recall Sir Thomas Wyatt's being "evicted" from his lands. Or not. If you're interested, you can read about the incident on page 530 of volume 6 of

Barrel aging at Yellow Springs produces some highly distinctive varieties.

the *Journals of the House of Lords*. But the brewery may have something else in mind. Regardless, this beer, English to the core (British ale yeast, Kent Golding hops, Golden Promise malt), could offer the evicted Sir Thomas some posthumous consolation. The focus is "balance," the brewers say. And they have achieved it. For some reason, it is difficult to find an American brewed bitter that tastes like what you might find when ordering "a pint o' best" in a British pub. But this one comes close—good malt taste, pleasing floral aroma, and down-to-earth hops—a good beer with which to celebrate a Chelsea victory over Manchester United.

I did not taste the **Nitro Prowler Oatmeal Stout** (ABV 7.25 percent, ABV 55), per se, but I did enjoy a version that had been aged for six months in fifteen-gallon barrels. The brewery describes it as "smooth and elegant." It is certainly smooth. The oatmeal offers that advantage. But rather than "elegant," I would say assertive. Because the roasted malt presence is pronounced, the experience is one of energy and possibility.

Finally, I want to commend the **Kerfuffle English Mild** (ABV 3.1 percent, IBUs 15), a reliable interpretation of a beer once offered in nearly all British pubs. The malt used here, derived from Maris Otter barley, has helped to inspire the "real ale" (or cask-conditioned) movement in England and is widely regarded as a malt of the highest quality. Every sip bespeaks serious brewing with high-quality ingredients. Does this sound not enthusiastic enough? I'm not a fan of the style. But if you are, you should make your way to Yellow Springs Brewery, because they do this well.

The Food

In addition to some bar snacks (local cheese, homemade potato chips) food trucks visit. Check the brewery's Facebook page ("This Week in the Taproom") to see what's cooking. Sometimes what's cooking is a beer dinner. Be alert!

Newsworthy

In its first year, 2013, Yellow Springs Brewery took home a silver medal from the GABF for its Smokin' Handsome in the "smoke beer" category and caught the attention of *BeerAdvocate* magazine. • In 2014, a collaboration with Great Lakes brewer Luke Purcell led to Night Tide American Dark Ale for Dayton Beer Week and for keg release to a few taprooms and restaurants in the area. • In 2015, the brewery turned heads with its bottle release of Bromancing Bastogne, a 9.5 percent ABV Belgian ale aged in oak barrels. • The brewery's expansion (more than quintupling its present capacity) and the installation of a canning operation necessitated a two-month closing, but YSB reopened in fall 2015.

Other Stuff

The brewery serves as a community art gallery, much like Weasel Boy and Star City. There are books to read and games to play. You can pedal there on your bike, grab a pint, and proceed refreshed. • "This Week in the Taproom" on the brewery's Web site lists special events such as the tapping of a limited-release beer, the opening of a new art exhibition, and the presence of food trucks.

THE SKINNY

LOCATION	From U.S. 68, turn onto Yellow Springs Fairfield Road, just north of downtown, and take a left on Walnut Street. Look a sign on your left, Millworks Business Center. You will find the brewery is in the white building at the end of the long drive.
HOURS	Wed–Fri 3:00–10 P.M. • Sat 1:00–10:00 P.M. • Sun 1:00–6:00 P.M.
PARKING	It's easy in the large but not very well-graded lot. Watch your footing.
KIDS	Kids are welcome.
TAKEOUT	In addition to growler and howler fills, you can sometimes obtain bottled Yellow Springs Brewery beer.
DISTRIBUTION	You will find Yellow Springs Brewery beers in a number of bars in the area, from Dayton to Cincinnati to Columbus. A larger brewing system and a canning line should enable the brewery to continue expanding its coverage.

CONSIDER ALSO

CARILLON BREWING CO. (1000 Carillon Boulevard, Dayton, Ohio 45409) stands on the Carillon Historical Park in Dayton and offers historical beer styles "historically brewed" in a setting meant to recreate the ambience of nineteenth-century brewing. While it would surely be anachronistic to refer to Carillon as a "brewpub," the kitchen offers a limited menu of foods "that tell the stories of Dayton's earliest immigrants." Perhaps "saloon"? Telephone: 937-910-0722 Web: http://www.carillonbrewingco.org/

DAYTON BEER COMPANY (912 East Dorothy Lane, Kettering, Ohio 45419) was the first modern-era brewery to open in the Dayton area. Its taproom has been open Wednesday through Saturday. But there's now a production brewery and "Bier Hall" downtown at 41 Madison Street, where all the beers on tap are Ohio born and brewed. Local food trucks provide solid sustenance. Many of Dayton Beer Company's styles honor brands once associated with Dayton. But there are original styles as well. A coffee stout named The Java Man Cometh won a gold medal at the 2015 Best of Craft Beer competition. Telephone: 937-228-2337 Web: http://thedaytonbeerco.com

EUDORA BREWING CO. (4716 Wilmington Pike, Kettering, Ohio 45440) offers both a brew-your-own facility and a three-barrel nano-brewery and taproom. In late 2014 the brewery offered an oatmeal stout brewed with coffee from Wood Burl roasters. In twenty-two-ounce bottles, the beer was available only in a package with a logo mug. Taproom hours are Wednesday through Sunday. Telephone: 937-723-6863 Web: http://eudorabrewing.com/taproom/

Operating as a co-op (owned by its members), the FIFTH STREET BREWPUB (1600 East Fifth Street, Dayton, Ohio 45403) serves food, house-brewed beer, and guest beers (including those of neighbors Warped Wing, Dayton Beer, and Toxic) seven days a week. Lots of events ensure that this cozy spot in the St. Anne's Hill district remains a center of activity. If you enjoy the beer, you can become an owner! Telephone: 937-443-0919 Web: http://www.fifthstreet.coop/

HAIRLESS HARE BREWERY (738 West National Road, Vandalia, Ohio 45377) brews at least eight beers, including a Breakfast Brown Ale. The taproom offers a limited menu: pizzas and pretzels. It is located north of Dayton near the city's airport and is open Wednesday through Sunday.

In early 2015 there were plans for a new production brewery—location to be announced. Telephone: 937-387-6476 Web: http://www.hair-lessharebrewery.com/

LUCKY STAR BREWERY (219 South Second Street, Miamisburg, Ohio 45342) is just down the street from the Star City Brewing Company described above. There's a Southwest flavor to the menu (salsas, tortillas, quesedillas, chicken tortilla soup) and to some of the beers. Their Mexican lager is named Ojos Locos (crazy eyes) and an IPA is IP YaY. Telephone: 937-866-2739 Web: https://www.facebook.com/LuckyStarBrewery

PINUPS & PINTS (10963 Lower Valley Pike, Medway, Ohio 45341) combines a microbrewery with "Dayton's hottest entertainers" as "America's First Strip-Club Brew-Pub." Seriously? Can one "couch dance" while sipping a Kölsch? Alas, I may never know. But freelance reporter Kevin J. Gray, who covered the opening for the *Dayton City Paper,* quoted owner Scott Conrad: "We've been having people come out for the beer." Bartender Alisha added, "It's fun to have more to offer." Telephone: 937-849-1400 Web: http://www.pinupsandpints.com/

Two announced breweries had not yet opened as this book went to press. VITRUVIAN BREWING COMPANY (305 North Walnut Street, Suite C, Yellow Springs, Ohio 45387) has described a commitment to brewing "Renaissance" beer through "the blending of the arts and sciences, perhaps best envisaged by Leonardo da Vinci in his renderings of the Vitruvian Man." Plans to open a tasting room were approved by the city's planning commission in summer 2014. Telephone: N/A Web: https://www.facebook.com/Vitruvian.brew. CRAFTED PINTS BREWING COMPANY announced that it would brew gluten-free as well as traditional beers and local hard cider. A fruit farm near Lebanon, south of Dayton, north of Cincinnati, was to serve as the new brewery's location. Telephone: 937-612-2337 Web: https://www.facebook.com/craftedpints and www.craftedpints.com. While it is always a good idea to check the latest information when planning a visit to a brewery, it is especially important to do so when openings may still be projected.

[7]

WORK IN PROGRESS
SUSTAINED GROWTH IN THE BUCKEYE STATE

Ohio's Craft Beers describes an industry that continues to grow—in capacity, in locations, in variety of styles, in distribution, and in market share. That growth represents an invigorating challenge to anyone trying to keep up. As Lenny Kolada observes in his introduction, no publication can capture entirely a process of evolution that may still be in its early stages. Things change too often. For remaining up to date on the late-breaking news, there's the Internet, of course, and, as mentioned before, Rick Armon's superb daily blog for developments in Ohio. You'll find a selective list of Web sites and Ohio beer writers on pages 240–244. And Web sites for the breweries themselves are listed throughout the book.

Hence *Ohio's Craft Beers* emphasizes not the latest bulletins but what's notable about Ohio brewing—the creative brewers and entrepreneurs, the interesting locations, the successes of the past, the planning for the future. This chapter does not offer a change in that priority. But it can be interesting, as one way of appreciating the sustained growth of Ohio brewing, to examine a six-month period—in this instance, January 1 to June 30, 2015—and some of the major stories that emerged during that period. It may be true that "present performance is no predictor of future results," but you would have to be an inveterate pessimist not to find heartening the developments in just one six-month period.

Like the book as a whole, this chapter offers a sampler of such developments rather than a comprehensive chronicle and is organized by region. These notes should pique your curiosity to check out the blogs and Web sites and plan your itinerary. The essentials remain the same. By drinking Ohio's terrific craft beers, you are helping a growing industry continue to grow. By your willingness to follow their leadership in trying new styles and new variations on old styles, you are expanding your own horizons. And by visiting the brewers on their home turf and drinking their beer where they have brewed it, you are making new friends—brewers, other beer fans, and the beers themselves.

TEN BREWERIES I WANT TO VISIT (OR REVISIT) ASAP

- **Dayton Brewing Company** has opened its production brewery and Bier House in downtown Dayton. They're brewing many of the beers available on tap, but every beer on tap is brewed in Ohio. That's worth a toast with their award-winning coffee stout, The Java Man Cometh. Or with their Batch 100, a golden strong ale. Or with . . .
- Ditto for the **Canton Brewing Company** in Canton, an ambitious undertaking that promises to be a transformative presence downtown.
- I'm eager to visit **Carillon Brewing Company** in Dayton to watch nineteenth-century beer styles being crafted.
- **Lucky Star** in Dayton is serving Mexican food with beers inspired by the Southwest. Sounds like a very good alliance!
- I'm looking forward to visiting **Findlay Brewing Company** as it grows from its nano-brewery origins to become a microbrewery—not because a nano-brewery cannot offer consistently reliable and delicious beers, because it can, but because a microbrewery may be able to offer a broader variety of styles.
- Having visited **Jackie O's** in Athens prior to its expansion, I want to return to see both the production facility and the downtown brewery's recovery from the fire that temporarily interfered with operations in late 2014.
- **Brewery X** in Cincinnati has signed an agreement to open a brewery in the iconic Eden Park pump station. When it opens, I want to be there. Cincinnatians will rejoice to see this beautiful and conspicuous structure once again put to good use.
- I want to have a beer and a sandwich in the completed garden at the **Fifth Street Brewpub** in Dayton. I might even decide to become an owner! (It's Ohio's first co-op brewery.)
- Why I haven't visited **Trailhead** in Akron before now I can't imagine. But the chance to visit both Trailhead and R. Shea while parking only once is too compelling to miss.
- **Kelleys Island**—again. Not just because there have been a few changes, but because I can't imagine a more pleasant mission. This time, as a paying customer, I will be able to enjoy a pint!

WHAT'S AT STAKE NEAR THE LAKE:
CLEVELAND, AKRON, AND THE WESTERN RESERVE

From the subtle redesign of iconic labels to the reappearance of a familiar craft brewery to long-needed expansions in capacity, there's a lot that can happen in six months in Northeast Ohio brewing. In fact, a lot *did* happen during our chosen half year, as suggested by one selection of Cleveland as the No. 1 U.S. "beercation" destination. Building on the observations of Condé Nast travel writer Amy Plitt, the online HuffingtonPost.com anointed Cleveland "the San Francisco of craft beer." That's a curious comparison, in that San Francisco, apart from its precedent-setting Anchor Steam, has not really emerged as a trendsetter in craft brewing. And the remainder of the list—which fails to include such cities as Boulder, Cincinnati, or, for goodness sake, Portland, Oregon—is a bit peculiar. But Cleveland as No. 1? We'll take it.

The redesign is of course that of **Great Lakes Brewing Company.** Already well regarded for its artful and evocative label illustrations, Great Lakes celebrated its new look with a block party in May and the opening of a new visitor center. Big news? Yes, according to the June 2015 issue of *Beer Advocate,* which devoted most of a page to the story. Freelance writer Courtney Cox describes the process through which artist Darren Booth, whose style she describes as "painterly with fragmented collage elements," sought to depict on the labels "Great Lakes' rich culture." The new labels may at first have perplexed faithful Great Lakes fans grown comfortable with the more traditional illustrations that had been featured on the classic labels, but the new packaging is likely to give the brewery a more competitive presence in grocery store coolers, especially in areas where beer fans are becoming acquainted with Great Lakes for the first time. As the photo comparing the two labels of Commodore Perry and Burning River suggests, the new designs are bolder, more colorful, more direct. Label changes are like retirements of star athletes: better too early than too late.

The reappearance? **Ohio Brewing Company** announced plans to open a brewpub in the heart of Akron's Highland Square, at the corner of West Market and South Highland, in late summer 2015. That would make good on a promise posted in November 2013, when the brewery pulled out of its former 451 South High Street location: "Ohio Brewing Company is NOT CLOSING permanently." That's more good news for an area already known for its small cafés, coffee shops, and pubs. Before closing, Ohio Brewing had earned a reputation for its Cardinal Ale (an Irish red), for Verich Gold (a Kölsch), and O'Holly Ale (an IPA).

An expansion, which began just in time to make this six-month roundup, was announced at Akron's **Hoppin' Frog**. When I encountered owner and brewer Fred Karm at a June 2015 meeting of the Ohio Craft Brewers Association in Columbus, he explained that four new fermenters would enable the award-winning brewery to increase its capacity by 50 percent. In sum, "Yeah more beer." The brewer's image continues to expand as well, in part as a result of the many awards, national and international, that are noted in the profile. So when the Cleveland Cavaliers tangled with the Golden State Warriors in the NBA finals, Ohio Sen. Sherrod Brown agreed on a wager with California Sen. Barbara Boxer. Because Brown (alas!) lost the bet, alas, Senator Boxer was to receive a shipment of Hoppin' Frog.

Great Lakes Brewing Company's spring 2015 label redesign introduced stronger fonts, cleaner overall designs, and bolder, less detailed graphics.

One other Northeast Ohio brewery forged a connection to the exciting title effort by the Cavaliers, by the way. **The Brew Kettle** worked with the team to create a session IPA, All for One, which was offered at the brewery, in area stores, and, of course, at the "Q," the Quicken Loans Arena. Of course, the way the 2015 season developed, it might just as easily have been called One for All.

Other expansions? **The Brew Kettle** indicated that it would open a restaurant in Amherst—and that it was exploring the possibility of opening another in Ironton, a small city upriver from Portsmouth and across the Ohio from Ashland, Kentucky. **Thirsty Dog,** having added considerable space in its historic Akron location, has used part of that space to begin an ambitious sours program. Another part of the building now houses a new bottling line offering an eightfold increase in output. With the resulting growth in productivity, Thirsty Dog looks to expand distribution well beyond Ohio.

In addition to these major developments on the part of major breweries, there are some new names in town as well.

Royal Docks Brewing, which began construction in the spring due west of Canton, hard by Nobles Pond, has proclaimed, "The British are coming—and they're bringing beer." The name points to the "royal" docks of London's thriving Docklands area and suggests the kind of focus the brewery will bring to the area: beer brewed according to "classic brewing traditions of

England" tempered by awareness of current innovative styles. Even before its September 2015 opening, its Flemish black ale won a "people's choice" award in a competition in Canton. Perhaps it is only a coincidence, but the names of streets in the vicinity of the new brewery—Queensgate, Knightsbridge, Paddington Down—suggest that it is in the right place.

And there's **Forest City Brewery.** Located in Tremont, it did not open within our six-month window, but it nevertheless managed to attract beer fans with inaugural brews. First there was a black stout, offered at **Brick and Barrel Brewing** (see Chapter 2's Consider Also) on St. Patrick's Day. Then in June Forest City staged a "takeover" of the Brick and Barrel taps in order to introduce additional varieties: Duck Island Amber Ale, Gitesi Coffee Stout, The Wet Mustache Belgian Wit, and Sorachi Ace Ginger Ale. The brewery as planned "will include a 5,000 square foot brewpub, located in a timber frame warehouse, built in 1915 on the site of the Silberg Brothers Beer Garden (1880–1900). Part of the beer garden area still exists, so we will also rebuild the beer garden. The beer hall, beer garden and brewery will feel like you are walking into a 19th Century brewery." Get the latest at http://www.forestcitybrewery.com.

AT THE HEART OF IT ALL: COLUMBUS AND ENVIRONS

Want one story that captures the energy in Ohio's craft brewing boom? Consider the lead to an article in the May 17 *Athens News:* "Three local craft breweries, two of which are within the city of Athens, are well on their way to opening up shop in Athens County by mid to late summer." The three are **Devil's Kettle, Little Fish,** and **Multiple Brewing.** The co-owner of Little Fish, Jimmy Stockwell, aptly describes "a whole new, expanded brew scene in Athens." Perhaps not surprisingly, Sean White, Stockwell's colleague, credits Jackie O's for offering an opportunity to test the recipe for Lil Harvey's Milk Stout. That's one reminder of the collaborative culture of craft brewing. Another? The brewers said they were all looking forward to tasting each other's brews.

North of Columbus, another start-up opened in May in Delaware at 25 N. Sandusky Street. A brewpub serving "the kind of food you want when you're having a beer," **Restoration Brew Worx** (that's not a typo) announced hours Wednesday through Sunday. Nestled among the antique shops, pubs, and bistros in Delaware's charming downtown, the brewpub is just a couple of blocks from Ohio Wesleyan University and even closer to the **Staas Brewing Company** at 31 West Winter Street. A growing brewery district in a charming small town?

There's also **Lineage Brewing**, mentioned among the Consider Also entries in the Columbus chapter. It opened in spring 2015 and immediately began to draw beer fans to its Clintonville location on North High. For those new to Columbus, that's several blocks north of *the* Ohio State University.

Finally, there's **Knotty Pine Brewing** at 1765 West Third Avenue, west of Route 315, Grandview Heights. A reincarnation of a restaurant that closed in 2012, the brewpub offers an interesting menu that draws on many cuisines but makes sure of standards (wings, pizza, ribs) as well. Let them tell it: "Chef Bret Perichak brings a menu of trendy American foods with Italian flavors." Mirror Lake IPA appears to be the flagship brew. Closed Mondays. Telephone: 614-817-1515.

Expansions abound in Columbus. **Columbus Brewing**'s long-needed move to new facilities west of downtown, mentioned in the profile, was completed for the most part during our six-month window. And four other breweries announced or completed expansion plans during this period. **Four String** will expand both its capacity and its distribution area once its supplementary production facility opens—not far from Columbus Brewing's new site. Add to this list **North High**'s new production facility, a new production system at **Barley's**, and additional fermentation and conditioning tanks at **Wolf's Ridge** and you'll get the picture: success leads to growth, and growth to increased success.

Perhaps the best way to summarize the good news coming out of the Columbus area is to point the way to the Columbus Ale Trail, which opened during our period. You can plan an itinerary that will take you from one of the twenty listed breweries to the next using the small book and map available in participating taprooms and brewpubs. As you make your visits, you will receive a passport stamp at each stop. Four stamps will earn you a free pint glass at Experience Columbus (277 West Nationwide Boulevard, Suite 125). Visit all twenty and you will receive a free T-shirt to wear while you are enjoying your pint. You can get started by checking out the map at http://www.dispatch.com/content/topic/news/2015/05/columbus-ale-trail.html.

Another window on craft brewing in Columbus appeared during our time frame in *Crave,* a magazine that focuses on the city's restaurants. In the Summer 2015 edition, Nicholas Dekker provides capsule descriptions of four brewpubs (**Smokehouse, Elevator, Barley's,** and **Columbus**). He offers an interesting reminder of the variety of cuisines available, though the profile of "Columbus Brewing Company & Restaurant" might have done more to clear up the confusion between brewery and the brewpub detailed in the full profile of Columbus Brewing. And what about **Wolf's Ridge**? That sophisticated restaurant certainly deserves a mention—more than a mention.

Finally, it says a lot about the brewery scene in Columbus that international brewers see opportunities there. **BrewDog**, a progressive and creative brewery based north of Aberdeen, Scotland, amid a "harsh and rugged landscape," boasts that it is "one of the most technologically advanced and environmentally friendly breweries in the world." Funded in part by the investments of more than fifteen thousand beer fans, the brewery's growth since its founding in 2007 enabled the opening of its new Scottish plant in 2013. Now there's to be a new house for the Brew-Dog in the United States. Writing in the *Columbus Dispatch* in June, J. D. Malone described plans for a "100,000-square-foot production brewery and canning line" as well as "a complex that also will include a restaurant, taproom and offices for its U.S. headquarters." Can you say *slàinte?*

SOUTHERN EXPOSURE: CINCINNATI AND THE SOUTHEAST

"More options than ever before for those who want to drink beer that's brewed here." Shauna Steigerwald's review in February for the *Cincinnati Enquirer* offers brewers' capsule descriptions of their most distinctive brews—and a reminder that every month brings Cincinnati-area beer fans more of an opportunity to discover a style that's new to them.

The deep roots of the Queen City's brewing tradition became more accessible in April with the installation of the first three kiosk trail markers for the Cincinnati Brewing Heritage Trail at the Great American Ball Park. A three-page spread in the *Enquirer* describes plans for a 2.3-mile trail that will feature signs, public art, and directional markers. The story gives considerable credit to Greg Hardman, who is president of the Brewery District board and, as noted in Chapter 4, the owner of the **Christian Moerlein Brewing Company.**

Start-ups continue to emerge. One of the most recent is **Urban Artifact**, which specializes in "tart and wild" beers. Don't say, "sour." Instead, say, "Wild, funky, tart, mouthwatering and gossip worthy." The taproom at 1660 Blue Rock Street, Cincinnati, 45223, is open seven days a week. To quote the brewery, "We're in the Northside neighborhood of Cincinnati—quick access from the Colerain Ave exit off of I-74, the Mitchell Ave exit off of I-75, or a one or two block walk from Hoffner Park on Hamilton Avenue." Beers from Urban Artifact are becoming easier to find in Queen City bars and restaurants. Rick Armon notes that this is the third Ohio brewery to locate in a deconsecrated church, the other two being **Taft's Ale House** in Over-the-Rhine and **Father John's Brewing Company** in Bryan. Amen to that.

Another new entry, **Woodburn Brewery**, began working during our six-month window toward a fall 2015 opening in East Walnut Hills, 2800

Woodburn Avenue. After completing restoration and retrofitting of a hundred-year-old former cinema, the brewery was planning to install a brewing system manufactured in Ohio—a further commitment to "local sourcing." Announced initial offerings were intriguing: a hybrid red ale/porter, a Cedar IPA, a pineapple saison, and a pilsner.

No less important, many of Cincinnati's established brewers are expanding.

As reported by WCPO (Cincinnati) in June, **Rivertown**'s founder and owner Jason Roeper has secured an additional eight thousand square feet in the brewery's present location in Lockland. A new fifty-barrel brewing system, once installed, will replace the current system. Visitors to a new two-story taproom will be able to observe operations through large windows.

In Over-the-Rhine, the **Rhinegeist** success story continues to develop as a new brewing system will supplement the present one, enabling close to a tripling of capacity. According to the brewery's press release, "the hard-working, beer-loving team at Rhinegeist" is growing as well, "from 5 people in early 2013, to over 50 today." Plans call for a team "over 100" by 2017. The brewery is expanding its 1910 Elm Street footprint as well. Just south of the taproom, a space capable of accommodating up to 250 for private events will open. And overhead, there will be a large roof deck with great views of OTR and downtown Cincinnati. In the Rhine-geist profile, I describe scrambling up a fire escape to make my first visit. Obviously, the ghostly brewers have come a long way!

NORTH BY NORTHWEST: THE ISLANDS AND GREATER TOLEDO

One of the smaller craft breweries in the state, **Kelleys Island**, has shown remarkable consistency in offering one of the more pleasant brewpub experiences. But that doesn't rule out a commitment to improvement. In an April Facebook posting, owner and brewer Doug Muranyi announced plans for a new beer, Devil's Shadow, " brewed in June and not ready until October." As noted earlier, at least one version of this beer poured in July. He mentioned as well a "makeover": "our menu, our view, lots of changes." Heck. I suppose it will now be necessary to pay another visit to check out these changes—and to sip a pint with all of Lake Erie providing the atmo-sphere. And then to return in October to try the new brew. Work, work.

Back on the mainland, **Black Cloister** (mentioned in the Consider Also notes) opened its tasting room in March. The space is remarkable. The Brew Review Crew Web site (http://www.brewreviewcrew.com/black-cloister-open/) reports that the brewery's "century" building was the first in the city to have electricity. I quote: "Beautiful brick-carved arches lace throughout and an oversized mural that simply stuns spans the entirety of the back wall." The beers include some unusual varieties, such as a raspberry chocolate imperial milk stout, a black saison, and two choices for fans of lager, a Vienna style and a Munich Helles style.

Finally, **Catawba Island Brewing Company** picked up the 2015 Entrepreneur Award for Ottawa County—a reminder, if one were needed, of just how much craft brewers contribute to their local economies through the jobs they provide, the tourists they attract, the hospitable spaces they create, and the taxes they pay.

THE SURPRISING SOUTHWEST: DAYTON AND ENVIRONS

What's remarkable about Dayton brewing?

For one thing, synergy. With **Dayton Beer Company**'s opening of its new downtown location in April, a beer fan can now stroll comfortably among three craft breweries, each with its own distinctive character: the neighborly intimacy of **Toxic Brew**, the industrial chic of **Warped Wing**, and now the beer-hall feel of Dayton Beer. And all are within walking distance of Fifth Third Field, home of the Dragons.

For another, recognition. Consider **Dayton Beer** again. Dayton entered the May 2015 Commonwealth Cup competition in Lexington, Kentucky, going up against 350 other beers from fifty-one other breweries with its Batch 100 golden strong ale. The *Herald-Leader* headline is a keeper: "Ohio microbrewery wins Alltech beer competition." A couple of months earlier, Dayton had won a gold medal for The Java Man Cometh (a coffee stout) at the Best of Craft Beer competition in Bend, Oregon. Winning competitions while addressing all the issues that arise with the opening of a new location has to be considered remarkable.

Finally, range. While Ohio as a whole is remarkable for introducing new brews, Dayton offers a microcosm of experimentation that offers a breadth of experience for beer fans. Here's a short list of styles: English mild (**Yellow Springs**), cream ale (**Star City**), Belgian quad (**Toxic Brew**), bourbon barrel-aged stout (**Dayton Beer**), saison with dried coffee fruit (**Warped Wing**), rye Pale Ale (**Hairless Hare**), and coriander ale (**Carillon**). A longer list would be easy—but you get the idea. While you could mount a similar list for any of Ohio's metropolitan areas, Dayton's recent, speedy rise to prominence makes its story particularly notable.

PRESENT PERFORMANCE, FUTURE PROSPECTS

Like the book as a whole, this chapter has offered a sampler for its six-month period rather than a comprehensive chronology. But just like a sampler can offer an impression of what a brewery can do, this January-to-June flyover gives at least some idea of how broadly and how quickly craft brewing in Ohio continues to develop. Of course, as in the stock market, it is wise to be prudent about extrapolating. But there's no justification for pessimism, either.

In his series of interviews with Ohio brewers, Rick Armon regularly asks whether the craft-brewing industry is becoming overextended, whether there's a bubble developing that may burst. Many predict a shakeout of some kind, as in any growing industry, but a widely shared view is that demand is more than keeping pace with supply. Every town of any size wants its own brewpub, mainline grocery chains are expanding their craft beer displays, distributors are enabling brewers to broaden their sales horizons, new festivals appear on the calendar every year, new Web sites track brewers and brewing, banks and investors get in line to support promising start-ups, and successful breweries are finding ways to expand.

In sum, while "present performance" is well worth celebrating, "future prospects" look good—very good, indeed.

A BEER FAN'S WORD LIST

This is not a beer dictionary. That would be another book. But to avoid having to define a term every time it appears, I have compiled this list of beer terms *as they are used in this book*. Perhaps it will offer some defense against beer geeks and beer snobs—both of which are defined below. Words *italicized* in these entries have an entry of their own. Very few beer styles are defined as their inclusion would double the length of the list, but there are leads to several useful Web sites under What to Read Next.

THE BREWING PROCESS

First, a quick review of the brewing process. The preliminary steps of (1) germination and (2) drying (kilning) of the grain, usually barley or wheat, take place in a malt house. At the malt house or brewery, (3) **milling** cracks the grain, enabling it to absorb water. The resulting **malt** is then (4) added to **hot liquor** (that is, hot water) in the **mash tun** to create a slurry called **mash**. During **mashing**, the starches in the grain turn into sugar. (5) Separating the resulting sweet liquid from the grain solids, a process referred to as **lautering**, creates **wort**. At this stage the brewer will **sparge** the grist with very hot water to capture all of the wort that results from mashing. (6) **Hops** are "pitched" (added to the wort) as the wort boils in the kettle for an hour or so. Once the wort is strained or spun to remove the hops and other solids, (7) it is piped into a **fermentation vessel** and allowed to cool (or is chilled) to a fermentation temperature consistent with the style being brewed. (8) Now it is time for the **yeast**: a top-fermenting yeast for ales, a bottom-fermenting yeast for lagers. Following **fermentation** the beer may (or may not) be filtered before it is (9) transferred (or **racked**) to a chilled **bright (conditioning) tank** for natural clarification, maturing, and, perhaps, for the infusion of additional carbonation. (10) After one or two (or many more) weeks, the beer is transferred to kegs or casks for serving, sent to a bottling or canning line, or placed in barrels for further aging.

ABV

Alcohol by volume (the percentage of alcohol in a beer relative to the volume) is a number that deserves respect, for it signals the alcoholic strength of a beer. In practical terms, if the ABV is below 5.0 percent, many beer drinkers may responsibly consider enjoying a second. Beers with ABVs between 5.0 percent and 8.0 percent? Consider very carefully. Those above 8.0 percent? Consider a designated driver.

adjuncts

Adjuncts are fermentable ingredients used in the brewing process other than water, malt, yeast, and hops. As rice, corn, or corn syrup may offer cost savings as well as clarity and lightness, they are associated primarily with American lagers, but not necessarily. Honey used in some of Ohio's holiday beers may be added to the brew kettle as an adjunct or introduced later in the brewing process as a flavoring. Other ingredients that may be used in the brewing process or added to the completed beer, such as coffee beans, raspberries, peanut butter (seriously), spices, hot peppers, and walnuts, are not adjuncts because they are not fermentable.

alcohol

In the brewing process, *yeast* converts the sugars in the *wort* into alcohol. Craft beers may present less than 3 percent *alcohol* (by volume—see above) or more than 10 percent. Most fall between 5 percent and 8 percent. If you drink more than one pint of 14 percent ABV beer, you may fall as well.

ale

One of two broad categories of beer—by far the oldest, the largest, and the most diverse. Having been brewed for several thousand years, ales are fermented with *yeast* that collects at the top of the fermentation tank and enjoys warm temperatures. (The other category is *lagers*.) Because ales may be brewed more quickly and economically, craft brewers usually brew them before considering lagers.

alt

Call a German etymologist! Because the literal translation of *alt* is "old," Altbiers are German brown ales *conditioned* (i.e., *lagered*) for a longer time than most other beers. But because *altus* in Latin means "high," perhaps the term refers instead (or also) to the yeast that rises in the top-fermented beer. Whatever your preference so far as the term is concerned, you will find Altbiers to be smooth and subtle, combining the best features of ales and lagers, with a gratifying softness produced by a balance between *malts* and *hops*—and by the additional *conditioning*.

BA

The Association of Brewers (craft brewers) and the Brewers Association of America (regional brewers) merged in 2005 to form the Brewers Association, which represents and advocates craft brewing in the United States. The BA sponsors the *GABF*, an annual convention of craft brewers, and the *World Beer Cup*.

barley

Milling barley provides the *base malt* for nearly all beers. In other words, barley is the principal go-to cereal grain for brewing beer. The terms "two-row" and "six-row" barley refer to the number of rows of corn down the length of the ear of grain. Because the corns on six-row barley tend to be inconsistent in size, many brewers prefer two-row for malting. But six-row barley has a couple of advantages. Midwest growers have found six-row barley to be more resistant to disease, and its higher enzyme strength can offer an advantage to brewers who use *adjuncts*.

barrel

You might think that "barrel" as a measurement of quantity would correspond to the capacity of "barrels" used to age beers. Not necessarily. When used to denote the productivity of a brewery, a barrel is equivalent to thirty-one-and-a-half gallons in the United States or to four-and-a-half liters elsewhere. Barrels used to age beer come from a variety of sources—distilleries, vineyards, even barrel manufacturers—and come in different volumes. "Barrel" is also used as a measure of a brewery's size. Using a ten-barrel brewing system, a brewery can brew ten barrels (or about 315 gallons) of beer at one time.

barrel-aged
In addition to serving beer as soon as it is ready to drink, many craft brewers now reserve some beer for aging in barrels, some of which may have once been used to age bourbon, gin, or even wine. The results can be fascinating—or terrible.

base malt
The primary *malt* chosen by the brewer for a beer. *Barley* is usually the base malt of choice. Even if *wheat* malt provides the base for brewing a wheat beer, barley malt will still represent a significant proportion of the malt used. Smaller quantities of more distinctively flavored malts, "specialty malts," may be added as well.

beer geek
An enthusiastic beer drinker who knows more about beer than you do.

beer snob
An enthusiastic beer drinker who knows more about beer than you do and who flaunts his or her superiority.

bitter
There are two distinct meanings. Bitter is an important element in the flavor of a beer, most notably in beers such as *IPAs* that may justify high *IBUs.* But in the United Kingdom and in some other countries, bitter refers to a popular style that is the staple in most pubs. Paradoxically, you are likely to find that a "pint o' bitter" in the United Kingdom tastes far *less* bitter than most American *IPAs.* Another twist: When bottled, the beer served on tap as "bitter" is labeled "Pale Ale."

body
The way a beer feels in the mouth—light and effervescent, say, or heavy and viscous. Some *beer geeks* discuss body in terms of *mouthfeel.*

boil
Boiling the *wort* arrests the conversion of malt proteins into sugar, cleanses the liquid of undesirable elements, sterilizes it, provides an opportunity to add hops, and creates an aroma in the brewery that is a beer drinker's perfume. Perhaps the time has come for a "boiling wort" air freshener?

bottle-conditioned
During the bottling process, additional sugar or *wort* may be added to the beer. The subsequent *fermentation* creates additional *carbonation.*

bottom fermentation
Unlike *ale yeasts,* which typically collect at the top of the tank, *lager yeasts* typically sink to the bottom of the tank during fermentation. Easy mnemonic: *ale* is on the "top" of the alphabet. See *lager* and *top fermentation.*

brew kettle
Once the *wort* has been separated from the *mash*, it is transferred to a brew kettle for boiling. To understand why brew kettles are sometimes referred to as "coppers," find the photo of Maumee Bay Brewing Company's brew kettle.

Brewers Association
A not-for-profit trade association with headquarters in Boulder, Colorado, dedicated to the support and promotion of craft brewing. The BA sponsors the annual *Great American Beer Festival* every year and the *World Beer Cup* every other year. The American Homebrewers Association is a division of the BA.

brewpub
Although some states have legal definitions for a brewpub, the term in *Ohio's Craft Beers* refers to a brewery that operates (or includes on its premises) a more or less full-service restaurant. *Taprooms* and *tasting rooms* may invite food trucks to hover, encourage patrons to bring food, offer access to deliveries from nearby restaurants, serve pizza, or allocate part of their space to an independent food service. That does not make them brewpubs.

bright (or brite) tank
A pressurized tank that can be temperature controlled to which freshly brewed beer is transferred to undergo natural *carbonation* and clarification. As solids fall to the bottom as sediment, the beer becomes "bright," that is, clear. Alternate terms: *conditioning* tank, serving tank.

canning
Jackie O's, Rivertown, Four String, Rocky River, and MadTree are among the increasing number of Ohio craft brewers that have either experimented with or committed to canning their beers. MadTree's brewers point out that canning more securely preserves the beer from the effects of light and oxygenation. Moreover, cans allow for compact storage and easier shipment. There is also the advantage that a canning plant can be more economical to purchase or rent. One firm in particular, Buckeye Mobile Canning, has made it possible for smaller brewers to move into canning without making a large investment in equipment and staff. There is one caveat so far as canned beer is concerned: Do not drink good beer from the can! Notwithstanding the nostalgic memories some may have about popping the top of a Stroh's or Schlitz in the pre-craft era, attempting to drink a good craft beer directly from the can will bring brewers to tears.

carbonation
There are several approaches to creating the fizz or sparkle in beer. Conditioning the beer in a pressurized *bright tank* is one. In *bottle-conditioning*, adding sugar or *wort* to beer during bottling prompts further *fermentation*, which creates additional carbonation. A similar result can be obtained by adding beer at the early stages of its *fermentation* to mature beer—a process called *kraeusening*. Or the finished beer can be infused with carbon dioxide.

cask

A small *barrel* in which freshly brewed beer may continue to mature and from which cask-conditioned beer may be served. While there is a variety of cask sizes, the most common is that of the *firkin,* 10.79 gallons (in U.S. measurements) or one-fourth of a barrel. See also *pin.*

cask-conditioned

Allowing unfiltered and unpasteurized beer in a *cask* to mature for a few days (or longer) in a cool space enables natural *carbonation* to develop through a secondary *fermentation.* Once the cask is tapped, the beer is pumped by hand and should be drunk within a few days. Cask-conditioned beers are served cool rather than cold, and they are less effervescent. Fans of a particular style often find that cask conditioning produces a more flavorful result.

color

The sidebar concerning myths about craft beer upends the notion that the color of a beer necessarily predicts its taste. It may, but it may not. And color has nothing at all to do with a beer's calorie count or alcoholic strength. What creates the color of a beer is the roast of the grain used to create the *malt,* any *adjuncts* that may be used, and any colorful ingredients (coffee, chocolate, fruit, syrups, etc.) that may be added during the brewing process.

conditioning

The process through which freshly brewed beer achieves *carbonation* and improves in other ways through storage in a tank or *cask.*

craft brewing, craft brewery

While there are technical and legal definitions based principally on brewery system capacity and output, *Ohio's Craft Beers* defines craft brewing principally in terms of a shared focus on brewing good beers by good methods for good people. Craft brewers tend to share as well a commitment to quality achieved through traditional brewing methods, a focus on continuing product development and refinement, engagement with the community, the local sourcing of ingredients for food and beer where possible, a concern for the ecology and for sustainability, and, where appropriate, an interest in architectural restoration.

dry hopping

Think of hops in a "tea bag" placed in the kettle during or following the boil—or even into a *conditioning* tank—so as to enhance the aroma of the beer without dramatically increasing its bitterness. Thus, the addition of hops to beer that has been or is being fermented.

fermentation

The process that takes place after *yeast* is added to the *wort.* The yeast converts sugars created in the mashing process into carbon dioxide and *alcohol.* Usually, the yeast is introduced by hand, i.e., *pitched.* Ale yeasts ordinarily create *top fermentation,* while lager yeasts produce *bottom fermentation.* For some beers (such as *lambics*) the brewer may open the kettle to the air and invite any wild yeasts that may be hanging around in the vicinity to join the beer. This can be risky, but the results can be surprisingly good, as in many Belgian ales. There is a distinction as well between **primary** fermentation, which occurs once the *wort* is transferred to the fermentation vessel (or "fermenter"), and **secondary** fermentation, which may take place in a cask or in bottles. See also *kraeusening.*

filtered and unfiltered
Some brewers filter some of their beers in order to remove any solids (such as yeast particles) that may still be present. Some styles, such as Hefeweizens, are meant to be served cloudy. Some brewers prefer to serve all beers unfiltered. In *bright tanks,* fresh beer naturally becomes clearer ("bright") as suspended solids settle to the bottom.

fining
To assist beer in casting off its unwanted solids (see *filtered and unfiltered*) a brewer may add an inert substance such as silica gel or gelatin. The particles attract and bind the unwanted substances and the whole lot sinks to the bottom.

firkin
A *cask* with roughly an eleven-gallon capacity used for conditioning, storing, and serving beer. Some breweries make a custom of tapping a fresh beer on "firkin nights." Barley's Brewing Company in Columbus advertises its (ahem) Firkin Good Ales. See also *pin.*

fresh hopping (aka wet hopping)
Increasingly popular within craft brewing—and impractical for mass-production brewing—the introduction of *hops* grown and picked locally and used before drying, while they remain "wet," imparts a fresh, often grassy taste that many (not all) beer drinkers find appealing. This process depends on local sourcing and a prompt response as fresh hops left undried will soon deteriorate.

GABF
The oldest and most prestigious of beer competitions, the Great American Beer Festival began in Denver in 1982, sponsored by the not-for-profit *Brewers Association.* The more than fifty thousand beer fans who now visit the Colorado Convention Center each year may sample more than three thousand beers submitted by more than seven hundred U.S. craft breweries. They can thus second-guess the judges who award the coveted medals. Note that skateboards and roller skates, which might facilitate mobility at the festival site, are expressly prohibited. Ohio medalists in 2015 included seven breweries and ten beers.

grist
Grain that has been milled. Also, a mixture of milled grains compounded for a particular beer recipe.

growler
A relatively new phenomenon in Ohio, growlers are glass jugs (typically but not necessarily sixty-four ounces) that beer drinkers may have filled with draft beer at properly equipped taprooms, beer bars, and grocery stores. There are creative names for smaller take-out vessels: howlers, torpedoes, bullets, etc. The term originally referred to a small pail used to transport beer from a corner tavern to

a kitchen table. There is no consensus on the etymology of the name. One theory is that carbon dioxide escaping from the pail created a growl. Another is that customers would growl as they walked along because beer would occasionally slosh over the side of the pail.

hophead
A beer drinker who prefers heavily hopped beers such as IPAs and imperial IPAs. Not meant as derisive.

hops
One of the four traditional ingredients of beer (the others being water, *malt,* and *yeast*), hops have the strongest influence on the taste and aroma of some beers. The soft cones (sometimes erroneously called flowers) produced by the hops vine may be picked when ripe and added directly to beer being brewed (*fresh hopping*) but are more often dried and perhaps compressed into pellets. There are four critical questions in choosing the hops for a beer: (1) For what purpose are the hops to be introduced: to add bitterness, to enhance flavor, or to create aroma? (2) How heavily hopped is the beer to be? For example, a brown ale is lightly hopped, while an India Pale Ale (*IPA*) is heavily hopped. (3) Which hops to use? There are more than one hundred available with new varieties being developed all the time in Europe and the United States. (4) When will the hops be introduced? *Pitched* early in the boil? Introduced to the beer (*dry hopping*) in a large porous bag? Though some authorities observe that dry hopping has a minimal influence on taste, beer drinkers know that the nose (aroma) of a beer may be integral to the experience it provides. Hops also have a preservative influence. See *IPA* and *IBUs.*

IBUs
International bitterness units offer a technical measure in milligrams of the amount of a bitterness-producing alpha acid in a liter of beer. However, according to the *OCB,* the IBU "is a laboratory construct that was never meant to leave the laboratory." The problem is that posted IBUs may not come close to indicating how bitter a beer *tastes.* That depends on the balance between hops and malts and on other factors as well, including the temperature at which the beer is served. Some lightly hopped beers (brown ales, some lagers, porters) may test at IBUs of 10 or below. Some *IPAs* and *imperial IPAs* may test at IBUs approaching or even exceeding 100. Pale Ales are usually somewhere in between.

imperial
This useful but only approximately defined term invites beer drinkers to "extreme" *IPAs* and other styles heavy in *alcohol* (see *ABV*). The term also offers fair warning. Origins of the term lie in the efforts of English breweries to meet Russian demand for porters. When the first shipments spoiled in transit, breweries increased both the hops and the alcoholic content. Success! Russian imperial stout!

IPA
There's a well-established account: Seeking to slake the thirst of troops in India, the British discovered that heavily hopped ales brewed with a higher alcoholic content were more likely to survive the long ocean voyage around the Horn of Africa to India. Alas, according to the *OCB,* nearly every element of this story

is wrong. "Of all beer styles," the *OCB* says, "IPA is the most romanticized, my-thologized, and misunderstood." This is not the place to reprint the "real story," which is complicated, but there are a few more details in the sidebar "10 Myths About Craft Beer." For practical purposes, an IPA typically presents a hefty ABV (6.0 percent and above) and a high level of IBUs (typically 50+). They can be quite bitter. A few brewers have lately begun to experiment with *session* IPAs, tasty beers with ABV levels below 5 percent.

keg

You know this one, right? It is a steel or aluminum container used for storing beer ready to serve. Kegs come in different sizes designated by their relation to a *barrel*. The size most often tapped in U.S. bars and restaurants (and perhaps remembered fondly from college parties) is a half barrel. There are also quarter-*barrel* kegs and some that are one-sixth of a *barrel*. Outside the United States, *barrels* are described according to metric measurements. The popularity of the "kegerator," a refrigerated cabinet for storing and serving beer in the home, has increased demand for smaller keg sizes.

kraeusening

One approach to *conditioning. Wort* in the active, early stages of fermentation is added to maturing beer to stimulate the production of *carbonation* through a secondary *fermentation.*

lager

In contrast to *ales,* which are brewed with *top-fermenting yeast* and aged at rela-tively warm temperatures, lagers are brewed with *bottom-fermenting lager yeast* and *lagered* at relatively cold temperatures for at least several weeks. Because la-gers "tie up the tanks" and require refrigeration, craft brewers with small-capacity systems usually specialize in ales. While ales have been brewed for thousands of years, lagers have been brewed for only about five hundred.

lagering

The process of storing brewed lager at relatively cold temperatures for at least several weeks, during which time the beer may improve in taste as it becomes clearer. In German, *Lager* means "bed," and a *Lagerhaus* is any kind of warehouse.

lambic

A Belgian wheat beer fermented with "wild *yeasts*" by opening the fermentation vessel to the open air or by adding yeasts that have been captured and care-fully preserved. There are several highly differentiated styles. The term may be applied more broadly by brewers such as Rivertown in Cincinnati, which brew beers that express this distinctive Belgian tradition.

lautering

Following mashing but before the boil, the wort must be separated from the grain residue by allowing it to filter through the husks. A lauter tun, a tank with a kind of strainer, offers an efficient apparatus for this operation. In German, lauter means "clear" or "pure" and can also mean, figuratively, "sincere."

lawn mower beer
You're hot. You're thirsty. For the moment, anyway, you aren't really interested in subtlety or complexity. Your criteria: Is it cold? Will it quench my thirst? You want a mass-produced lager.

liquor
Water—especially hot water—used in brewing. Brewers frown at novices who refer to "water" while visiting a brewhouse. Novices frown when they hear brewers mentioning "liquor."

malt
One of the four traditional ingredients in beer. The choice of one or more malts is a principal determinant of the taste of a beer. The process that produces malt from grain is described in "The Brewing Process" above.

mash
The slurry created by mixing hot *liquor* (hot water) with *malt* in a mash tun. The foam that may form on the surface of the liquid as the grain starches are converted into sugars may recall the "slurry with the fringe on top." Not really.

milling
To produce *malt,* one of the four essential ingredients of beer, millers grind *barley, wheat,* or some other grain so as to crack the kernels and expose the starch inside without pulverizing them into powder. Rather like opening very, very tiny pistachio nuts? The milled grain can then absorb *liquor.*

mouthfeel
The term concerns questions such as: How fizzy (or carbonated) does the beer feel on the tongue? How viscous is it? Thick (like some stouts) or thin (like many lagers)? How "alcoholic" does the beer seem to be? Does the beer (like some sours) pucker your mouth? It is possible and perhaps more seemly to discuss any of these questions by referring to a beer's *body.*

nitro
Ordinarily, carbon dioxide propels beer from the keg to the tap. When a beer is "on nitro," gas combining carbon dioxide and nitrogen performs this function. The result is a less effervescent, very smooth beer with a creamy, long-lasting head. Once reserved for stouts and porters, many brewers will now serve almost any style on nitro, at least occasionally. While most nitrogenated beers are available only on draft, some may be found in cans and bottles.

noble hops
Czech and German hops that are go-to varieties for brewing European styles. German hops include Spalt, Tettnang, and Hallertau. Saaz is a Czech noble hop. Though often thought to be associated with a long tradition of brewing, the term itself is a fairly recent coinage. The *OCB* describes it as "merely a marketing tag."

OCB

Edited by Garrett Oliver, brewmaster at the Brooklyn Brewery, the *Oxford Companion to Beer* is the single most useful reference for the serious beer consumer.

OCBA

Founded in 2008, the Ohio Craft Brewers Association (http://ohiocraftbeer.org/) took a major step forward in 2013 with the appointment of an executive director. The OCBA offers a "unified voice" for Ohio's craft brewers as they seek to "contribute to systemic, local community development by driving economic and job growth, while creating experiences that bring people together." The OCBA sponsors, supports, or endorses several events each year.

pin

A small *cask* equal to about one-eighth of a *barrel,* ideal for serving experimental brews.

pitching

The word suggests throwing *hops* into the *wort* after it has cooled sufficiently. In practice, the process is less athletic, more delicate, and more methodical.

Real Ale

Let's allow Cleveland's Indigo Imp, which serves Real Ale in its Real Ale Room, to assist in defining the term: "It is a beer that has been naturally carbonated in the container [e.g., a traditional English cask] from which it is served." The natural *carbonation* results from a secondary fermentation prompted by adding sugar or unfermented beer to the freshly fermented (green) beer. Applied to beer in bottles as well as in casks, the process can create a highly flavorful beer with "smooth carbonation."

Reinheitsgebot

Beer should be made solely with water, *malt, hops,* and *yeast.* Anything else—and you're violating this ancient consumer protection legislation, the German purity law. Although many Ohio craft brewers comply with this convention at least so far as some of their beers are concerned, it is not a law in the United States or in most other countries. Many Ohio beers are not in compliance, but that is because they include other ingredients such as spices or peanut butter or fruit. Not because they are "impure."

session beer

Regional brewer Schaefer once advertised its *lager* as "the one beer to have when you're having more than one." That is not a bad definition of a session beer—one sufficiently low in *alcohol* so that you can enjoy "more than one." A recent phenomenon is the "session IPA," the brewing of a low-alcohol beer that is meant to taste like a style more often defined by moderate (7 percent and above) *alcohol* levels.

sparging

Once the *mashing* is complete, the *grist* is irrigated with very hot *liquor* (water) to capture all of the sugars that result from *mashing*—that is, to obtain all of the *wort.*

taproom or tasting room

A space usually closely adjacent to a brewing system where customers can enjoy the results.

top fermentation

As *ale yeast* ferments the *wort,* it gathers on the surface, where it can be harvested for later use. *Yeasts* that sink to the bottom are associated with the fermentation of *lagers.*

tun

A term used by some brewers to refer to any large vessel.

water

Do you really need a definition of water? No. But you may be interested to know that some beers are defined by characteristics of the water used in brewing. A Gose tastes slightly salty because the style was first brewed in Goslar, Germany, a city that depended on a water supply with more than a hint of salinity. Other beers owe some of their characteristics to water with high mineral content.

wheat

A cereal grain that can be malted and used for brewing beer. While a beer may be brewed entirely with *barley malt,* it is difficult to brew with wheat malt only, as wheat lacks the coarse husks that serve as a filter during *lautering.*

World Beer Cup

Like the *GABF* (see above), the World Beer Cup is sponsored by the *Brewers Association* (see above). Unlike the *GABF,* the WBC invites international competitors. In 2014, more than 4,700 beers were entered by 1,403 breweries from fifty-eight countries. The judges represented thirty-one countries. Ohio winners in 2014 included Willoughby Brewing Co., Thirsty Dog Brewing Co. (Akron), Fat Head's (two awards, Middleburg Heights), and Columbus Brewing Co.

wort

The liquid that results from mixing *malt* with hot *liquor* in a brewing vessel known as a *mash tun.* Brewers may distinguish between "sweet wort" (produced in the mash tun), "brewed wort" (produced in the brew kettle), and "fermenting wort" (produced in the fermenter).

yeast

One of the four basic ingredients in beer, together with water, *malt,* and *hops,* yeast is critical. Without it, there would be no beer. Yeast transforms sugars present in the *wort* into *alcohol* and carbon dioxide.

WHAT TO READ (OR DOWNLOAD) NEXT

Some beer fans want to be left alone. They know what they like and where to find it. In the words of the well-known commentator who thought himself "good enough and smart enough," that is OK. Doggone it, people like them. May even elect them to the United States Senate. But you may find beer an unfolding adventure. You may believe that knowing more about the beer you drink will enhance your enjoyment and expand your experience. If you belong to the former group, "live long and prosper." If you want to know more, you should live long, prosper, and consider glancing at some of the resources listed here. They may enrich your experience.

INTERESTING WEB SITES

Beer Advocate
http://www.beeradvocate.com/
A site rich in information, news, and products, with a link to subscribing to the magazine and a downloadable app.

Beerpulse.com
http://beerpulse.com/
The "world's #1 daily beer news website" offers a "30-second daily e-mail" service.

Brew Professor ("On sabbatical" as of fall 2015)
http://brewprof.com/
The brew professor focuses on "Cincinnati craft beers and local breweries, home brewing, and the occasional beer review."

Brew Review Crew
http://www.brewreviewcrew.com/
A stylish and colorful site offering lots of information plus the views of "two teachers who love to drink, review, and talk all things craft beer."

Brewers Association
http://www.brewersassociation.org/
The Web site of the Brewers Association ("A Passionate Voice for Craft Brewers") reports news of interest to craft beer fans.

CraftBeer

http://www.craftbeer.com/

An online magazine publishing articles devoted to craft beer.

Drink Up Columbus

http://drinkupcolumbus.com/

A remarkably detailed and informative site that announces events, reports on releases, categorizes bars, and provides a directory of Columbus breweries, distilleries, and wineries.

German Beer Institute

http://www.germanbeerinstitute.com

Detailed descriptions of German brewing methods, ingredients, beer styles.

Great American Beer Festival

http://www.greatamericanbeerfestival.com/

Information about competing in the GABF or simply attending the festival.

Hoperatives.com

http://www.hoperatives.com

Focused primarily on but not limited to craft brewing in the Cincinnati area.

North American Guild of Beer Writers

http://nagbw.org/

Web site of the North American Guild of Beer Writers listing its members and announcing events.

OhioBreweriana.com

http://www.ohiobreweriana.com

Historical information on Ohio brewing.

Ohio Craft Beer

http://www.ohiocraftbeer.com/breweries/index.cfm

A list of Ohio breweries, with addresses, telephone numbers, an interactive map, and a tab leading to additional details.

Pat's Pints

http://patspints.com/

A labor of love (of beer) that offers posts according to nine categories for "ordinary folks who enjoy good beer." Focus is primarily but not exclusively on Central Ohio.

Queen City Drinks

http://queencitydrinks.com/

As the name suggests, a platform for news and reviews concerning brewing, mostly in Cincinnati.

RateBeer

http://www.ratebeer.com
A membership site that invites members to review the beers they are experiencing.

RateBeer Beer Styles

http://www.ratebeer.com/BeerStyles.asp
A useful reference that defines each beer style and offers lists of examples.

Untappd

https://untappd.com/
A multifaceted site that includes a time line for members, lists of top rated beers, etc.

RELEVANT APPS

I'm not endorsing apps for your mobile device, as some of them come with a fee, but there are some interesting resources available on iTunes and Google Play. For example:

Any Beer ABV

When you type in your beer by name, this app will probably be able to give you its alcohol content.

BeerAdvocate

Reviews and articles by the magazine of the same name.

Brewery Map

What it sounds like. Type in where you're leaving from and going to and find the breweries along your route.

RateBeer

The popular ratings service that reflects the tastes of beer fans.

Untappd

No, there's no e. But there's lots of information in an accessible format.

OHIO BEER WRITERS

Rick Armon is Ohio's most authoritative reporter and commentator on beer. His articles in the *Akron Beacon Journal* are engaging and informative, and you can subscribe to his daily beer blog through http://www.ohio.com/blogs/the-beer-blog. His 2011 *Ohio Breweries* (Mechanicsburg, Penn.: Stackpole Books) remains highly useful. Other Ohio beer writers (or writers who sometimes write about beer) include the following:

- Marc Bona of the Northeast Ohio Media Group/*Cleveland Plain Dealer*
- Karen Bujak of the Examiner.com and *Great Lakes Brewing News*
- Dan Eaton of *Columbus Business First*
- Cheryl Harrison of *Drink Up Columbus*

- J. D. Malone of the *Columbus Dispatch*
- Amelia Robinson of the *Dayton Daily News*
- Shauna Steigerwald of Cincinnati.com and the *Cincinnati Enquirer*
- Tom Streeter and Carla Gesell-Streeter of Hoperatives.com

BOOKS

The single most authoritative and useful guide to beer is The *Oxford Companion to Beer* (New York: Oxford University Press, 2012) edited by Garrett Oliver, brewmaster at the Brooklyn Brewery. It covers in detail every stage of brewing processes, ingredients, prominent breweries, and beer styles while offering engaging articles on the history of brewing. Other books worth a look include the following:

Acitelli, Tom. *The Audacity of Hops: The History of America's Craft Beer Revolution.* Chicago: Chicago Review Press, 2013.

Bernstein, Joshua M. *Brewed Awakening: Behind the Beers and Brewers Leading the World's Craft Brewing Revolution.* New York: Sterling Publishing, 2011.

———. *The Complete Beer Course: Boot Camp for Beer Geeks.* New York: Sterling Publishing, 2013.

Calhoun, Doug. *The Beer Lover's Guide to Beer Books: A Bibliography of Brewers, Brewing, Pubs, and Other Beer Related Subjects, Published in Books and Pamphlets and Printed in English Over the Last 550 Years or So.* Malibu, Calif.: Athanor Books, 2011.

Hales, Steven D., ed. *Beer & Philosophy.* New York: Free Press, 2004.

Mosher, Randy. *Radical Brewing: Recipes, Tales, & World-Altering Meditations in a Glass.* Boulder, Colo.: Brewers Association, 2004.

———. *Tasting Beer: An Insider's Guide to the World's Greatest Drink.* North Adams, Mass.: Storey Publishing, 2009.

Musson, Robert A., M.D. *Brewing in Cleveland.* Charleston, S.C.: Arcadia Publishing, 2005.

Perozzi, Christina, and Hallie Beaune. *The Naked Pint: An Unadulterated Guide to Craft Beer.* New York: Penguin, 2009.

Tolzmann, Don Heinrich. *Christian Moerlein: The Man and His Brewery.* Milford, Ohio: Little Miami Publishing Co., 2012. (Foreword by Gregory Hardman, founder of Cincinnati's Moerlein Lager House and Moerlein Malt House.)

MAGAZINES

Finally, there are the magazines. The top national magazines are *Draft* (bimonthly), *Beer Advocate* (monthly), *Beer Magazine* (bimonthly), *All About Beer* (bimonthly), and *Beer Connoisseur Magazine* (quarterly), all of which offer some information useful to home brewers but speak to beer aficionados above all. You may find free copies of *Great Lakes Brewing News* at your beer store or pub. Grab one. =